CogLab Manual

Cognitive Psychology
Connecting Mind, Research, and Everyday Experience

THIRD EDITION

E. Bruce Goldstein

CogLab Material by

Daniel VanHorn
Purdue University

With CogLab contributions from

Greg Francis

Ian Neath

WADSWORTH
CENGAGE Learning

Australia • Brazil • Japan • Korea • Mexico • Singapore • Spain • United Kingdom • United States

ISBN-13: 978-0-8400-3354-3
ISBN-10: 0-8400-3354-0

Wadsworth
20 Davis Drive
Belmont, CA 94002-3098
USA

Cengage Learning is a leading provider of customized learning solutions with office locations around the globe, including Singapore, the United Kingdom, Australia, Mexico, Brazil, and Japan. Locate your local office at: **www.cengage.com/global**

Cengage Learning products are represented in Canada by Nelson Education, Ltd.

To learn more about Wadsworth, visit
www.cengage.com/wadsworth

Purchase any of our products at your local college store or at our preferred online store
www.cengagebrain.com

Printed in the U.S.A.
7 8 9 15 14 13

Table of Contents
(This Table of Contents has been updated to reflect the correlation of exercises in the 3rd edition
of *Cognitive Psychology*)

Chapter 12: Problem Solving
None

Chapter 13: Reasoning and Decision Making

WADSWORTH CogLab™ 2.0
Online Laboratory

Introduction to CogLab

Welcome to the Cognitive Psychology Online Laboratory (CogLab), a set of Web-based demonstrations of classic experiments and concepts from cognitive psychology. CogLab allows students to experience a variety of important experimental studies. This experience will help you understand each experiment, the data, and the significance of the study.

CogLab can be accessed anywhere in the world through the Internet with a Web browser that adequately supports the Java programming language. For Microsoft Windows, most recent Web browsers will work just fine. CogLab has been successfully used with the Firefox, Internet Explorer, and Opera Web browsers on Windows XP. For Mac OS X, Safari is the recommended browser (for MacOS X 10.2 or more recent), but Opera also works quite well. Other Web browsers and operating systems may also work, but have not been thoroughly tested.

CogLab Demonstrations include:

Attention	Perception	Neurocognition
Attentional Blink	Apparent Motion	Brain Asymmetry
Change Detection	Garner Interference	Blind Spot
Simon Effect	Muller-Lyer Illusion	Receptive Fields
Spatial Cueing	Signal Detection	
Stroop Effect	Visual Search	
Sensory Memory	**Short-Term Memory**	**Working Memory**
Metacontrast Masking	Brown-Peterson	Irrelevant Speech Effect
Modality Effect	Position Error	Memory Span
Partial Report	Sternberg Search	Operation Span
Suffix Effect		Phonological Similarity Effect

Memory Process	Metamemory	Imagery
Encoding Specificity	False Memory	Link Word
Levels of Processing	Forgot-It-All-Along Effect	Mental Rotation
Serial Position	Remember/Know	
Von Restorff Effect		
Speech & Language	**Concepts**	**Judgment**
Categorical Perception – Identification	Absolute Identification	Monty Hall
Categorical Perception – Discrimination	Implicit Learning	Decision Making
Lexical Decision	Prototypes	Risky Decisions
Word Superiority		Typical Reasoning
		Wason Selection Task

Getting Started with CogLab

To get started using CogLab, follow these steps.

STEP 1: GET A COGLAB REGISTRATION CODE

The registration code can come in several forms. If you purchased a new printed version of this CogLab Student Manual, the registration code should be on the inside front cover, under a scratch-off surface. If the registration scratch-off surface has already been removed, it is likely that your registration code will not work because a registration code can be used only once. You should return the book and demand a refund or a replacement manual. **Do not purchase used CogLab Student Manuals.** Alternately, the registration code may have been bundled as a postcard inside your textbook. If you purchased a used textbook, it is likely that the registration code has already been used. If your textbook is brand new, this should not be a problem. The third place to get a registration code is from the Thomson Learning electronic catalogue. This source provides what is called a CogLab e-Pin. The e-Pin is the same thing as a registration code.

STEP 2: GET THE STEP-BY-STEP INSTRUCTIONS FROM YOUR INSTRUCTOR

Your instructor will give you a printout or direct you to a Web page (see below for an example) that gives you step-by-step instructions for setting up your CogLab account. With this account, you will be listed as part of your instructor's CogLab group. Your instructor will be able to verify that you completed your CogLab assignments on time and can give you the appropriate credit for the assignment. Follow all of the steps in these instructions and you should be ready to start running CogLab experiments.

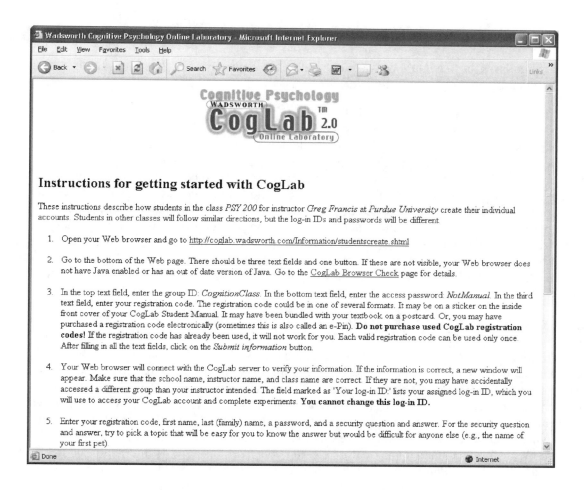

Instructions for getting started with CogLab

These instructions describe how students in the class *PSY 200* for instructor *Greg Francis* at *Purdue University* create their individual accounts. Students in other classes will follow similar directions, but the log-in IDs and passwords will be different.

1. Open your Web browser and go to http://coglab.wadsworth.com/Information/studentscreate.shtml

2. Go to the bottom of the Web page. There should be three text fields and one button. If these are not visible, your Web browser does not have Java enabled or has an out of date version of Java. Go to the CogLab Browser Check page for details.

3. In the top text field, enter the group ID: *CognitionClass*. In the bottom text field, enter the access password: *NotManual*. In the third text field, enter your registration code. The registration code could be in one of several formats. It may be on a sticker on the inside front cover of your CogLab Student Manual. It may have been bundled with your textbook on a postcard. Or, you may have purchased a registration code electronically (sometimes this is also called an e-Pin). **Do not purchase used CogLab registration codes!** If the registration code has already been used, it will not work for you. Each valid registration code can be used only once. After filling in all the text fields, click on the *Submit information* button.

4. Your Web browser will connect with the CogLab server to verify your information. If the information is correct, a new window will appear. Make sure that the school name, instructor name, and class name are correct. If they are not, you may have accidentally accessed a different group than your instructor intended. The field marked as 'Your log-in ID:' lists your assigned log-in ID, which you will use to access your CogLab account and complete experiments. **You cannot change this log-in ID.**

5. Enter your registration code, first name, last (family) name, a password, and a security question and answer. For the security question and answer, try to pick a topic that will be easy for you to know the answer but would be difficult for anyone else (e.g., the name of your first pet)

Running a CogLab Experiment

Point your Web browser to coglab.wadsworth.com. Select the experiment that you want to perform by clicking on the appropriate link.

STEP 1: RUNNING THE EXPERIMENT

Each experiment's Web page has unique instructions that describe details of experimental stimuli and the experimental task. To properly complete a demonstration, you *must* read and understand the instructions. You will not be able to complete an experiment unless you understand the instructions. After logging in, click on the *Start experiment* button to begin the experiment. Your computer will connect with the CogLab computer to download the necessary files. This may take a minute or more, depending on the speed of your Internet connection. A window will appear where experimental stimuli will be presented and your responses will be measured. A smaller window will also appear with a shortened set of instructions. Close the instructions window before starting the experiment. Most experiments require you to press a key or click on a button to start an experimental trial. You must read the instructions to know what is required to get the experiment running.

STEP 2: FINISHING THE EXPERIMENT

When you finish an experiment, the experiment window may close and a small window will appear to explain that your data is being sent to the CogLab computer. Perhaps after a short delay, an explanation of the experiment and a summary of your data will appear in your Web browser. Your computer will connect to the CogLab computer through the Internet to store your data. That data is available for both you and your instructor to download later. You will know that your data is stored when your Web browser loads the experimental results and the small window disappears. Wait for the data to appear before closing your Web browser. If Internet usage is heavy, it may take a few minutes for the data to appear in your Web browser. This screen shot shows part of what is seen after completing the Attentional Blink experiment. The data is the average for all students in your class. A link to another page that shows only your personal data also appears on the data page.

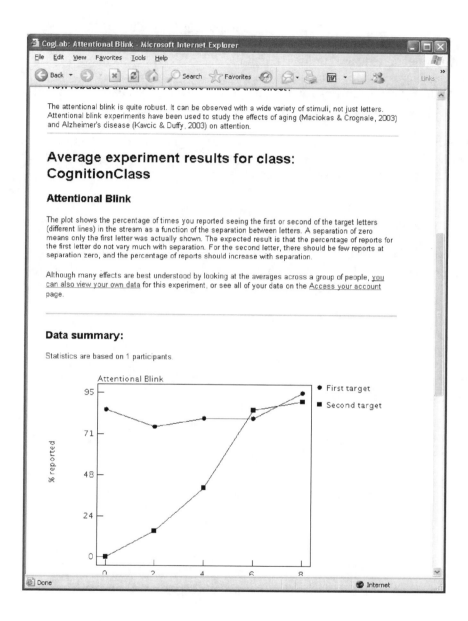

CogLab: Attentional Blink - Microsoft Internet Explorer

File   Edit   View   Favorites   Tools   Help

Back | Search   Favorites | Links

The attentional blink is quite robust. It can be observed with a wide variety of stimuli, not just letters. Attentional blink experiments have been used to study the effects of aging (Maciokas & Crognale, 2003) and Alzheimer's disease (Kavcic & Duffy, 2003) on attention.

Average experiment results for class: CognitionClass

Attentional Blink

The plot shows the percentage of times you reported seeing the first or second of the target letters (different lines) in the stream as a function of the separation between letters. A separation of zero means only the first letter was actually shown. The expected result is that the percentage of reports for the first letter do not vary much with separation. For the second letter, there should be few reports at separation zero, and the percentage of reports should increase with separation.

Although many effects are best understood by looking at the averages across a group of people, you can also view your own data for this experiment, or see all of your data on the Access your account page.

Data summary:

Statistics are based on 1 participants.

Attentional Blink

• First target
■ Second target

% reported

Done   Internet

Ways of Summarizing CogLab Data

Your experimental data are summarized at the end of each experiment. CogLab also provides average data across all the students in the class and average data across a global set of students who volunteer their data from around the world. In every case, experimental data is provided in either a graphic (plot) or a text (table) format.

Data plot: This is a graphical description of the experimental data. An example is for the Attentional Blink experiment, as shown on page 5. Below the data plot is a data table with the same information. This allows you to create your own plot if you wish.

Data table: Experiments that do not show a data plot present a data table. The window below shows an example of a data table that appears after the Stroop Effect experiment.

Trial-by-trial data: Below the data table is a listing of information for every trial of the experiment. This provides details about the stimulus shown on that trial and your response. This information is useful for in-depth analysis of the experimental results.

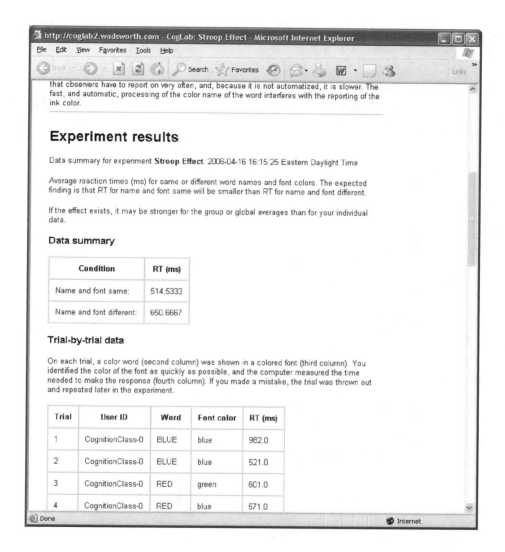

Sources of CogLab Data

If you want to look at data from an experiment that you previously completed, follow the *Access your account* link on the CogLab home page under Account Information - Students. Enter your log-in information and then click on the *Access account* button. A new window will appear that lists details about your CogLab account and a list of the labs you have completed will appear on the right hand side of the window. Select a lab and then click on one of the buttons below. A new

Web page will appear with an explanation of the experiment and data summary. You have the following choices:

Get your data: This is the data you generated when you finished the experiment. If you do an experiment more than once, only your data from the first time will be saved. However, the data shown at the end of an experiment is always the data that was just generated.

Get group averages: The CogLab program automatically combines your data with the data of other students in your class to compute class average data. This choice displays those average results. A data table below the average data also gives the standard deviations of the data across the students in the class. The standard deviations are useful for some types of statistical analyses.

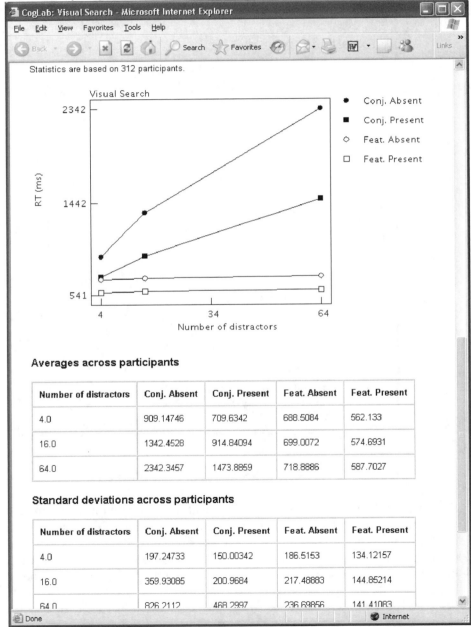

Statistics are based on 312 participants.

Averages across participants

Number of distractors	Conj. Absent	Conj. Present	Feat. Absent	Feat. Present
4.0	909.14746	709.6342	688.5084	562.133
16.0	1342.4528	914.84094	699.0072	574.6931
64.0	2342.3457	1473.8859	718.8886	587.7027

Standard deviations across participants

Number of distractors	Conj. Absent	Conj. Present	Feat. Absent	Feat. Present
4.0	197.24733	150.00342	186.5153	134.12157
16.0	359.93085	200.9684	217.48883	144.85214
64.0	826.2112	468.2997	236.69856	141.41083

Get global averages: This is the same type of data as for the group averages, but it is data that students volunteered to submit to a global data set. The graph at the right shows global average data for the Visual Search experiment.

Working with CogLab Data

If you want to use your CogLab data for a report or to do further analysis, you need to save the data to your local computer. Your data will always be saved on the CogLab server as well.

PRINTING YOUR DATA
To print the explanation page and the data that are generated at the end of an experiment, use your Web browser's *Print* feature.

SAVING YOUR DATA
To save the entire explanation page, use your Web browser's *Save As...* feature. Depending on your Web browser, this may or may not save the graphics along with the Web page.

To save a graphic, such as a data plot, place your mouse pointer over the graphic and right-click (control click on a Mac). A small set of menu options should appear; select the option *Save Picture As...* or something similar (it varies depending on your Web browser). You will then be prompted to name the file and identify where you want to save it on your file system.

IMPORTING YOUR DATA INTO ANOTHER PROGRAM
Many programs, such as MS Word and MS Excel can read html files. If you saved your data as a complete html page, you can directly read in that file in to these programs.

You can also copy and paste selected parts of your data page into these (and other) programs. To copy a graphic, such as a data plot, from the explanation page, place your mouse pointer over the graphic and right-click (control click on a Mac). A small set of menu options should appear; select the option *Copy* or something similar (it varies depending on your Web browser). Now go to the program in which you want to place the graphic and paste the copied image by using either the menu options (*Edit and Paste*) or the keyboard shortcuts appropriate for your operating system.

To paste a data table or trial-by-trial data, highlight the text on the Web page by selecting it with your mouse cursor. Copy the text using either the menu options (*Edit and Copy*) or the keyboard shortcuts appropriate for your operating system. Now go to the program in which you want to place the data table. Paste the text by using either the menu options (*Edit and Paste*) or the keyboard shortcuts appropriate for your operating system. If the program you paste into deals with tables of information, such as MS Excel, SPSS, or SigmaPlot, the data should appear with each cell of the table arranged appropriately for the program. The figure below shows the data table for the Attentional Blink experiment as it appears after being pasted into MS Excel.

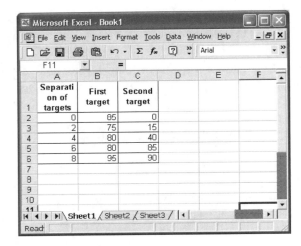

CogLab Help

If your question is not answered below, please request free on-line Tech Support from the CogLab Web site.

My Web browser hangs when I try to log in.

The most likely situation is that there is a firewall between your computer and the Internet. A firewall is a security program that prevents unauthorized communications between computers over the Internet. The firewall is usually set up by the computer people who maintain the network through which your computer connects to the Internet. You need to ask the computer staff to make a pinhole in the firewall to allow read/write access to coglab.wadsworth.com. This should be fairly easy for them to do.

It says my registration code is already used!

This most commonly occurs when you have purchased a used copy of the CogLab Student Manual or other textbook that has CogLab bundled with it. The registration code will not work because it can be used only once. You should return the used manual and demand a refund from whoever sold it to you. You will need to purchase a new registration code.

How can I get a new registration code?

The fastest way is to order a CogLab registration code on-line. Go to the How to Order page. On that page is a link to the Thomson Learning Electronic catalogue. Once there, do a search for CogLab. There will be several choices listed. You want the CogLab (e-Pin Code Version). You will receive the e-Pin Code, which is the same thing as a registration code, as soon as your credit card is charged.

I forgot my password/log-in ID; what can I do?

Go to the Look up password or log-in ID page. Enter either your log-in ID or your registration code, and then answer the security question. You will then be given your information. Be sure to print out or save the Web page that shows your log-in information.

How can I verify that my data was saved?

From the CogLab home page, follow the Access your account link under Students. Log in and then click on the Access account button. A window will appear that lists your account information. On the right is a list of all the labs you have completed. Select a lab and then click on one of the buttons below to see whatever type of data you want.

Which Web browsers work best?

Almost any recent Web browser that has Java enabled will work. You can test your browser on the Browser check page.

Why doesn't the experiment begin?

If a window appears to start the experiment but nothing seems to happen, make certain that you are following the directions. Most experiments require you to press a key (usually the space bar) or click on a button to start an experiment. If the instructions ask you to press a key to start a trial, but nothing happens after the key press, your Web browser may be causing a minor problem. Some Web browsers fail to properly direct keyboard input to the designated window. Using your mouse, click once in the middle of the window. (Be sure to move the mouse cursor out of the way of any stimuli that may be presented.) Pressing the appropriate key should now produce a response from the window.

Why aren't some of the experiments working on my Linux system?

Some combinations of Linux, X Windows, and certain window managers do not update the Java window correctly. One result of this is that text is often not drawn to the screen unless some other activity (e.g., moving the mouse) forces a window update. The best solution is to try a different window manager.

Why doesn't the Trials to go menu item count down?

Some experiments require that you provide a correct answer(s) on each trial. When mistakes occur, the trial is repeated later in the experiment. If you never answer correctly, the Trials to go menu label properly shows that you have not completed any trials. Until you provide the correct answers for the trials, the experiment will not end. Make sure you read the instructions for the experiment.

I didn't save my data to the global data set; do I have to redo the lab?

No. Submitting your data to the global data set is entirely optional. There is no way to tell whether a particular individual has submitted his/her data. Regardless of whether you submit your data or not, you do not have to redo the lab. As soon as you see the results page appear, you know that the system has recorded that you have finished the lab.

Experiments

Mental Rotation

Minimum time to complete this experiment: 30 minutes

Background

When we carry out some cognitive tasks, we seem to use mental images. For example, how many windows are in your house or apartment? To answer this question, most people seem to recall a mental map of their homes and, mentally, move through the map as they count windows.

Although everyone seems to experience something that we call mental imagery, it is difficult to draw conclusions from such introspections. For example, some people report that their mental images are very sketchy and ill defined, while others report their mental images are detailed and crisp. Based solely on these reports, it is impossible to know whether people's mental images really differ or if subjects just describe the mental images differently.

To explore mental images more objectively, researchers give subjects tasks that seem to require the use of mental images. As a critical part of the task is varied, some characteristics of mental images can be deduced. Roger Shepard and his colleagues (e.g., Shepard & Metzler, 1971) designed one of the most often-used tasks. In this task, subjects were shown two novel visual stimuli and were asked to determine whether the stimuli had the same shape or different (mirror image) shapes. The shapes (random block shapes) were rotated around the vertical axis. Subjects reported that they mentally rotated a shape in their head until the two stimuli were oriented the same way, and then made their judgments.

When subjects were asked to make their responses as quickly as possible, the reaction-time increased with the angle of rotation between the shapes. This suggests that it takes time to mentally rotate an image, and implies that mental images are much like real images. Shepard further found that every 50 degrees of physical rotation required one second of mental rotation before subjects could respond. This suggests that the rate of mental rotation is at a constant velocity.

Shepard's findings have had a large influence on theories of mental representation. This experiment allows you to participate in the mental rotation task.

Instructions

1. In the text fields below, enter your CogLab log-in ID and password. If you do not have a log-in ID and password, see your instructor for information on how to get one for your class.
2. Click the Submit information button.
3. If the information is correct, the Start experiment button will become activated. Click the button to begin the experiment.

A window will appear that fills nearly the entire screen, and a smaller window will appear with abbreviated instructions. Close the instructions window. You can open it again later from the CogLab Info. menu.

Start a trial by pressing the space bar. Two 3-D block shapes will appear on the screen, one to the left and one to the right. Each block shape is within a circle. The two shapes are either identical, or different (one is a mirror image of the other). One shape is also rotated around the vertical axis. The rotation is 0, 20, 40, 60, 80, 100, or 120 degrees relative to the orientation of the other shape. Your task is to determine whether the two shapes are the same or not. Respond as quickly as possible by pressing the / key (for same) or the z key (for different). You will receive feedback on whether you were correct. When you are ready for the next trial, press the space bar again.

There is a minimum of 70 trials. For each pair of same and different stimuli, five trials are presented for each rotation angle. If you make a mistake (e.g., say the stimuli are different when they were actually the same), the trial will be repeated (with different stimuli) later in the experiment. In this way, only reaction-times for which you were correct are used. If you find you are often making mistakes, you should try slowing down on your responses and/or try harder.

At the end of the experiment, you will be asked if you want to save your data to a set of global data. After you answer the question, a new Web page window will appear that lists your class averages for this experiment. On that page is also a link to your personal data.

Additional References

Ginn, S., & Pickens, S. (2005). Relationships between spatial activities and scores on the mental rotation test as a function of sex. *Perceptual and Motor Skills, 100*, 877-881.

Nakatani, C., & Pollatsek, A. (2004). An eye movement analysis of "mental rotation" of simple scenes. *Perception & Psychophysics, 66*, 1227-1245.

Olivier, G., Velay, J., Labiale, G., Celse, C., & Faure, S. (2004). Mental rotation and simulation of a reaching and grasping manual movement. *Perceptual and Motor Skills, 98*, 1107-1116.

Heil, M. (2002). The functional significance of ERP effects during mental rotation. *Psychophysiology, 39*, 535-545.

Basic Questions

1. Were your personal experimental results similar to the predicted experimental results? Explain your answer.

2. Why did Shepard & Metzler's (1971) findings suggest that mental images were similar to real images?

3. In demonstrations like this, participants often report that they mentally rotate the objects in their minds in order to make their same/different judgments, so why did researches decide to take reaction-time measurements also?

Advanced Questions

1. Using the global data, predict the reaction-time for making a same response if someone was shown two identical shapes but one of the shapes had been rotated 140 degrees on the y-axis.

2. In this demonstration, why did you have to repeat the trial if you made an incorrect same/different judgment?

3. You are trying to get a new mattress through your front door. Currently, the mattress is laying flat on your front porch. You look at the mattress and mentally rotate the object in your mind to figure out how it might fit through the doorway. There are two ways the mattress could conceivably fit through the doorway: it could be slightly tilted to one side or it could be stood up on end. Using what you have learned in this demonstration, which of these two possibilities are you more likely to come up with first? Why?

Discussion Question

1. Describe some cognitive tasks (not already mentioned in the text) in which one might utilize mental imagery.

Receptive Fields

Minimum time to complete this experiment: 25 minutes (often more)

Background

A fundamental tenet of cognitive science is that the mind can be understood by studying the brain. The brain consists of billions of individual cells (neurons), whose combined behavior corresponds to what we call cognition. Because of the immense number of neurons and their complicated connections, it is difficult to relate the behavior of an individual neuron with human behavior (e.g., seeing a red apple).

A concept that helps make that connection, in certain cases, is the receptive field. Basically, the receptive field of a neuron consists of any stimulus that changes the neuron's firing rate. By definition, every neuron has a receptive field, although the receptive fields for some neurons are very complicated. The concept of a receptive field is most useful in those parts of the brain that are tied to specific senses (e.g., touch, audition, vision, taste) or to motor control. For neurons sensitive to visual information, for example, the receptive field describes how spatial patterns of light influence the neuron's behavior. It is often the case that a neuron responds only when light falls within a certain part of the visual field. Moreover, the light can have excitatory or inhibitory effects, depending on where it falls in the receptive field. Identifying the region of the receptive field and the excitatory and inhibitory parts provides a good deal of information about the role of the neuron in visual perception.

In a neurophysiological study of visual receptive fields (and there are many), a researcher typically inserts an electrode into a neuron to record its electrical potential (including action potentials). The researcher then presents visual stimuli to the animal and records the cellular responses. By noting changes in the electrical potential (or in the number of action potentials), the researcher can determine if light at a particular location is: (a) excitatory, (b) inhibitory, or (c) outside the receptive field and thus neither excitatory nor inhibitory. By carefully watching the cell's behavior as the stimulus changes, the researcher can map out the receptive field of a neuron.

Knowledge about neural receptive fields is of great significance for understanding perception. For example, neurons close to the retinas of your eyes have (relatively) circularly shaped receptive fields. For some neurons, the center of this circle is excitatory, while the surround is inhibitory. Other neurons switch the locations of excitation and inhibition. Some neurons in area V1 of the cortex are sensitive to light-to-dark edges of a specific orientation. Other neurons in area V1 are sensitive to light-to-dark edges but are also sensitive to dark-to-light edges of the same orientation. The properties of these neurons play a fundamental role in theories of visual perception.

This experiment provides you with the opportunity to map out receptive fields. Your task is to find a stimulus that drives an unknown receptive field. Do not take the properties of the virtual neurons too literally. The receptive fields are caricatures of true receptive fields; they do not take into account much of the underlying neurophysiology. This caveat aside, this experiment will introduce you to the concept of receptive fields.

Instructions

1. In the text fields below, enter your CogLab log-in ID and password. If you do not have a log-in ID and password, see your instructor for information on how to get one for your class.
2. Click the Submit information button.
3. If the information is correct, the Start experiment button will become activated. Click the button to begin the experiment.

A window will appear that includes a plot, a large black area, and buttons. A smaller window will also appear with abbreviated instructions. Close the instructions window. You can open it again later from the CogLab Info. menu.

On the main window, the large black area is a canvas for showing the stimulus. Here you place stimuli that are to be presented to the virtual visual system. On the top left is a plot that shows the response of the cell to the drawn stimulus. The plot is updated every half a second. Position the stimulus by dragging the mouse in the black drawing canvas. Change the stimulus shape by selecting from the pull-down choices. Adjust the stimulus size with the sliders.

Your task is to create and position a stimulus that generates a response from the neuron that is at least 50% of its maximal response. Once you have that stimulus, you can move on to the next trial. This is more difficult than it sounds. You must first identify where the receptive field is located on the canvas. It may be best to use a small filled dot to do this. The text in the upper right part of the window identifies the type of receptive field present, and it gives information about how strongly the current drawn pattern drives the cell.

8

The first four trials are for practice. The practice trials are just like the test trials, except you can always reveal the true shape of the receptive field by clicking on the Show RF button. Use the practice trials to see the receptive field and explore how light patterns correspond to electrical potentials. A shown receptive field is represented on the drawing canvas by a green (excitatory) region and a red (inhibitory) region. The locations of the green and red pixels correspond to the location in visual space of the receptive field. With the mouse, place a filled circle in the middle of the green region. You should see that the plot of electrical potential rises and the number of spikes increases. The spikes plotted intermittently correspond to action potentials. Action potential frequency increases as electrical potential increases, but action potentials can also occur without a stimulus.

Try changing the size of the circle so that it fills most of the green area. You should find that the neuron gives a strong response. When the response is above 50% of the cell's maximum response, the Next trial button becomes activated. Before starting the next trial, increase the size of the filled circle to cover some of the red region as well. You will find that the electrical potential is smaller and there are fewer action potentials. When the stimulus covers all of the red and the green, you should find that the neuron does not respond to the stimulus any differently than it responds to a blank screen.

The receptive field types and their shapes are shown below. The simple and complex receptive fields have similar shapes, but the complex receptive field is actually more complex than can be drawn. A complex receptive field can respond to light on either side of its receptive field, but it does not respond well to light on both sides of its receptive field. A simple receptive field is sensitive to light on only one, fixed side.

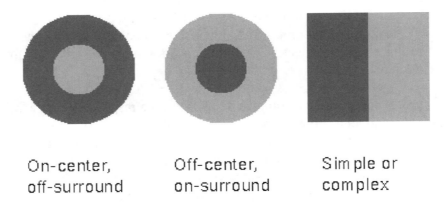

On-center,   Off-center,   Simple or
off-surround   on-surround   complex

The receptive field will be randomly located on the canvas drawing surface. Your task is to find its location and choose a stimulus shape and size that will get the neuron to respond strongly. Only then can you move on to the next trial. Each receptive field is presented once, in random order.

At the end of the experiment, you will be asked if you want to save your data to a set of global data. After you answer the question, a new Web page window will appear that lists your class averages for this experiment. On that page is also a link to your personal data.

Additional References

Schefrin, B., Hauser, M., & Werner, J. (2004). Evidence against age-related enlargements of ganglion cell receptive field centers under scotopic conditions. *Vision Research, 44*, 423-428.

Georgeson, M., & Scott-Samuel, N. (2000). Spatial resolution and receptive field height of motion sensors in human vision. *Vision Research, 40*, 745-758.

Wiesel, T., & Hubel, D. (1963). Single-cell responses in striate cortex of kittens deprived of vision in one eye. *Journal of Neurophysiology, 26*, 1002-1017.

Basic Questions

1. In this demonstration, which cell's receptive field was the most difficult to map? Does your data support your assessment? Why?

2. What physiological measure is used to identify a neuron's activation?

3. What shape of light induced high levels of activation for each of the following types of cells: on-center, off-surround cells, off-center, on-surround cells, simple cells, and complex cells?

Advanced Questions

1. What feature of an object or a picture would simple cells be useful in identifying?

2. When trying to find various constellations in the night sky, which type of receptive field would be most responsive?

3. Consider a white square on a black background. Where would you place an on-center, off-surround cell if trying to maximize its response activation?

Discussion Question

1. This demonstration showed that certain neurons in the visual system are sensitive to specific patterns of light. What stimulus properties might trigger responses in neurons related to other modalities (i.e., audition, smell, taste, and touch)?

Brain Asymmetry

Minimum time to complete this experiment: 10 minutes

Background

You may have heard that each person has two distinct hemispheres of the brain, each with different capabilities. For example, the sensory signals from the left side of your body are sent to the right hemisphere of your brain and the sensory signals from the right side of your body are sent to the left hemisphere of your brain. Likewise, control of your right arm and leg is via your left hemisphere and control of your left arm and leg is via your right hemisphere. More notable cognitive differences also exist.

The left hemisphere is said to deal with language and analytical thought, while the right hemisphere is said to deal with spatial relations and creativity. The basis for these claims about cognition comes from investigations of clinical patients who, usually to control a serious case of epilepsy, underwent surgery that separated their left and right hemispheres. (This surgery prevented epileptic seizures from passing from one hemisphere to the other.) Careful studies of these split-brain patients revealed fascinating properties about how the brain is organized. A patient asked to fix on a spot on a screen could verbally report words flashed on the right side of the screen. (Those words were sent to the left hemisphere.) The patient could not say the word if it was flashed on the left side of the screen (thus sent to the right hemisphere). Notably, the patient could identify, by picking up with the left hand, a physical item matching a word flashed on the left side of the screen.

Subsequent work showed a variety of differences between the brain hemispheres, and some researchers concluded that even people without split brains effectively have two competing brains. These conclusions were picked up by the popular press, and one now sees a variety of claims that schools should nurture one brain side instead of another, or that different types of therapy should be used to strengthen an undeveloped hemisphere.

Some of these claims appear in very odd places. For example, unrelated research suggests that Mozart's music stimulates creativity and intelligence in children. One CD jacket claims that Mozart's music stimulates the left brain to improve logical skills. It suggests positioning the speakers on the child's right side (presumably so the sound goes to the left brain). It is nice music and may help improve logical skills, but the left brain/right brain difference does not necessarily have anything to do with it. Moreover, sound will go in both ears and reach both hemispheres, so positioning the speakers on one side versus another cannot possibly make much difference.

As it turns out, many experiments fail to find much difference at all between the two hemispheres in normals (individuals without split-brain surgery). This is not to suggest that there are no differences, but the functional significance of these differences may be very slight. Moreover, when such differences do exist, they tend to be strongest for right-handed males. Females and left-handed individuals tend to not show brain-side effects nearly as well.

This experiment uses a technique devised by Levy, Heller, Banich, & Burton (1983) (also see Rueckert, 2005) for demonstrating differences between the hemispheres of a normal subject's brain. The stimuli involve chimeric faces. A chimeric face is made by taking two different faces, dividing them in half, and combining the left side of one face with the right side of the other face to make a combined, chimeric, face.

The subject then views two such chimeric faces and must decide which one more strongly demonstrates a particular quality (e.g., happiness, age, attractiveness). If the chimeric faces are constructed so that the two halves differ in the quality of the rated characteristic and so that the information goes to different brain hemispheres, then the choices made by subjects should show a bias toward information that goes to the right hemisphere, which seems to be more involved than the left hemisphere in making judgments about faces.

Significantly, the expected effect should be weaker for left-handed people than for right-handed people because the former show fewer differences between the left and right hemispheres.

Instructions

1. In the text fields below, enter your CogLab log-in ID and password. If you do not have a log-in ID and password, see your instructor for information on how to get one for your class.
2. Click the Submit information button.
3. If the information is correct, the Start experiment button will become activated. Click the button to begin the experiment.

A small window will appear that asks you to indicate whether you are right-handed or left-handed. There are several definitions of handedness, but you might report which hand you typically use to write. After answering the handedness question, a window will appear that fills nearly the entire screen, and a smaller window will appear with abbreviated instructions. Close the instructions window. You can open it again later from the CogLab Info. menu.

Click on the space bar to start a trial. Two chimeric faces will appear. Choose the face that seems youngest. To indicate that the chimeric face on the top appears younger, press the *i* key. Press the *k* key to indicate that the chimeric face on the bottom appears younger. With your keypress, a green box will be drawn around the selected chimeric face. This indicates that the computer noted your choice. You can change your choice if you wish.

You will not receive feedback on whether you were correct in your choice. Indeed, there are no absolutely correct or incorrect answers. Simply report what seems correct to you. After you are satisfied with your choice, press the space bar for the next trial.

At the end of the experiment, you will be asked if you want to save your data to a set of global data. After you answer the question, a new Web page window will appear that lists your class averages for this experiment. On that page is also a link to your personal data.

References

Rueckert, L. (2005). A web-based study of cerebral asymmetry for perception of emotion. *Behavior Research Methods, 37 (2),* 271-276.

Kanwisher, N., McDermott, J., & Chun, M. (1997). The fusiform face area: A module in human extrastriate cortex specialized for face perception. *The Journal of Neuroscience, 17 (11),* 4302-4311.

Levy. J., Heller, W., Banich, M., & Burton, L. (1983). Asymmetry of perception in free viewing of chimeric faces. *Brain & Cognition, 2,* 404-419.

Gazzaniga, M. S., Bogen, J. E., & Sperry, R. W. (1965). Observations on visual perception after disconnection of the cerebral hemispheres in man. *Brain, 88,* Part 2, 221-236.

Basic Questions

1. Does your data provide evidence that you have an asymmetric brain? Explain your answer. Do the same for the global results.

2. Describe another experiment that would test for brain asymmetry. It should be different from this experiment and the split-brain language experiment already described.

3. What skills/processes are primarily associated with the left hemisphere? What about the right hemisphere?

Advanced Questions

1. What types of professions might benefit from using what we know about brain asymmetry?

2. Describe a task that might be more difficult for a split-brain patient than a normal individual.

3. The interpretation of the experimental results relies on a comparison between the data from right-handed participants as well as left-handed participants. Why is this the case?

Discussion Question

1. Why might it be advantageous for us to have a brain in which some processes are specific to one hemisphere?

Change Detection

Minimum time to complete this experiment: 15 minutes

Background

In this demonstration, the picture on the right shows a street in Vancouver, Canada, alternating with a light gray background. (The picture changes and so cannot be printed in this manual. Please go to the CogLab web site to see this picture.) There are actually two different photographs of the road. Can you spot what is changing?

Chances are, you don't see anything changing right away, and it should take you a while to spot the change. Once you know what to look for, however, the change is obvious. (The answer is at the bottom of the page.)

The picture illustrates change detection (Rensink, 2002) or, more accurately, how difficult it can be to detect change. The basic idea is that people do not store many details of a scene in memory. Rather, the critical factor seems to be attention: In order to see an object change, it is necessary to attend to the object.

The animated image illustrates Rensink's flicker paradigm in which an original image is followed by a blank image (a mask) and is then followed by a changed image (and another mask). The blank image swamps the local-motion signal that would ordinarily be caused by a change in an object, so attention is not drawn to the change. The presence of the mask prevents automatic detection of change. Change must now be detected by a slower, higher-level process. Basically, you have to search the scene, object by object, until you happen to find the changed object.

Failing to detect that an object has changed has been called change blindness. Researchers think that change blindness is a leading cause of many car accidents. Glancing away from the road and then back is equivalent to seeing a scene, followed by a blank field, followed by a changed scene: The change is very difficult to notice, so your car hits another car.

Instructions

1. In the text fields below, enter your CogLab log-in ID and password. If you do not have a log-in ID and password, see your instructor for information on how to get one for your class.
2. Click the Submit information button.
3. If the information is correct, the Start experiment button will become activated. Click the button to begin the experiment.

A window will appear that fills nearly the entire screen, and a smaller window will appear with abbreviated instructions. Close the instructions window. You can open it again later from the CogLab Info. menu.

Press the space bar key to start a trial. You will see a message that the images are being loaded. Depending on the speed of your Internet connection, this may take 10-30 seconds. You will then see two pictures alternating. Sometimes the pictures will be separated by a gray field; sometimes they won't. Your task is to decide if anything is changing between the two versions of the picture. If something is changing, press the *c* key. If nothing is changing, press the *n* key. You should try to respond as quickly and as accurately as you can.

There are 16 trials, half with a change and half without a change, and half with flicker (the gray field) and half without.

At the end of the experiment, you will be asked if you want to save your data to a set of global data. After you answer the question, a new Web page window will appear that lists your class averages for this experiment. On that page is also a link to your personal data.

Additional References

Eimer, M., & Mazza, V. (2005). Electrophysiological correlates of change detection. *Psychophysiology, 42*, 328-342.

Cole, G., Kentridge, R., Gellatly, A., & Heywood, C. (2003). Detectability of onsets versus offsets in the change detection paradigm. *Journal of Vision, 3*, 22-31.

Simons, D. (2000). Current approaches to change blindness. *Visual Cognition, 7*, 1-15.

Basic Questions

1. Was it harder for you to detect a scene change in the trials with or without a flicker between photographs? Does your data support your evaluation? Explain.

2. What effect does the flicker have on attention?

3. What type of search strategy is commonly used in the no-flicker condition? What type of search strategy is commonly used in the flicker condition?

Advanced Questions

1. Why is reaction-time reported with your experimental results, instead of just reporting your percent correct?

2. Which condition of the demonstration is equivalent to the following driving situations: looking down to turn the radio station, picking up your cell phone, or checking your speedometer? What types of problems can arise from these behaviors?

3. The flash used in the flicker condition is also used to divert or attract your attention in many experiences you have probably had. Describe an experience you have had that utilized a flash. What was the effect of the flash?

Discussion Question

1. Identify and describe at least two factors that will determine one's ability to detect a change in a scene?

Apparent Motion

Minimum time to complete this experiment: 15 minutes

Background

If two stimuli are briefly flashed in rapid succession, observers will sometimes report seeing motion between the two stimuli. Reports of this type of apparent motion were investigated near the beginning of the 20th century by Gestalt psychologists (most notably Wertheimer). They noticed, among other things, that the timing of the flashes was important in determining whether or not motion was seen. If the time between the offset of the first stimulus and the onset of the second stimulus (called the interstimulus interval or ISI) is very short, observers simply see two dots presented nearly simultaneously. If the ISI is very long, observers see one dot flash on and off and then the other flash on and off. For intermediate ISIs, the first dot seems to turn off, move through the space between the dots, and appear at the position of the second dot.

Korte (1915) noted that the ISI thresholds for seeing motion versus being too short varied with the spatial separation of the stimuli. The farther apart the stimuli were, the longer the ISI needed to be for a good motion percept. These findings, and others, were formulated in a set of "Korte's laws" that have been used to describe aspects of apparent motion.

Instructions

1. In the text fields below, enter your CogLab log-in ID and password. If you do not have a log-in ID and password, see your instructor for information on how to get one for your class.
2. Click the Submit information button.
3. If the information is correct, the Start experiment button will become activated. Click the button to begin the experiment.

A window will fill the entire screen, and a smaller window will appear with abbreviated instructions. Close the instructions window. You can open it again later from the CogLab Info. menu.

Press the space bar key to start a trial. After pressing the space bar, a small fixation square will appear in the middle of the screen. Stare at this square. It will disappear after one and a half seconds. Less than a second later, a dot will appear on the right and disappear, and then a dot will appear on the left and disappear. These stimuli will then cycle back and forth repeatedly. Each of the dots is presented for 150 milliseconds. The duration of the blank between dots (the ISI) is variable.

Your task is to adjust the ISI until the motion percept is as strong as you can make it. You can increase the ISI by 20 milliseconds by pressing the *i* key. You can decrease the ISI by 20 milliseconds by pressing the *k* key. The ISI can never become negative.

After you are satisfied that the motion percept is as strong as you can make it, press the space bar to start the next trial. The spacing of the dots will vary from trial to trial. There are five spacings and five replications for each spacing for a total of 25 trials.

At the end of the experiment, you will be asked if you want to save your data to a set of global data. After you answer the question, a new Web page window will appear that lists your class averages for this experiment. On that page is also a link to your personal data.

Additional References

Muckli, L., Kiregeskorte, N., Lanfermann, H., Zanella, F., Singer, W., & Goebel, R. (2002). Apparent motion: Event-related functional magnetic resonance imaging of perceptual switches and states. *Journal of Neuroscience, 22*, 3342-3444.

Koriat, A. (1994). Object-based apparent motion. *Perception & Psychophysics, 56*, 392-404.

Anstis, S., Giaschi, D., & Cogan, A. (1985). Adaptation to apparent motion. *Vision Research, 25*, 1051-1062.

Basic Questions

1. What is an ISI? How does it relate to apparent motion?

2. Using your personal data, which dot distance did you assign the shortest ISI? Which distance did you assign the longest ISI? Describe the relationships between the dot distances and the ISIs you assigned (linear, exponential, logarithmic, etc.).

3. What does one experience when an ISI is too slow? What does one experience when an ISI is too fast?

Advanced Questions

1. Using your personal data, what would you predict your optimal ISI to be if the flashing dots had a distance from the center of .40? Make a prediction for the group data as well.

2. Name two things that use apparent motion that are not already mentioned in the text.

3. Apparent motion is dependent on factors other than ISI. Describe the various factors that would affect one's ability to perceive apparent motion. For each factor you identify, describe a situation in which it would facilitate apparent motion perception and one in which it would impair apparent motion perception.

Discussion Question

1. Describe some of the properties and/or limitations of the visual system that are consistent with the finding that apparent motion is often perceived in the same way as real motion.

Blind Spot

Minimum time to complete this experiment: 35 minutes

Background

Your eyes contain a dense set of receptors that are sensitive to light energy. These receptors convert light energy into electrical energy, which eventually is transferred to your nervous system and your brain. These receptors, however, are not distributed evenly across your eye. There is a central location, called the fovea, where the receptors are very densely packed. Generally, when you stare at an object you are arranging your eyes so that the object's image falls on the foveae of your eyes. There are fewer receptors outside the fovea. In fact, in some places there are no receptors at all.

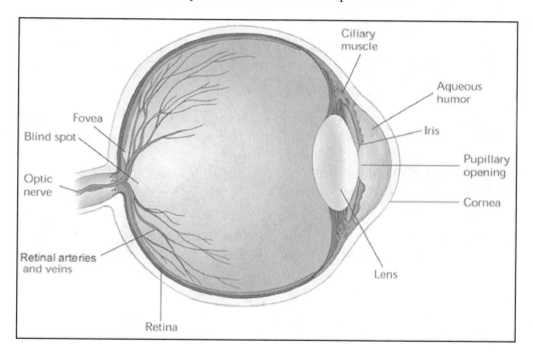

There is a place in each eye where the optic nerve exits the back of the eye to send information to the brain. This hole is called the optic disk. It contains no light-sensitive receptors. As a result, any light that falls on this part of the eye is undetected and invisible to you. Functionally, this location in the eye is called the blind spot.

You probably have never noticed your blind spots (one in each eye). There are several reasons for this. First, each blind spot is far away from its eye's fovea. Because the fovea is typically where you are "looking," you would not generally notice that something has disappeared into a blind spot. Second, when you view the world with two eyes, one eye can compensate for the other eye's blind spot. Light that falls into the blind spot of one eye generally does not fall on the blind spot of the other eye. Third, your brain only processes the presence of information, not the absence. Your brain does not notice a hole in the information it receives from the eye. It simply works with the information it receives. In a similar way, the brain does not observe that we are unable to view ultraviolet light. It has no knowledge about missing information.

With the proper experiment, however, it is possible to identify and map the blind spot, which is the purpose of this experiment. You probably will be surprised at how large the blind spot is. It covers a large part of your visual field. The experiment used here is similar to a test used by eye doctors to identify visual scotomas (damaged spots in the retina of your eye). Should you consistently find holes in your data other than the blind spot, you may want to see an eye doctor.

Instructions

1. In the text fields below, enter your CogLab log-in ID and password. If you do not have a log-in ID and password, see your instructor for information on how to get one for your class.
2. Click the Submit information button.
3. If the information is correct, the Start experiment button will become activated. Click the button to begin the experiment.

A window will fill the entire screen, and a smaller window will appear with abbreviated instructions. Close the instructions window. You can open it again later from the CogLab Info. menu.

A small blue fixation square will appear on the far left of the screen. The experiment is designed to map the blind spot of your right eye. Close your left eye or cover it with your hand or a patch. Fix on the small square with your right eye. Try to sit so that your head is centered directly in front of the fixation square. Press the space bar key to start a trial. A white dot will appear somewhere on the screen. Simultaneously, the fixation point will turn green. Your task is to report whether or not you see the dot, all while keeping your right eye fixed on the fixation square.

If you see the dot, press the *m* key. If you do not see the dot, press the *n* key. Either of the keys you press will produce written feedback at the location of the fixation point. This is simply to indicate that the computer received your response. If the response is not what you intended (e.g., you pressed *m* when you meant to press *n*), just press the intended key. The computer will keep your last response as the response for that trial. Do not move your eye from the fixation square when you make this judgment. Press the space bar key to start the next trial when you are ready.

There are a total of 300 trials. That may sound like a lot, but each trial takes only a couple of seconds. You can take a break if you wish, but try to stay seated in the same position when you resume the experiment. If you move around, your blind spot will move with you and the data will be a mix of the two positions you take. Also, be careful to make accurate judgments of whether you see or do not see the dot. If you try to go too fast, the computer will warn you to slow down. Most importantly, keep your right eye fixed on the small blue square. If you move your eye around, be sure to go back to the fixation square before making your judgment about seeing or not seeing a dot.

At the end of the experiment, you will be asked if you want to save your data to a set of global data. After you answer the question, a new Web page window will appear that lists your class averages for this experiment. On that page is also a link to your personal data.

The data themselves are given in two different formats. First, the experimental window will show a full array of dots colored green and red. These dots are in the locations you just viewed during the experiment. Any dot colored green is one that you reported as visible. Any dot colored red is one that you reported as not visible. You should find that there is a patch of red dots near the middle of the array. These are dots whose images fell on the blind spot of your eye. Its precise location varies a bit among observers and varies a lot depending on how far you are seated from the monitor. The same data is also presented in a new Web browser window as a data table. Here 1s and 0s are used to indicate seen and not seen dots in the array, respectively.

Additional References

Matsumoto, M., & Komatsu, H. (2005). Neural responses in the macaque V1 to bar stimuli with various lengths presented on the blind spot. *Journal of Neurophysiology, 93*, 2374-2387.

Kawabata, N. (1982). Visual information processing at the blind spot. *Perceptual and Motor Skills, 55*, 95-104.

Cumming, G., & Friend, H. (1980). Perception at the blind spot and tilt aftereffect. *Perception, 9*, 233-238.

Basic Questions

1. Describe the location of your blind spot identified by this demonstration. Was its location consistent with the global data?

2. What is the cause of your blind spot?

3. In this demonstration, what would affect the size of an individual's blind spot?

Advanced Questions

1. Why is it important to keep your left eye closed for this demonstration to work?

2. Could you change anything about the target stimulus to overcome your blind spot? Explain.

3. Describe a situation in which an individual might be susceptible to missing something in the environment because of their blind spot.

Discussion Question

1. Your blind spot typically goes unnoticed. Describe a few of the reasons why this is the case.

Metacontrast Masking

Minimum time to complete this experiment: 35 minutes

Background

Masking refers to a class of phenomena in which presentation of one stimulus (the mask) can impair performance on some task that requires judgment about another stimulus (the target). Visual masking plays two roles in cognitive science. First, masking is used to investigate properties of the visual system. By identifying the way in which the target and mask stimuli influence each other, vision scientists are able to deduce details about the underlying mechanisms involved in visual perception. Second, visual masking is used to indirectly restrict systems involved in information processing of visual stimuli.

The logic of this type of approach is that the mask can halt further processing of the target and one can thereby explore the order and time course of many information-processing systems. A special subset of this approach is based on evidence that people with various types of cognitive disorders may respond differently than normal people under some masking conditions. Thus, masking has been proposed as a simple method for detecting some disorders and as a means of specifying the underlying mechanisms for those disorders.

Both the target and mask stimuli are usually very brief (often less than 200 milliseconds). Despite its short duration, if the target stimulus is presented by itself, it is clearly visible and it is easy for observers to perform whatever judgment is required of them. What is interesting is that the subsequent presentation of a mask stimulus, even a hundred milliseconds after the target has turned off, can make the observer's task of judging something about the target exceedingly difficult. When this effect was first noted by Stigler (1910), it forced the field of perceptual psychology to realize that the processing of visual information took time and could be interrupted. Backward masking has been used to identify details of the perceptual and cognitive processes involved in building percepts and judgments.

Metacontrast masking is a specific type of masking in which the target and mask have no overlapping contours and the mask follows the target in time. A surprising finding in studies of metacontrast masking is that when performance on some judgment about the target is plotted against the stimulus onset asynchrony (SOA) between the target and mask, the resulting curve is U-shaped. Performance is generally quite good when the mask immediately follows the target. Performance is also generally good for very long (greater than 200 milliseconds) SOAs. For SOAs between 60 and 100 milliseconds, however, performance is often quite poor. Some observers even report that they do not see the target at all.

The effect of the mask on the target sometimes gets stronger as the target and mask are separated in time, which is contrary to many simple models of visual perception. Investigations of the U-shaped metacontrast masking function are numerous and have identified a variety of characteristics about the visual system.

Instructions

1. In the text fields below, enter your CogLab log-in ID and password. If you do not have a log-in ID and password, see your instructor for information on how to get one for your class.
2. Click the Submit information button.
3. If the information is correct, the Start experiment button will become activated. Click the button to begin the experiment.

A window will appear that fills nearly the entire screen, and a smaller window will appear with abbreviated instructions. Close the instructions window. You can open it again later from the CogLab Info. menu.

Click on the space bar to start a trial. A small fixation square will appear in the middle of the screen. Fix on this square. Half a second later, four rectangles will appear at the corners of an imaginary square around the fixation point. Three of the rectangles will be squares, while one will be a bit thinner than a square. The rectangles will be shown for only 30 milliseconds. In addition, a box will be drawn around each of the rectangles. The boxes will also be shown for 30 milliseconds. The timing between the rectangles and boxes varies from trial to trial. It is characterized by the stimulus onset asynchrony (SOA). This is the time between the onset of the target (rectangles) and the mask (boxes). When SOA equals zero, the rectangles and boxes will appear together. On other trials, the boxes will obviously follow the rectangles.

Your task is always the same: Report the location of the thin rectangle. Make your selection by a key-press to indicate the location. Press the *u* key to indicate the top-left position. Press the *i* key to indicate the top-right location. Press the *k* key to indicate the bottom-right location. Press the *j* key to indicate the bottom-left position. With each key-press, a rectangle will appear that corresponds to the selection you are making. You can change your choice by pressing another key. When you are satisfied with your choice, press the space bar key to start the next trial. Before the next trial begins, you will be given feedback on whether your choice was correct. You will notice an error when the rectangle corresponding to your choice changes to the actual location.

There are seven SOAs, and 30 trials for each SOA. This makes a total of 210 trials. That may sound like a lot, but each trial only takes a few seconds, so the entire experiment will not take very long. Moreover, you can take a break between trials if needed. There may be some trials in which the rectangles do not seem to appear at all. Likewise, there may be trials in which you have absolutely no idea where the thin rectangle is located. On such trials, guess the location. Do not be concerned if you often have to guess.

At the end of the experiment, you will be asked if you want to save your data to a set of global data. After you answer the question, a new Web page window will appear that lists your class averages for this experiment. On that page is also a link to your personal data.

Additional References

Francis, G., Rothmayer, M., & Hermens, F. (2004). Analysis and test of laws for backward (metacontrast) masking. *Spatial Vision, 17*, 163-185.

Kondo, H., & Komatsu, H. (2000). Suppression on neuronal responses by a metacontrast masking stimulus in monkey V4. *Neuroscience Research, 36*, 27-33.

Francis, G. (2000). Quantitative theories of metacontrast masking. *Psychological Review, 107*, 768-785.

Lachter, J., & Durgin, F. (1999). Metacontrast masking functions: A question of speed? *Journal of Experimental Psychology: Human Perception and Performance, 25*, 936-947.

Basic Questions

1. What is SOA?

2. Using your data, at what SOA was your performance the best? At what SOA was your performance the worst? Are your results consistent with the typical findings of a metacontrast masking experiment? Explain.

3. What do the findings of masking experiments tell us about visual perception?

Advanced Questions

1. Using your data, at what SOA would your performance be near perfect? Do the same for the group data.

2. In this demonstration, if you identified the thin rectangle correctly 25% of the time is your performance above random guessing, below random guessing, or equal to random guessing? Explain.

3. This demonstration used a specific type of visual masking, but masking can also be utilized in other modalities. Describe a situation in which auditory masking is used or would be useful.

Discussion Question

1. Why is performance high at long and short SOAs and low at medium SOAs in metacontrast masking?

Muller-Lyer Illusion

Minimum time to complete this experiment: 25 minutes

Background

This experiment serves two purposes. First, it introduces a well-known perceptual illusion called the Muller-Lyer illusion. Second, it demonstrates a psychophysical experimental method called the method of constant stimuli.

The Muller-Lyer illusion is easily demonstrated. There are three horizontal lines in the figure. Two of the lines contain a pair of wings. The wings are drawn outward or inward from the line ends. The illusion is that the line with the outward-drawn wings tends to look longer than the line with the inward-drawn wings. The line without wings tends to look smaller than the line with outward-drawn wings and bigger than the line with inward-drawn wings. It is an illusion because the lines are actually all the same length, which you can verify with a ruler.

This experiment is not directly about experiencing the illusion, which can be done just by looking at the figure, but is about using the illusion to demonstrate a common experimental technique: the method of constant stimuli.

It is fun to look at visual illusions and realize how our perceptions differ from reality. To guide the development of theories on cognition and perception, however, we need more-specific data. We need to know, for example, just how long does the line with the outward-drawn wings look? The more general question is, "How do we measure characteristics of percepts?" We cannot measure them directly because a perception is a particularly subjective experience.

The field of psychophysics deals with precisely this question. It attempts to relate reported characteristics of perception to physical properties. Instead of just asking an observer to look at and comment on stimuli, specific judgments are required and the stimuli are systematically varied. For the Muller-Lyer illusion, we will have observers compare the perception produced by a line with outward-drawn wings to the perception produced by lines with no wings. We will systematically vary the length of the line without wings to see when the perceived line lengths match. We can then look at the physical length of the matching line without wings and use that as a measure of the strength of the Muller-Lyer illusion. There are several ways to go about making such comparisons. One of the simplest and most powerful is the method of constant stimuli.

We will generate a large set of lines without wings of varying lengths and have the observer compare each one with a standard line with wings. For each comparison, the observer notes whether the line without wings is perceived to be bigger or smaller than the line with wings. Unlike some other psychophysical methods (such as the method of adjustment), the stimuli are not changeable by the observer, thus they are constant stimuli. The observer's task is just to report on the perception.

The goal of this type of experiment is to produce a psychometric function, that is, a set of values that describes the probability of a certain response as a physical characteristic is varied. For the Muller-Lyer experiments, we will find the proportion of reports in which the line without wings seemed bigger than the standard as a function of the physical length of the line without wings. With such a curve, you can often identify critical values, such as the point of subjective equality, where the line without wings seemed to be the same size as the line with wings (e.g., 50% of the time it is described as bigger and 50% of the time is described as smaller).

Instructions

1. In the text fields below, enter your CogLab log-in ID and password. If you do not have a log-in ID and password, see your instructor for information on how to get one for your class.
2. Click the Submit information button.
3. If the information is correct, the Start experiment button will become activated. Click the button to begin the experiment.

A window will appear that fills nearly the entire screen, and a smaller window will appear with abbreviated instructions. Close the instructions window. You can open it again later from the CogLab Info. menu.

Press the space bar key to start a trial. After pressing the space bar, two vertical lines will appear. The line on the lower right has outward-drawn wings. The line on the upper left has no wings. Your task is to choose which vertical line is longer. Press the z key if the line on the left seems longer. Press the / key if the vertical line on the right appears longer. A box will be drawn around your selection. You can change your response if you wish. When you are satisfied with your response, press the space bar key to start the next trial.

There are a total of 150 trials. Each trial only takes a few seconds to complete. Do not go too fast though, or the computer will tell you to slow down and take time to make an accurate judgment of relative line lengths.

At the end of the experiment, you will be asked if you want to save your data to a set of global data. After you answer the question, a new Web page window will appear that lists your class averages for this experiment. On that page is also a link to your personal data.

Additional References

Predebon, J. (2005). A comparison of length-matching and length-fractionation measures of Muller-Lyer distortions. *Perception & Psychophysics, 67*, 264-273.

Welch, R., Post, R., Lum, W., & Prinzmetal, W. (2004). The relationship between perceived length and egocentric location in Muller-Lyer figures with one versus two chevrons. *Perception & Psychophysics, 66*, 1095-1104.

Morikawa, K. (2003). An application of the Muller-Lyer illusion. *Perception, 32*, 121-123.

Brosvic, G., Dihoff, R., & Fama, J. (2002). Age-related susceptibility to the Muller-Lyer and the horizontal-vertical illusions. *Perceptual and Motor Skills, 94*, 229-234.

Basic Questions

1. How difficult did you find this task? How accurate do you think you were in this task? Looking at your individual data, do your results support the feelings you had about your performance? Explain.

2. When the line without wings and the line with wings were the same size, how often did you report the line without wings as being bigger?

3. What is the method of constant stimuli? How is it different from other psychophysical methods?

Advanced Questions

1. Describe what your data would look like if you suppose that the wings of the comparison line were drawn inward instead of outward in this demonstration.

2. In this demonstration, the method of constant stimuli was used to measure the effect of a particular type of illusion. What else could this method be used to measure?

3. Compare your data with the global data. Did you show more or less of an illusory effect than the average participant? (Use an objective means of comparison.) Explain how you came to your conclusion.

Discussion Question

1. Experience teaches us to expect certain perceptual relationships among stimuli. Illusions often take advantage of these expectations. Think of an everyday situation that could partly explain the Muller-Lyer illusion.

Signal Detection

Minimum time to complete this experiment: 15 minutes

Background

Much of cognitive psychology involves gathering data from experimental participants. Gathering good data is not always easy, especially when one uses a variety of people as participants. Researchers often must design an experiment carefully to be certain that participants are following the instructions and are motivated to try their best. Even despite these efforts, experimental results can be contaminated by individual differences if the researcher does not properly analyze the data.

For example, consider two participants in visual detection of a faint target. The researcher wants to explore a property of the visual system, so he/she presents a visual stimulus and asks the participants to report whether they saw the target. After 50 trials, participant A reports seeing the target 25 times and participant B reports detection 17 times. Did participant A do better? Not necessarily. Perhaps participant A is simply more prone to report seeing the target and participant B is more conservative. That is, the two participants may have equivalent visual systems, but differences in reporting. Reports of simple detection do not allow the researcher to compare participants' results.

A better experiment is a modification of the one above. Have two kinds of trials, one with the target present and one with the target absent. Again have subjects report whether they saw the target. There are four statistics to be calculated from this experiment. Trials in which participants correctly detects the target are called hits. The trials in which the target was there but participants did not detect it are called misses. If a participant reports seeing the target when it was not actually there, he/she has made a mistake (false alarm). A trial in which the participant correctly reports that the target was not present is a correct rejection.

Suppose that after 100 trials (50 for target present and 50 for target absent) the researcher again finds that on the trials in which the target was in fact present, participant A reports seeing it 25 times and participant B 17 times. Who is doing better? It depends on the frequency of false alarms. If participant A has 25 false alarms and participant B has 5 false alarms, then B is better than A at distinguishing the trials in which the target is present from the trials in which the target is absent. That is, in this case, A seems to often guess that the target is there, but he/she is wrong (false alarm) as often as right (hit). B is more selective about saying he/she detects the target, but rarely says the target is there when it is not. Thus, B is doing better.

This type of analysis suggests that you need to consider two numbers, hits and false alarms, to really be able to compare performance across subjects. Fortunately, you can combine the numbers in a careful way to produce a single number that gives an indication of the sensitivity of the participant to the presence of the target. The calculation is structured so that, with certain assumptions, it will not matter whether a participant takes a conservative or liberal approach to claiming to detect the target. There are two measures of sensitivity that are often used. One is called d' (d-prime) and is based on signal detection theory. The other is called log(alpha) and is based on choice theory. For most situations, the two measures give very similar results, although there are quantitative differences.

A discussion of the algorithms for calculating sensitivity is beyond the scope of this experiment [see Macmillan & Creelman, (1991) for further discussion]. Instead, you will participate in an experiment that measures sensitivity.

Instructions

1. In the text fields below, enter your CogLab log-in ID and password. If you do not have a log-in ID and password, see your instructor for information on how to get one for your class.
2. Click the Submit information button.
3. If the information is correct, the Start experiment button will become activated. Click the button to begin the experiment.

A window will appear that fills nearly the entire screen, and a smaller window will appear with abbreviated instructions. Close the instructions window. You can open it again later from the CogLab Info. menu.

Press the space bar to start a trial. A group of randomly placed dots (sort of like a star field) will appear. The number of random dots varies from trial to trial. Also, on some trials (target present) an additional set of ten dots arranged in a straight line that slants downward from left to right is randomly placed within the dot field. On the other trials (target absent), the line is not included. Your task is to report whether the target is present or absent.

If you think the target is present, press the / key. If you think the target is not present, press the z key. You will be given feedback on whether you were correct. In addition, on the trials in which the target was actually present, a green line will connect the target dots after you make your decision. Look for the dots along this line so you will learn what the target looks like but the target will be randomly placed on the screen from trial to trial. There are a total of 60 trials, 20 trials for each number of random dots. Half of the trials have the target present, while the target is absent in the other half of the trials.

At the end of the experiment, you will be asked if you want to save your data to a set of global data. After you answer the question, a new Web page window will appear that lists your class averages for this experiment. On that page is also a link to your personal data.

Additional References

Santhi, N., & Reeves, A. (2004). The roles of distractor noise and target certainty in search: A signal detection model. *Vision Research, 44*, 1235-1256.

Maylor, E., & Rabbitt, P. (1987). Effect of alcohol on rate of forgetting. *Psychopharmacology, 91*, 230-235.

Kerkhof, G., & Uhlenbroek, J. (1981). P3 latency in threshold signal detection. *Biological Psychology, 13*, 89-105.

Basic Questions

1. Define the following terms in relation to signal detection theory: hit, miss, false alarm, and correct rejection.

2. Compare your individual sensitivity measures for each of the three conditions with those of the global average? Are your sensitivity measures higher or lower than the global average? What does this mean?

3. If an individual's hit rate is .79 and his/her correct rejection rate is .71, what is his/her miss rate and his/her false alarm rate?

Advanced Questions

1. While going over some experimental results from a signal detection study, you notice an individual's hit rate is .98. What does this tell you about his/her sensitivity measure?

2. Signal detection theory assumes that a signal is always accompanied by a certain amount of noise. Identify at least two sources of noise for the detection of an audio signal.

3. Name at least three jobs that must accurately detect signals to effectively do the job. This means that signal detection methods could be used to evaluate performance.

Discussion Question

1. The C statistic is also known as the response criterion. This is the amount of evidence an individual requires to make a target-present response. What does a negative C statistic mean? What does a positive C statistic mean? What factors can influence someone's response criterion?

Visual Search

Minimum time to complete this experiment: 20 minutes

Background

This experiment explores aspects of attention in a visual-search task. It is a classic experiment that makes strikingly clear the time needed to bring attention to bear on different regions of visual space. The basic idea is to ask a participant to search a visual image for a particular item and to respond as quickly as possible once they find the item, or to respond as quickly as possible when they are certain the item is not in the image. This type of experiment was used to develop a popular theory of attention (Treisman & Gelade, 1980).

Searches are divided into two types, those that require selective use of attention and those that do not. In the latter, the target item seems to pop out of the display and the participant can respond quickly. Notably, this pop out effect allows the participant to respond quickly even when the number of other (distractor) items is increased. In the other type of display, it seems as though the participant is forced to study each item individually until the target item is found. In these cases, the target item does not pop out and search time increases with the number of distractor items. Controlling whether or not attention is needed is accomplished by the types of target and distractor items.

In this experiment, the target is always a green circle. For the feature condition, the distractors are always blue squares. As you will see, the green circle seems to pop out of the image to quickly identify the location of the target. To require attention, the distractor items are made more complex. Some of the distractors are green squares while others are blue circles. Because some of the distractors are green, the green target circle no longer pops out and the participant must search through all of the items to find the one that is both green and a circle. This type of search is called a conjunctive search because the target is a conjunction of features in the distractors.

Instructions

1. In the text fields below, enter your CogLab log-in ID and password. If you do not have a log-in ID and password, see your instructor for information on how to get one for your class.
2. Click the Submit information button.

3. If the information is correct, the Start experiment button will become activated. Click the button to begin the experiment.

A window will appear that fills nearly the entire screen, and a smaller window will appear with abbreviated instructions. Close the instructions window. You can open it again later from the CogLab Info. menu.

Press the space bar to start the first trial. A fixation dot will appear in the middle of the window. Stare at it. A short time later (less than a second), circles and squares of various colors will appear on the screen. Your task is to determine if there is a green circle among the shapes. When you see a green circle, press the / key on your keyboard as quickly as possible. When you are certain there is not a green circle in the window, press the z key on your keyboard, again as quickly as possible.

After pressing the z or / key, press the space bar to start the next trial. If you wish, before pressing the space bar, but after pressing the z or / key, you can check how many trials remain for the current experiment with the pull-down menu.

The feature and conjunctive trials consist of approximately 48 trials each. If you make a mistake (e.g., say "Present" when you should have said "Absent"), that trial is repeated later in the experiment, so you may actually run more than 48 trials. You can also discard a trial by pressing the t key instead of z or /. Discarding is appropriate if, after starting a trial, you sneeze, zone out, or are otherwise distracted. Discarded trials will be repeated later.

In every trial, your goal is simply to determine if a green circle is present. If it is press /, if it is not press z. If you are frequently incorrect (feedback is given when you are incorrect), try to delay your response until you are more certain that you are correct.

At the end of the experiment, you will be asked if you want to save your data to a set of global data. After you answer the question, a new Web page window will appear that lists your class averages for this experiment. On that page is also a link to your personal data.

Additional References

Herd, S., & O'Reilly, R. (2005). Serial visual search from a parallel model. *Vision Research, 45*, 2987-2992.

Bichot, N., Rossi, A. & Desimone, R. (2005). Parallel and serial neural mechanisms for visual search in macaque area V4. *Science, 308*, 529-534.

Wolfe, J. (1994). Guided search 2.0: A revised model of visual search. *Psychonomic Bulletin & Review, 1*, 202-238.

Wolfe, J., Cave, K., & Franzel, S. (1989). Guided search: An alternative to the feature integration model for visual search. *Journal of Experimental Psychology: Human Perception and Performance, 15*, 419-433.

Basic Questions

1. Did you find the feature search or the conjunctive search to be more difficult? Why?

2. A common observation within visual-search tasks, such as the one in this demonstration, is that the conjunctive absent condition takes about twice as long as the conjunctive present condition. Why would this be the case?

3. Why does increasing the number of distractors typically slow reaction-times in a conjunctive search but not in a feature search?

Advanced Questions

1. Identify two products/items in which applying the concepts of visual search would be useful.

2. Visual search is a process we use many times throughout the day. Go back through your day and identify a few of the instances in which you had to employ a visual search process.

3. For each of the instances you identified in advanced question two, identify the features of your target and categorize them as unique to the target or shared by the distractors. How many distractors were there? How long did your search take and was this search time consistent or inconsistent with the predictions of visual search?

Discussion Question

1. What role does attention play in visual search?

Garner Interference

Minimum time to complete this experiment: 25 minutes

Background

In many perceptual tasks, people are asked to judge a stimulus on one dimension. For example, they might be asked to indicate whether the stimulus is light or dark (varies in terms of brightness). We can measure how quickly and accurately people make these decisions.

Sometimes, people are asked to make a decision, but the stimulus also varies along a second dimension. For example, the subject might be asked to judge the brightness of the stimulus (light or dark), but the stimulus might also vary in size. The size of the stimulus is irrelevant, only the brightness matters. In this type of situation, researchers are interested in whether the variation along the irrelevant dimension causes interference (i.e., a decrease in speed of responding and accuracy).

According to Garner (1974), some dimensions are separable (i.e., no interference), whereas others are integral (i.e., there is interference). As the names suggest, people seem capable of processing two separable dimensions as two dimensions; however, people seem to process two integral dimensions as one dimension, hence the interference.

In this experiment, you are asked to judge either the brightness (light or dark) or size (big or small) of a stimulus. In addition, the stimulus sometimes varies in saturation (how colorful the stimulus is, relative to plain gray). The computer will measure the time needed for you to make the judgment. Try to be as fast as possible, but do not go so fast that you make a lot of mistakes.

The experiment is broken in to several parts. In some parts, referred to later as a baseline condition, the stimulus is only one saturation, either high or low (the stimulus looks less or more gray). In other parts, called the correlated conditions, the stimulus can have high or low saturation. How it varies always matches with your task (to judge either the brightness or size of the stimulus). Thus, a high-saturated stimulus might always be small and a low-saturated stimulus might always be large. In the last condition, called the filtering condition, the stimulus varies in saturation, but can be paired with either other trait of the stimulus.

If the relevant and irrelevant stimulus dimensions are separable, the visual system represents them independently. As a result, it will be fairly easy to focus your attention on just the dimension that matters for the judgment. The saturation of the stimulus should not interfere. The reaction-time and percentage of correct judgments should not vary much across the different conditions.

In contrast, if the relevant and irrelevant stimulus dimensions are integral, the visual system represents them together. As a result, it will be difficult to focus your attention on just the dimension that matters for the judgment. In the version of the experiment with integral dimensions, the time needed to make the judgment (and possibly the accuracy of the judgment) will depend on the condition of the experiment. The reaction-time should be shortest (and accuracy highest) for the correlated condition. In this condition, you could pay attention to either dimension and know how to respond. The reaction-time might be a bit longer for the baseline condition because only the relevant dimension gives you the information you need. The other dimension does not help or hurt because it is always the same.

The slowest reaction-time (and poorest percentage correct) should be found for the filtering condition in which both dimensions are randomly paired together. Because the dimensions are integrally related, it is difficult to focus on one and ignore the other. This should make the task more difficult and lead to a longer reaction-time (or poorer percentage correct). The increase in reaction-time for the filtering condition relative to the baseline condition is called Garner Interference.

Instructions

1. In the text fields below, enter your CogLab log-in ID and password. If you do not have a log-in ID and password, see your instructor for information on how to get one for your class.
2. Click the Submit information button.
3. If the information is correct, the Start experiment button will become activated. Click the button to begin the experiment.

You will be randomly assigned to either the integral or separable version of the experiment. A window will appear that fills nearly the entire screen, and a smaller window will appear with abbreviated instructions. Read these instructions carefully, because they vary depending on which version of the experiment you are assigned. Close the instructions window. You can open it again later from the CogLab Info. menu.

Click on the space bar to start a trial. A reminder of which keys to press will appear at the top of the window. This is always the same. Less than a second later, the target stimulus will appear. Depending on the version of the experiment, your task is to judge either the size or brightness of the stimulus.

You want to respond as fast as possible, so keep your fingers over the response keys. After you respond, you will be given feedback on whether you judged correctly or incorrectly. If you find you are making many mistakes, you should slow down.

At the end of the experiment, you will be asked if you want to save your data to a set of global data. After you answer the question, a new Web page window will appear that lists your class averages for this experiment. On that page is also a link to your personal data.

Additional References

Patching, G., & Quinlan, P. (2002). Garner and congruence effects in the speeded classification of bimodal signals. *Journal of Experimental Psychology: Human Perception and Performance, 28,* 755-775.

Huettel, S., & Lockhead, G. (1999). Range effects of an irrelevant dimension on classification. *Perception & Psychophysics, 61,* 1624-1645.

Melara, R. (1989). Dimensional interaction between color and pitch. *Journal of Experimental Psychology: Human Perception and Performance, 15,* 69-79.

Basic Questions

1. Which version of the experiment did you complete (integral, separable)? Did you find some trials were more difficult than others?

2. Look at the global data for the integral version of the experiment. Using what you know about Garner Interference, do the data follow the predicted pattern? Explain your answer.

3. According to the ideas presented on Garner Interference, what determines whether two stimulus dimensions are integral or separable?

Advanced Questions

1. Using your trial-by-trial data, compute your standard deviation for the baseline and filtering conditions.

2. Considering the global data for the integral version, does the proportion-of-correct measure seem to support or contradict the reaction-time measure for each of the conditions? Why or why not?

3. You are planning on painting your living room, so you go to the local hardware store to buy some paint. You want a color that gives you a perception of a specific kind of blue. The sales clerk lets you brush some of the paint you are interested in on an available piece of drywall. The color matches exactly what you had in mind. Can you now purchase the paint with confidence? Why or why not?

Discussion Question

1. What can the typical findings with Garner Interference tell us about people's perceptual judgments? Explain.

Stroop Effect

Minimum time to complete this experiment: 20 minutes

Background

When you first learned to tie your shoelaces, you needed to think carefully through each step of the process. Now, you probably do not even think about the steps, but simply initiate a series of movements that proceed without any further influence. When a behavior or skill no longer requires direct interaction, cognitive psychologists say it is automatized.

Many behaviors can become automatized: typing, reading, writing, bicycling, piano playing, driving, etc. Automatization is interesting because it is an important part of daily life. We perform a variety of automatized behaviors quickly and effortlessly. In some cases, people report that they do not consciously know how the behavior is performed, they just will it to happen and it does happen.

To explore properties of automatized behaviors, cognitive psychologists often put observers in a situation in which an automatized response is in conflict with the desired behavior. This allows researchers to test the behind-the-scenes properties of automatized behaviors by noting their influence on more easily measured behaviors. This demonstration explores a well-known example of this type of influence, the Stroop Effect.

Stroop (1935) noted that observers were slower to properly identify the color of ink when the ink was used to produce color names different from the color of the ink. That is, observers were slower to identify red ink when it spelled the word blue. This is an interesting finding because observers are told to not pay any attention to the word names and simply to report the color of the ink. However, this seems to be a nearly impossible task, as the name of the word seems to interfere with the observer's ability to report the color of the ink.

A common explanation for the Stroop Effect is that observers (especially college undergraduates) have automatized the process of reading. Thus, the color names of the words are always processed very quickly, regardless of the color of the ink. On the other hand, identifying colors is not a task that observers have to report on very often and, because it is not automatized, it is slower. The fast and automatic processing of the color name of the word interferes with the reporting of the ink color.

Instructions

1. In the text fields below, enter your CogLab log-in ID and password. If you do not have a log-in ID and password, see your instructor for information on how to get one for your class.
2. Click the Submit information button.
3. If the information is correct, the Start experiment button will become activated. Click the button to begin the experiment.

A window will appear that fills nearly the entire screen, and a smaller window will appear with abbreviated instructions. Close the instructions window. You can open it again later from the CogLab Info. menu.

Start a trial by pressing the space bar. A fixation dot will appear in the middle of the window. Stare at it. A short time later (less than a second), a word (RED, GREEN, or BLUE) will appear on the screen, and the word will be printed in either red, green, or blue. Your task is to classify, as quickly as possible, the font color, regardless of the word name. If the font color is red, press the *h* key; for green, press the *j* key; for blue, press the *k* key. It may take a bit of practice to remember which key corresponds to which font color.

After pressing a key to identify the font color, you will receive feedback on whether you were correct. If you were incorrect, the trial will be repeated later in the experiment. If you find you are making lots of mistakes, you should slow down or make certain you understood which key goes with which font color. Press the space bar to start the next trial. If you wish, before pressing the space bar but after identifying the font color, you can check how many trials remain for the current experiment with the pull-down menu.

There are at least 45 trials, 30 in which the font colors and word names are different, and 15 in which the font colors and color names match (e.g., the word RED is in red font color). You can also discard a trial by pressing the *t* key instead of identifying the font color. Discarding is appropriate if, after starting a trial, you sneeze, zone out, or are otherwise distracted. Discarded trials will be repeated later.

At the end of the experiment, you will be asked if you want to save your data to a set of global data. After you answer the question, a new Web page window will appear that lists your class averages for this experiment. On that page is also a link to your personal data.

Additional Resources

Henik, A. & Salo, R. (2004). Schizophrenia and the Stroop Effect. *Behavioral and Cognitive Neuroscience Reviews, 3*, 42-59

Durgin, F. (2000). The reverse Stroop effect. *Psychonomic Bulletin & Review, 7*, 121-125.

Green, E. & Barber, P. (1981). An auditory Stroop effect with judgments of speaker gender. *Perception & Psychophysics, 30*, 459-466.

Basic Questions

1. Look at your individual data. Were you faster on congruent trials or incongruent trials? Does this surprise you? Why or why not?

2. What is the most commonly accepted explanation of why most people are slower on incongruent trials than on congruent trials in the Stroop task.

3. Imagine that in this demonstration you were asked to read the color words and to ignore the ink color in which the words are written. Using the explanation of the Stroop Effect given in the text, do you think your reaction-times on the incongruent trials would be faster, slower, or similar to the congruent trials?

Advanced Questions

1. What strategy could one use to overcome the Stroop Effect observed in this demonstration?

2. Name three tasks that are automatic for most people.

3. The data for this demonstration displays mean reaction-times and mean standard deviations. Usually subjects have a greater standard deviation on the incongruent trials than on the congruent trials. Why do you think this might be?

4. At a cross walk, there is often a signal that tells pedestrians when to walk and when not to walk. Typically these signals use an upright hand to represent do not walk and a human figure to indicate when walking is permitted. What colors are usually associated with these symbols? Do the colors and symbols seem congruent (support a correct response) or incongruent (inhibit a correct response)? Explain.

Discussion Question

1. What types of effects would you predict if a subject were given extensive training in a Stroop task before being tested? Why?

Spatial Cueing

Minimum time to complete this experiment: 20 minutes

Background

A spotlight is a metaphor that nicely captures many characteristics of the focus of visual attention: It is a beam that is moved spatially, that may not be divided, and that enhances the detection of events falling within it.

Some of the strongest evidence supporting the unitary concept of attention comes from the luminance-detection paradigm (e.g., Posner, 1980). In such experiments, subjects are first cued with the likely spatial location of a target and then respond as rapidly as possible when the target appears at any location in the display. For example, in a typical display, the stimuli are arranged horizontally with a fixation point in the center, which is also the location where the cue appears. The cue is either valid, correctly identifying the spatial location of the target, or invalid, incorrectly identifying the location of the target. Following the presentation of the cue, a single target stimulus is illuminated (usually about 1000 ms after the onset of the cue) and subjects respond as soon as they detect the target, regardless of its location. Relative to a neutral cue condition, responses are faster when the target appears in the cued location (a valid trial) and slower when the target appears in a non-cued location (an invalid trial).

Demonstrations of these patterns of results occur independently of eye movements. In other words, when an eye tracker verifies that your eyes are still fixed on the center, your focus of attention can be off to the right, or off to the left. While other interpretations of these findings are possible, they are consistent with the notion of a focused beam of attention that may be moved to distinct spatial locations - incorrectly in the case of the an invalid trial and correctly in the case of a valid trial.

Instructions

1. In the text fields below, enter your CogLab log-in ID and password. If you do not have a log-in ID and password, see your instructor for information on how to get one for your class.
2. Click the Submit information button.
3. If the information is correct, the Start experiment button will become activated. Click the button to begin the experiment.

A window will appear that fills nearly the entire screen, and a smaller window will appear with abbreviated instructions. Close the instructions window. You can open it again later from the CogLab Info. menu.

Start a trial by pressing the space bar. A fixation dot will appear in the middle of the window. Stare at it. A short time later, a cue will appear. If the arrow points to the right, 80% of the time the target will appear on the right. If the arrow points to the left, 80% of the time, the target will appear on the left. If no arrow appears, the target is equally likely to appear on the left or right. A short time after the cue disappears, a red square will appear.

Your task is to respond as quickly as possible when you see the square appear, regardless of its location. To respond, press the *n* key.

After pressing the *n* key, press the space bar to start the next trial. If you wish, before pressing the space bar, but after pressing the *n* key, you can check how many trials remain for the current experiment with the pull-down menu. There are at least 80 trials. If you respond too soon or too late, the trial will be discarded and will be repeated later in the experiment.

At the end of the experiment, you will be asked if you want to save your data to a set of global data. After you answer the question, a new Web page window will appear that lists your class averages for this experiment. On that page is also a link to your personal data.

Additional Resources

Richards, J. (2005). Localizing cortical sources of event-related potentials in infants' covert orienting. *Developmental Science, 8*, 255-278.

Golla, H., Ignashchenkova, A., Haarmeier, T., & Thier, P. (2004). Improvement of visual acuity by spatial cueing: A comparative study in human and non-human primates. *Vision Research, 44*, 1589-1600.

Theeuwes, J. (1989). Effects of location and form cueing on the allocation of attention in the visual field. *Acta Psychologica, 72*, 177-192.

Basic Questions

1. Does visual attention always follow a person's eye movements? Explain.

2. What was the independent variable in this demonstration? What was the dependent variable?

3. In this demonstration, the cue arrows are examples of an endogenous cue. What is an endogenous cue? What is an exogenous cue?

Advanced Questions

1. In soccer, goalies find themselves in a difficult position during a penalty kick. In this situation, they often observe the opposing player as he/she approaches the ball to try and find an indicator of the direction the ball might go. Why would a goalie take this strategy and what are its implications?

2. Name a profession (other than a professional soccer player) in which an individual might give an invalid spatial cue. Why do they use these invalid cues?

3. Envision an experiment similar to the one you just completed in which you have to make a response in relation to the location of a target. In this experiment you are given either a blue or a red square as a target. Furthermore, instead of being given a location cue you are given a cue about the color of the upcoming target. Do you think your valid-cue condition reaction-times would increase, decrease, or stay the same as compared to an uncued condition?

Discussion Question

1. In this demonstration, the arrow predicted the location of the target with 80% accuracy. What do you think the results would have looked like had the arrow predicted the target location with 50% accuracy? What about with 20% accuracy?

Attentional Blink

Minimum time to complete this experiment: 30 minutes

Background

Cognitive mechanisms can handle only limited amounts of information. In many situations, there are more stimuli and mental events than resources for processing. As a result, some stimuli are processed and some are not. Selectively choosing some stimuli and ignoring others is called attention. Many studies of attention investigate how mental resources are switched from one stimulus to another. This experiment explores some properties of attention with rapidly changing stimuli. It shows that there is a brief time after paying attention to one stimulus when attention cannot be focused on a subsequent stimulus. This duration is called an attentional blink because it is analogous to being unable to see objects during an eye blink.

In the experiment, many letters are shown in rapid succession, with each letter overwriting the previous letter. The observer's task is to watch the entire sequence and then indicate whether certain target letters were in the sequence. The sequences are carefully constructed to systematically vary the temporal separation between two target letters. Thus, if the target letters are J and K, a sequence with the letters ". . . JXTVRK . . ." places K five letter-spaces beyond J.

The notable finding is that identification of the second target letter is very low when it quickly follows the first target letter. As temporal separation increases, identification of the second letter improves. This finding suggests that when the observer sees the first target letter, he/she must attend to it to ensure that it will be remembered later. The focusing of attention to that letter apparently requires time and, if the second target letter appears during that time, it is not attended and not reported. By looking at recognition of the second letter as a function of separation, we can estimate the time required to focus and break attention for stimuli.

Instructions

1. In the text fields below, enter your CogLab log-in ID and password. If you do not have a log-in ID and password, see your instructor for information on how to get one for your class.

2. Click the Submit information button.

3. If the information is correct, the Start experiment button will become activated. Click the button to begin the experiment.

A window will fill the entire screen, and a smaller window will appear with abbreviated instructions. Close the instructions window. You can open it again later from the CogLab Info. menu.

Start a trial by pressing the space bar. A sequence of 19 letters will appear, with each new letter overwriting the previous one. Each letter is presented for only 100 milliseconds. After the letter sequence is finished, you will be prompted to make a response. Do not enter a response before the sequence is finished or the trial will have to be discarded (and run again).

Your task is to determine whether the letter J and/or K were in the sequence of letters just presented. You indicate the presence of a J by pressing the *j* key and you indicate the presence of the K by pressing the *k* key. If you see both letters, press each in any order. If you did not see either letter, do not press either key. The screen will present the key you press, but this is only so you know the program received your key press; it is not feedback on whether you were correct. When you are ready for the next trial, press the space bar again.

If, for some reason, you need to discard a trial (e.g., you sneezed, your attention drifted, you "zoned out," et cetera), press the *t* key before pressing the space bar for the next trial. This will discard the just-run trial. (It will be re-run later in the experiment.)

At the end of the experiment, you will be asked if you want to save your data to a set of global data. After you answer the question, a new Web page window will appear that lists your class averages for this experiment. On that page is also a link to your personal data.

Additional References

Dell'Acqua, R., Jolicoeur, P., Pesciarelli, F., Job, R., & Palomba, D. (2003). Electrophysiological evidence of visual encoding deficits in a cross-modal attentional blink paradigm. *Psychophysiology, 40*, 629-639.

Maki, W., Frigen, K., & Paulson, K. (1997). Associative priming by targets and distractors during rapid serial visual presentation: Does word meaning survive the attentional blink? *Journal of Experimental Psychology: Human Perception and Performance, 23*, 1014-1034.

Raymond, J., Shapiro, K., & Arnell, K. (1992). Temporary suppression of visual processing in an RSVP task: An attentional blink? *Journal of Experimental Psychology: Human Perception and Performance, 18*, 849-860.

Basic Questions

1. What is the main function of attention?

2. What does attentional blink tell us about attention?

3. Human behavior is often broken down into three stages: perception, cognition, and response execution. With what stage is attentional blink associated?

Advanced Questions

1. Use your personal data plot to calculate your attentional blink (in ms) for this activity. Do the same for the global data.

2. What are some occupations in which a workers' performance could be adversely affected by attentional blink?

3. Using the occupations identified in question 2, what types of problems/mistakes might occur?

Discussion Question

1. In this demonstration, letters were used as targets. The target used can influence the duration of one's attentional blink. What other targets could have been used for this experiment? Predict the effects each of these targets would have on the duration of one's attentional blink as compared to the activity you recently completed. Explain the reasoning behind your predictions.

Simon Effect

Minimum time to complete this experiment: 15 minutes

Background

The Simon Effect refers to the finding that people are faster and more accurate when responding to stimuli that occur in the same relative location as the response, even though the location information is irrelevant to the actual task (Simon, 1969). Studying the Simon Effect gives us insight into a stage of decision making called "response selection." According to information-processing theory, there are three stages of decision making: stimulus identification, response selection, and response execution or the motor stage.

Superficially, the Simon Effect may seem similar to the Stroop Effect. However, it is generally accepted that the interference that occurs in the Stroop Effect comes from the stimulus identification, while the interference that occurs in the Simon Effect occurs in the response-selection stage. During response selection, a person uses a rule to translate the relevant stimulus dimension, usually shape or color, to the correct left or right response. However, the location dimension of the stimulus (its position on the screen) overlaps with the relevant stimulus dimension (left or right). Because of this, the irrelevant location dimension of the stimulus activates the corresponding response and interferes with making a response to the non-corresponding side. As a result, same-side responses are faster and more accurate than opposite-side responses.

In the real world, the Simon Effect has important implications. Primarily, it shows that location information cannot be ignored and will affect decision making, even if the user knows that the information is irrelevant. The Simon Effect (and related phenomena) must be taken into account in design of man-machine interfaces. Good interfaces display information in ways that match the types of responses people should make. For example, imagine that you are flying a plane and the left engine has a problem. The indicator for that engine should be to the left of a corresponding indicator for the right engine. If it is the other way around, you may respond incorrectly to the indicator and adjust the wrong engine. That could be problematic.

Instructions

1. In the text fields below, enter your CogLab log-in ID and password. If you do not have a log-in ID and password, see your instructor for information on how to get one for your class.

2. Click the Submit information button.

3. If the information is correct, the Start experiment button will become activated. Click the button to begin the experiment.

A window will appear that fills nearly the entire screen, and a smaller window will appear with abbreviated instructions. Close the instructions window. You can open it again later from the CogLab Info. menu.

Position your hands so the index finger of your left hand is on the *v* key and the index finger of your right hand is on the *m* key. Press the space bar to start a trial. A fixation dot will appear in the middle of the window. Stare at it. A short time later (less than a second), you will be shown a red or green square to the left or right of fixation dot. Your task is to press the *v* key if the square is green and to press the *m* if the square is red.

After each trial, you will be given feedback about whether your response was correct or incorrect, and how fast your reaction-time was in milliseconds. If you respond before the stimulus appears or too long after the stimulus appears, you will be prompted to slow down or speed up.

There are at least 100 trials. If you make a mistake (e.g., report a green square as red), the trial will be repeated later in the experiment. You can discard a trial by pressing the *t* key instead of *v* or *m*. Discarding is appropriate if, after starting a trial, you sneeze, zone out, or are otherwise distracted. Discarded trials will be repeated later.

At the end of the experiment, you will be asked if you want to save your data to a set of global data. After you answer the question, a new Web page window will appear that lists your class averages for this experiment. On that page is also a link to your personal data.

Additional Resources

Urcuioli, P., Vu, K., & Proctor, R. (2005) A Simon Effect in Pigeons. *Journal of Experimental Psychology: General, 134*, 93-107.

Van der Lubbe, R., & Verleger, R. (2002). Aging and the Simon task. *Psychophysiology, 39*, 100-110.

Proctor, R., & Lu, C. (1999). Processing irrelevant location information: Practice and transfer effects in choice-reaction tasks. *Memory & Cognition, 27*, 63-77.

Basic Questions

1. The Simon Effect is the result of a conflict between two sources of information. Describe this conflict.

2. According to human information-processing theory, at what stage does the Simon Effect occur?

3. Compare your data to the global data. Did you display a smaller or larger Simon Effect than the group? Explain.

Advanced Questions

1. Consider the stove design below, using your knowledge about the Simon Effect. Identify a positive aspect of the design as well as an aspect with the design that could be problematic. (The knob on the far left corresponds to the stove coil on the bottom left, the knob second from the left corresponds to the stove coil on the top left, the knob second from the right corresponds to the stove coil on the top right, and the knob on the far right corresponds to the stove coil on the bottom right.)

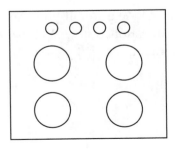

2. While you are driving, a pedestrian walks in front of your car from the right side and you do not have time to stop. Thinking only in terms of the Simon Effect, what would be your best course of action? Explain.

3. Many designs that utilize what is known about stimulus location and response compatibility (the Simon Effect) are evident in transportation. Think about the last few times you have been in a car and identify two of them.

Discussion Question

1. In this demonstration, you were shown targets to the left and right of your eye fixation and had to make a right or a left key press depending on the target. Describe another experimental setup in which you might find a Simon Effect. Be sure to identify the targets, responses, target locations, and the conflict that would cause the Simon Effect.

Von Restorff Effect

Minimum time to complete this experiment: 20 minutes

Background

When people are trying to remember a set of items, events, or people, they often report being able to recall the information more easily and more accurately if a particular item is distinctive or stands out in some way from similar items. This type of result is usually known as the Von Restorff Effect, named after Hedwig von Restorff who published her results in 1933.

In the typical von Restorff experiment, you might see a list of 7 items and your task is to recall the items in their original order. In the control condition, you might see a list such as RMSKQLF, where all the letters are black. In the experimental condition, you might see a list such as RMSKQLF, where the Q is red and all the other letters are black. The typical finding is that you would be more likely to recall the red Q than the black Q. This effect is also sometimes known as the isolation effect because the Q is isolated in the sense that it is the only item in a different color. Research has shown that you can observe the von Restorff or isolation effect when the first item in the series is the different one. This rules out explanations based on differential encoding of the item because at the time the first item is seen, it is not different.

These results are now usually interpreted in terms of distinctiveness (Neath & Surprenant, 2003): The unusual (relative to the list) item stands out from the other items.

Instructions

1. In the text fields below, enter your CogLab log-in ID and password. If you do not have a log-in ID and password, see your instructor for information on how to get one for your class.
2. Click the Submit information button.
3. If the information is correct, the Start experiment button will become activated. Click the button to begin the experiment.

After clicking on the Start experiment button, a window will appear with a blank area on the left and a number of buttons on the right. Start a trial by pressing the Next trial button. A sequence of 10 letters will appear on the left of the window, with each item presented for one second. After the full sequence has been presented, the buttons on the right will become active.

Your task is to click on the buttons for the items that were just shown. You can click on the buttons in any order. You are allowed to make only 10 responses. After you have clicked on 10 buttons, the remaining buttons will be disabled. After you have finished clicking on all of the buttons that you remember being in the sequence, click on Next trial to start the next sequence.

At the end of the experiment, you will be asked if you want to save your data to a set of global data. After you answer the question, a new Web page window will appear that lists your class averages for this experiment. On that page is also a link to your personal data.

Additional References

Hunt, R., & Lamb, C. (2001). What causes the isolation effect? *Journal of Experimental Psychology: Learning, Memory, and Cognition, 27*, 1359-1366.

Holmes, C., & Arbogast, R. (1979). An auditory von Restorff effect. *Journal of General Psychology, 101*, 199-204.

Deutsch, M., & Sternlicht, M. (1967). The role of "surprise" in the von Restorff effect. *Journal of General Psychology, 76*, 151-159.

Basic Questions

1. Does your personal data reveal a Von Restorff Effect? How do you know?

2. What was done in the experimental trials of this demonstration to distinguish one of the list items from the others?

3. Excluding the distinctive list item, for which two items do you show the highest recall? Why might this have been the case?

Advanced Questions

1. In this demonstration, some of the trials had one list item that stood out from the other list items because it had a feature that was unique. This item is typically remembered with a higher frequency than its matched control, and is called the Von Restorff Effect. What do you think would happen to this effect if two of the list items shared this distinctive feature instead of one?

2. You've just started a new job and on the first day you've been told you're going to meet twelve of the company's employees, one of whom is your new supervisor. Using what you've learned about the Von Restorff Effect, what can you do to make sure you remember your new supervisor's name?

3. You're a sports agent and your new client will be competing in an open tryout in front of professional scouts. Your client is a good athlete but not well known. What advice would you give to your client help him/her get noticed during the tryout?

Discussion Question

1. How might you explain the Von Restorff Effect using interference?

Partial Report

Minimum time to complete this experiment: 20 minutes

Background

In the beginnings of the study of psychology, researchers were interested in something called the perceptual span. Their quest was to determine how much information could be gathered in a single percept. For example, when you read text, how many letters can you interpret in a single glance? Or, how many coins can you distinguish if you briefly glance at them? The goal was to identify the limits of perceptual abilities. A variety of ingenious studies seemed to draw similar conclusions: People could accurately report about 4.5 items from a brief percept. This fact was built into many theories of cognition until a set of experiments by George Sperling (1960) proved it wrong.

Sperling suggested that the 4.5 item limit was imposed not by the capabilities of the perceptual system, but by observers' abilities to recall items that had been seen. To test this possibility, he designed a partial-report experiment. This laboratory allows you to participate in a version of this experiment.

In Sperling's original experiment, the observer saw a three by three matrix of random letters on each trial. The letters were flashed for a very short period of time (50 milliseconds). After the letter matrix turned off, one of three tones sounded, and the observer reported the letters from the row associated with the tone. If the tone was presented directly after offset of the letters, Sperling found that observers were nearly 100% accurate in reporting letters from the indicated row.

This result destroys theories that hypothesized that percepts hold only 4 or 5 items. Because the tone was sounded after the letters disappeared, observers must be focusing on the appropriate row as it is stored in some type of sensory store of perceptual information. Moreover, since perfect performance is found regardless of which row is indicated, the sensory store must contain a nearly perfect representation of the total visual percept. Thus, perceptual span was not 4.5 items, but essentially every item in the visual field.

What determined perceptual span in the earlier experiments was not the limits of the perceptual system, but the time needed to report the seen items. The duration of information in the sensory store is very brief (a few hundred milliseconds) so, as observers report what they see, items in the sensory store fade away. By the time observers report on 4 or 5 items, the sensory store information is gone and recall is finished.

Sperling also found a way to measure the duration of information in the sensory store. When he increased the time between the offset of the letter matrix and the onset of the tone cue, he found that recall of letters became worse. If the tone was delayed by a full second, recall was comparable to the 4.5 items found in other experiments.

When these experimental results were reported in 1960, they revolutionized both our understanding of perception and memory and the experimental methods with which cognitive psychology was studied. There have subsequently been thousands of studies on the sensory (also called iconic) store and it is a part of many theories of cognition.

Instructions

1. In the text fields below, enter your CogLab log-in ID and password. If you do not have a log-in ID and password, see your instructor for information on how to get one for your class.
2. Click the Submit information button.
3. If the information is correct, the Start experiment button will become activated. Click the button to begin the experiment.

This experiment requires a computer that can play sounds. We recommend using headphones so that you do not disturb other people. Please make sure the volume is not too loud before you put the headphones on.

After clicking on the Start experiment button, a window will fill the entire screen. Press the space bar to start a trial.

The first thing you will hear are the three tones so that you can tell which is the low pitched tone, which is the medium, and which is the high. After you have heard the tones, press the space bar to begin the experiment.

After you press the space bar, a small fixation point (an asterisk, *) will appear in the middle of the screen. Fix on this. It will disappear after one and a half seconds. Half a second later, a three by three matrix of letters will be flashed for 150 milliseconds. Some time after the offset of the letter matrix, a tone will be played that indicates:

A high-pitched tone means report the top row.
A medium-pitched tone means report the middle row.
A low-pitched tone means report the bottom row.

Type the letters from the indicated row. Guess if you do not know what the letters were. You can make up to three guesses for every trial.

When you are ready, press the space bar for the next trial. There are a total of 60 trials, with the same basic task in every one. Simply report the letters that flashed from the indicated row. As you go through the experiment, keep your eyes steady on the fixation mark and do not move them until after the matrix disappears. There is no method for discarding a trial in this experiment, so try to make certain you are ready as you start a trial.

At the end of the experiment, you will be asked if you want to save your data to a set of global data. After you answer the question, a new Web page window will appear that lists your class averages for this experiment. On that page is also a link to your personal data.

Additional References

Fenske, M., & Stolz, J. (2001). Disengaging attention: On the locus of the cue-duration effect in partial report. *Journal of Experimental Psychology: Human Perception and Performance, 27*, 1335-1346.

Gugerty, L. (1998). Evidence from a partial report task for forgetting in dynamic spatial memory. *Human Factors, 40*, 498-508.

Di Lollo, V., & Dixon, P. (1992). Inverse duration effects in partial report. *Journal of Experimental Psychology: Human Perception and Performance, 18*, 1089-1100.

Basic Questions

1. In this experiment, how would one measure the interstimulus interval (ISI)?

2. At what ISI did you show the most accurate recall? At what ISI did you show the least accurate recall?

3. In general, participant's recall accuracy decreases as ISI increases. Explain why this relationship exists.

Advanced Questions

1. In a partial report experiment like the one in this demonstration, you are shown a 4 x 4 matrix of letters and are cued to report the letters from the first row. Assuming you recalled three of the four letters in the cued row, how many of the letters in the matrix were available in your sensory memory at the offset of the letter matrix?

2. Using your personal data, what would you predict your recall accuracy would be with a 700ms ISI? Using the global data, make a prediction for someone's recall accuracy with a 700ms ISI.

3. You only briefly see a holiday shopping list for your family members before it gets taken away by a gust of wind. What strategy should you employ to maximize your accuracy in remembering what was on the list?

Discussion Question

1. Say you're watching television with a group of friends and something happens that makes everyone laugh but you. Afterward, everyone is talking about what made them laugh, but you do not remember seeing it at all. Is it that you did not see it or that you do not remember it? Explain.

Brown-Peterson

Minimum time to complete this experiment: 20 minutes

Background

In the 1940s, memory loss was widely considered to be the result of new information interfering with previously learned information. In the late 1950s, two groups of researchers (one named Brown and a husband and wife team named Peterson) published data that forced a new interpretation of human memory.

Parenthetically, it is interesting to note the instructions that Peterson & Peterson (1959, p. 194) gave to their subjects: "Please sit against the back of your chair so that you are comfortable. You will not be shocked during this experiment." One can infer that it was common to give electric shocks to human subjects back in the 1950s.

In the memory task, the participant viewed a trigram of consonants (e.g., GKT, WCH,...) and then performed a number of algebraic computations (e.g., counting backward by 3s) for less than 20 seconds. The data showed that recall of the trigram was less likely as the participant worked on the algebraic computations for longer durations.

Solving math problems seems to be very different from recalling consonant trigrams, so it was unlikely that there was any interference to disturb the memory of the trigram. The conclusion was that there exists a short-term memory (STM) system that holds information for several seconds. Without an active effort by the participant, information in STM fades away (but see Keppel & Underwood, 1962, for an alternate explanation). Performing the distractor task prevented the participant from actively rehearsing the trigram. STM is now a fundamental part of most theories of cognitive psychology.

Instructions

1. In the text fields below, enter your CogLab log-in ID and password. If you do not have a log-in ID and password, see your instructor for information on how to get one for your class.
2. Click the Submit information button.
3. If the information is correct, the Start experiment button will become activated. Click the button to begin the experiment.

A window will appear that fills nearly the entire screen, and a smaller window will appear with abbreviated instructions. Close the instructions window. You can open it again later from the CogLab Info. menu.

Click on the space bar to start a trial. Position your hands on the keyboard so that one finger can hit the *f* key and another can hit the *j* key. In the middle of the screen, a trigram of letters will appear for two seconds. You will then be given a sequence of letter strings and must classify each item as a word (press the *j* key) or a nonword (press the *f* key). The duration of time spent classifying the letter strings will vary from one to twenty-one seconds. You need to respond quickly enough to keep up with the sequence.

After correct completion of the classification task, you will be prompted to recall the consonant trigram. Using the keyboard, type in the letters, in the correct order, that appeared before the classification task. After you have entered your guess and are ready for the next trial, press the space bar again.

For the trial to count, you must have correctly classified all of the letter strings as words or nonwords. If you make any mistakes, the trial will be repeated later in the experiment. The rate of the sequence will change from trial to trial. It will become slower if you make a mistake and faster if you get it correct. To finish the experiment, you must apply yourself to the word-nonword classification task. There is a total of 18 trials that must be run to finish the experiment.

At the end of the experiment, you will be asked if you want to save your data to a set of global data. After you answer the question, a new Web page window will appear that lists your class averages for this experiment. On that page is also a link to your personal data.

Additional References

Sebastian, M., Menor, J,& Elosua, R. (2001). Patterns of errors in short-term forgetting in AD and aging. *Memory, 9*, 223-231.

Nairne, J., Whiteman, H., & Kelley, M. (1999). Short-term forgetting of order under conditions of reduced interference. *Quarterly Journal of Experimental Psychology A: Human Experimental Psychology, 52*, 241-251.

Puckett, J., & Lawson, W. (1989). Absence of adult age differences in forgetting in the Brown-Peterson task. *Acta Psychologica, 72*, 159-175.

Basic Questions

1. In the Peterson and Peterson (1959) study, what was equivalent to the word non-word distractor task used in this demonstration?

2. At what distractor duration was your performance best? What duration was your performance the worst?

3. What is the function of the distractor task in the Brown-Peterson paradigm?

4. To what was the Brown-Peterson data attributed?

Advanced Questions

1. Using your personal data, at would distractor duration would you predict your recall performance to be approximately 15%?

2. Utilizing your understanding of the Brown-Peterson data, what type of environment would you suggest for someone trying to learn new material?

3. Do you or anyone you know like to study with the television or the radio on? Now that you have done this experiment, what do you think about this practice? Explain

Discussion Question

1. Other than the explanation given in Basic Question # 4, what else could have explained the data?

Memory Span

Minimum time to complete this experiment: 15 minutes

Background

Many theories of cognition propose that there is a short-term or working memory system that is able to hold a limited amount of information for a short period of time. The memory-span experiment is one measure of working memory capacity. In this experiment, participants are given a list of items and asked to recall the list. The list length is varied to see at what list length participants will make few errors. That list length is the memory span for that subject on that task. Individuals with larger memory spans can better keep in mind different stimuli, and this seems to give them an advantage for a wide variety of cognitive tasks. Memory span has been linked to performance on intelligence tests, standardized tests, reading skills, problem solving, and a variety of other cognitive tasks.

The very existence of short-term memory is largely based on memory-span types of experiments, as it was noted that memory span was approximately seven (plus or minus two) for a wide variety of stimuli. This suggested a simple storage system that held approximately seven items. Later studies demonstrated that memory span could be systematically influenced by a variety of stimulus characteristics. For example, when the stimuli are letters that sound alike (e.g., d, b, p, t), memory span is shorter. Likewise, memory span is shorter for lists of long words (e.g., encyclopedia, refrigerator) than for lists of short words (e.g., book, stove). These findings have suggested that the capacity of short-term memory is controlled by verbal processes. This experiment allows you to measure your memory span for a variety of stimulus types.

Instructions

1. In the text fields below, enter your CogLab log-in ID and password. If you do not have a log-in ID and password, see your instructor for information on how to get one for your class.
2. Click the Submit information button.
3. If the information is correct, the Start experiment button will become activated. Click the button to begin the experiment.

Start a trial by clicking the Next trial button. On the left of the window, a sequence of items will appear, with each item presented for one second. After the full sequence has been presented, the buttons on the right will show labels for item names, including those just shown. Your task is to click on the buttons for the items just shown in the same order that the items were presented. After you have finished clicking on all the buttons to recreate the list, click on Next trial to start the next sequence.

The experiment includes five types of stimuli: numbers, letters that sound different, letters that sound the same, short words, and long words. In each case, your task is simply to report the items you saw, in the order they were presented. Each stimulus type will be presented five times, with varying list lengths.

List length is varied, for each type of stimuli, in order to find the longest list for which you can correctly recreate the sequence. Being correct means that you both recall all the items in the sequence and click on the buttons in the same order the items appeared in the sequence. Any mistake (recalling too many items, recalling too few items, or recalling items in the wrong order) counts as Incorrect. There is no way to correct mistakes in button presses, so be careful in your selections. After clicking on Next trial, you will be given feedback on your response to the previous sequence (Correct/Incorrect) before the next sequence is presented.

If you are correct for a given sequence, the next sequence for that stimulus type will be one item longer. If you are incorrect, the next sequence for that stimulus type will be one item shorter. In this way, the length of the sequence converges on the longest list length that you can reliably report back.

At the end of the experiment, you will be asked if you want to save your data to a set of global data. After you answer the question, a new Web page window will appear that lists your class averages for this experiment. On that page is also a link to your personal data.

Additional References

Kawai, N., & Matsuzawa, T. (2000). Numerical memory span in a chimpanzee. *Nature, 403*, 39-40.

May, C., Hasher, L., & Kane, M. (1999). The role of interference in memory span. *Memory & Cognition, 27*, 759-767.

Baddeley, A. (1994). The magical number seven: Still magic after all these years? *Psychological Review, 101*, 353-356.

Basic Questions

1. For which type of stimuli was your memory span the longest? For which was it the shortest?

2. What three types of mistakes could one make in recalling the stimulus sequence that would lead to it being scored as incorrect?

3. Approximately how many items can the average person hold in short-term memory?

Advanced Questions

1. Typically, when the stimulus sequence consists of long words, one's memory span is shorter than when the stimulus sequence consists of short words. Why might this be the case?

2. Typically, when the stimulus sequence consists of similar sounding letters, one's memory span is shorter than when the stimulus sequence consists of dissimilar sounding letters. Why might this be the case?

3. You have a friend who is taking Biology, Anatomy and Physiology, Comparative Politics, and American Government and he/she has tests in all of these classes on the same day, this upcoming Friday. Your friend decided to study for two of the exams on Wednesday and two of the exams on Thursday. Based on what you have learned about memory span, which classes would you advise him/her to study for on each of these days? Why?

Discussion Question

1. Memory span has been linked to intelligence. Suppose two individuals from different parts of the world were given the same memory test (in their respective native languages) and one individual showed a much longer memory span than the other. Using what you have learned from this demonstration, why is it unfair to say that the individual with the longer memory span is most likely more intelligent than the individual with the shorter memory span?

Phonological Similarity Effect

Minimum time to complete this experiment: 20 minutes

Background

When people are asked to recall a list of items, their performance is usually worse when the items sound similar than when the items sound different (Conrad, 1964). Although this effect has become known as the phonological similarity effect, a better term is the acoustic similarity effect because what matters is that the items sound similar to each other.

What is most surprising about the phonological similarity effect is that it occurs even when there is no auditory input, such as when you read the items silently to yourself. This result has been seen as suggesting that people recode the information. If you used only a visual representation, you would be more likely to confuse items that looked similar (e.g., E and F). This idea is central to Baddeley's (1986) conception of the phonological loop, one of the components of working memory. The phonological loop has two parts: the phonological store and the articulatory control process. The phonological store is a memory store that can retain speech-based (phonological) information for a short period of time. Unless rehearsed, the traces within the store are assumed to fade and decay within about 2 seconds, after which they are no longer usable. The second component is the articulatory control process, which is responsible for two different functions: It translates visual information into a speech-based code and deposits it in the phonological store; and it refreshes a trace in the phonological store, offsetting the decay process.

According to the phonological loop model, the reason that you get a phonological similarity effect when there is no auditory input is that the articulatory control process has converted the visual information into phonological form. One key prediction is that if you somehow prevent the articulatory control process from converting the information, the phonological similarity effect will be removed. In other words, recall of similar sounding and dissimilar sounding items will be equivalent. One way of preventing this recoding is to keep the articulatory control process busy doing something else.

This demonstration is based on an experiment reported by Murray (1968) and uses a technique called articulatory suppression to prevent the articulatory control process from recoding the visual information into phonological information. On half of the trials, you will see similar sounding letters and on the other half of the trials you will see dissimilar sounding letters. On some trials, you will be asked to say "One, two, three, four, one, two, three, four, ..." out loud, over and over. You should start speaking when told to start, and you should continue until you see the response buttons become active.

Instructions

1. In the text fields below, enter your CogLab log-in ID and password. If you do not have a log-in ID and password, see your instructor for information on how to get one for your class.
2. Click the Submit information button.
3. If the information is correct, the Start experiment button will become activated. Click the button to begin the experiment.

Start a trial by clicking once on the Next trial button. On the left of the window, a sequence of letters will appear, with each letter presented for one second. After the full sequence has been presented, the buttons on the right will show labels for the letters, including those just shown. Your task is to click on the buttons just shown in the same order that the letters were presented. After you have finished clicking on all the buttons to recreate the list, click on Next trial to start the next sequence.

Being correct means that you both recall all the items in the sequence and click on the buttons in the same order the items appeared in the sequence. Any mistake (recalling too many items, recalling too few items, or recalling items in the wrong order) counts as incorrect. There is no way to correct mistakes in button presses, so be careful in your selections.

Click on the Next trial button to start a trial.

On some trials, you will see the instruction "Speak" appear before the letters. You should repeatedly say "one, two, three, four, one, two, three, four, ..." out loud until you see the response buttons become active. You do not need to speak loudly, but you should try to speak quickly. (You should avoid doing this lab in a public space so that you do not disturb other people around you.) If you see the word "Quiet," do not say anything out loud.

The experiment includes 32 trials. Half involve articulatory suppression, and half do not. Half have letters that sound similar to each other and half have letters that all sound different.

At the end of the experiment, you will be asked if you want to save your data to a set of global data. After you answer the question, a new Web page window will appear that lists your class averages for this experiment. On that page is also a link to your personal data.

Additional References

Gupta, P., Lipinski, J., & Aktunc, E. (2005). Reexamining the phonological similarity effect in immediate serial recall: The roles of type of similarity, category cuing, and item recall. *Memory & Cognition, 33*, 1001-1016.

Li, X., Schweickert, R., & Gandour, J. (2000). The phonological similarity effect in immediate recall: Positions of shared phonemes. *Memory & Cognition, 28*, 1116-1125.

Nairne, J., & Kelley, M. (1999). Reversing the phonological similarity effect. *Memory & Cognition, 27*, 45-53.

Saito, S. (1993). Phonological similarity effect is abolished by a silent mouthing task. *Perceptual and Motor Skills, 76*, 427-431.

Basic Questions

1. In the phonological loop model, what is the phonological store?

2. What is the purpose of saying numbers aloud on half of the trials in this demonstration?

3. Did you show the phonological similarity effect? Explain.

Advanced Questions

1. Would it be harder to recall the word sequence of house, mouse, and spouse or the word sequence house, cabin, and mansion? Why?

2. In this demonstration, on half of the trials you were asked to count to four aloud over and over throughout the presentation of the sequence of letters. What other tasks could have taken the place of the counting task?

3. Using your trial-by-trial data, evaluate the types of errors you made on your first 10 trials. How many times did you fail to report a letter from the original list? How many times did you make an error in the order that you recalled the letters? Where did most of your errors occur (beginning, middle, or end of the list)?

Discussion Question

1. In a demonstration similar to this one, do you think you would be more likely to report seeing an item not on the original list in the similar quiet condition or in the dissimilar quiet condition? Explain.

Irrelevant Speech Effect

Minimum time to complete this experiment: 20 minutes

Background

When people are asked to recall a list of items, their performance is usually worse when the presentation of the list is accompanied by irrelevant speech. The speech does not need to be in a language that the subject knows, and doesn't even have to be real speech. Nonsense speech (such as "ba da ga") works just as well.

One reason that this phenomenon, known as the irrelevant speech effect, has attracted a lot of attention is because it seems strange that auditory information (the irrelevant speech stimuli) would interfere with visual information (the items you are trying to remember).

Although there is still no generally agreed upon explanation for this effect, there are at least three explanations (Neath, 2000). One theory attributes the disruption to interference in working memory. The visual items are translated into a phonological code that is stored in the same part of memory (the phonological store) as the irrelevant speech. Another attributes the effect to a disruption of order information. You remember the items, but it is information about the order that is lost. A third attributes the effect to a combination of two factors, an attentional component and an interference component.

Instructions

1. In the text fields below, enter your CogLab log-in ID and password. If you do not have a log-in ID and password, see your instructor for information on how to get one for your class.
2. Click the Submit information button.
3. If the information is correct, the Start experiment button will become activated. Click the button to begin the experiment.

This experiment requires a computer that can play sounds. We recommend using headphones so that you do not disturb other people. Please make sure the volume is not too loud before you put the headphones on.

A window will appear, and a second smaller window will appear with abbreviated instructions. Close the instructions window. You can open it again later from the CogLab Info. menu.

Click on the Next trial button to start a trial.

On each trial, you will see a sequence of letters presented in random order. Then you will see the response buttons become active. Your task is to click on the buttons in the same order that the letters were presented. After you have finished clicking on all the buttons to recreate the list, click on Next trial to start the next sequence.

The experiment includes two types of trials: Some trials are presented with irrelevant speech (a passage from Franz Kafka in German) and some are presented with no irrelevant speech. The order of the conditions is random.

Being correct means that you click on the buttons in the same order the items appeared in the sequence. There is no way to correct mistakes in button presses, so be careful in your selections. There are 30 trials.

At the end of the experiment, you will be asked if you want to save your data to a set of global data. After you answer the question, a new Web page window will appear that lists your class averages for this experiment. On that page is also a link to your personal data.

Additional References

Toppino, T., & Pisegna, A. (2005). Articulatory suppression and the irrelevant-speech effect in short-term memory: Does the locus of suppression matter? *Psychonomic Bulletin & Review, 12*, 374-379.

Neeley, C., & LeCompte, D. (1999). The importance of semantic similarity to the irrelevant speech effect. *Memory & Cognition, 27*, 37-44.

LeCompte, D., Neely, C., & Wilson, J. (1997). Irrelevant speech and irrelevant tones: The relative importance of speech to the irrelevant speech effect. *Journal of Experimental Psychology: Learning, Memory, and Cognition, 23*, 472-483.

Basic Questions

1. In this demonstration, did you show the Irrelevant Speech Effect? Explain how you know.

2. How is visual information stored in working memory, and how might this explain the Irrelevant Speech Effect?

3. Irrelevant Speech is thought to impair one's ability to recall list items and/or impair one's ability to recall list items in the correct order. Based on your experience with this demonstration, which of these two hypotheses do you think is most accurate? Why?

Advanced Questions

1. You have an important exam tomorrow and your roommates ask you if they can have people over for a small party. They promise that you can have the whole upstairs to yourself so no one will bother you. Will this allow you to effectively study for your exam? Why or why not?

2. If you get a phone call while watching television, you always make a point to mute the television. You have always thought this allowed you to hear the person you were talking to more clearly. After having done this demonstration, can you think of another reason why muting the television allows you to communicate on the phone more effectively?

3. In this demonstration, if you were presented with auditory tones instead of irrelevant speech when being shown the sequence of numbers, do you think your recall performance would be improved, further impaired, or the same? Why?

Discussion Question

1. How might attention play a role in the Irrelevant Speech Effect?

Modality Effect

Minimum time to complete this experiment: 20 minutes

Background

People often have to recall a series of items in order, such as a phone number. When the list of items is heard (as opposed to read silently), people usually are very good at remembering the final list item. This advantage in recalling just the last one or two items when the list is heard is called the modality effect.

Modality effects can be seen with presentation modalities other than auditory (hearing). Lists that are lip-read or silently mouthed also produce an advantage for the last one or two items compared to silent visual presentation.

These effects have an enormous influence on the development of sensory memory. This memory system is supposed to store raw, unanalyzed sensory input. It can be thought of as a back-up system: If the information in this store is useful, recall can be enhanced.

The best explanation is that auditory presentation leads to an additional type of information compared to visual (Neath & Surprenant, 2003). When trying to recall the last item in the list, you are more likely to be successful if you also have some information about how the list sounds.

Instructions

1. In the text fields below, enter your CogLab log-in ID and password. If you do not have a log-in ID and password, see your instructor for information on how to get one for your class.
2. Click the Submit information button.
3. If the information is correct, the Start experiment button will become activated. Click the button to begin the experiment.

This experiment requires a computer that can play sounds. We recommend using headphones so that you do not disturb other people. Please make sure the volume is not too loud before you put the headphones on.

A window will appear, and a second smaller window will appear with abbreviated instructions. Close the instructions window. You can open it again later from the CogLab Info. menu.

Click on the Next trial button to start a trial.

On each trial, you will either see or hear the digits 1 through 9 in random order. Then you will see the response buttons become active. Your task is to click on the buttons in the same order that the numbers were presented. After you have finished clicking on all the buttons to recreate the list, click on Next trial to start the next sequence.

Being correct means that you click on the buttons in the same order as the items appeared in the sequence. There is no way to correct mistakes in button presses, so be careful in your selections. There are 30 trials.

At the end of the experiment, you will be asked if you want to save your data to a set of global data. After you answer the question, a new Web page window will appear that lists your class averages for this experiment. On that page is also a link to your personal data.

Additional References

Beaman, C. P. (2002). Inverting the modality effect in serial recall. *Quarterly Journal of Experimental Psychology A: Human Experimental Psychology, 55,* 371-389.

Crowder, R. (1986). Auditory and temporal factors in the modality effect. *Journal of Experimental Psychology: Learning, Memory, and Cognition, 12,* 268-278.

Engle, R., & Roberts, J. (1982). How long does the modality effect persist? *Bulletin of the Psychonomic Society, 19,* 343-346.

Basic Questions

1. Describe your personal data. For which list position was your recall performance the highest? For which was it the lowest?

2. Does your data show the modality effect? Why or why not?

3. What is sensory memory?

Advanced Questions

1. Using what you have learned from this demonstration, what study tips would you give to a friend who has an important exam coming up?

2. When looking up a phone number in the yellow pages, what can you do to improve your recall of that phone number later?

3. What occupations might be able to use the findings from experiments on the modality effect in their work? Explain.

Discussion Question

1. Why does the modality effect only show up for the last one or two items in the list?

Operation Span

Minimum time to complete this experiment: 15 minutes

Background

Recent conceptions of memory have suggested that memory consists of a flexible workspace that not only stores information but also plays an active role in processing and manipulating information. This active process, however, seems to have a limited amount of resources to work with. One question that has been posed is whether the capacity is specific to verbal tasks or if there is a general pool of resources that is used in every working-memory task. Most previous researchers have used only verbal materials in measuring working-memory capacity.

To determine whether there is a general capacity for all working-memory tasks, Turner and Engle (1989) developed a task called operation-word-span (OSPAN). In this task, subjects are asked to read and verify a simple math problem (such as $(4/2) - 1 = 1$) and then read a word after the operation (such as SNOW). After a series of problems and words has been presented, the subjects recall the words that followed each operation. The number of operation-word strings in a sequence is increased and decreased to measure the subject's operation span. Operation-span measures predict verbal abilities and reading comprehension even though the subjects are solving mathematical problems. Engle and his colleagues have argued that this implies a general pool of resources that is used in every type of working-memory situation.

This demonstration allows you to measure your operation span using the procedure of Conway & Engle (1996).

Instructions

1. In the text fields below, enter your CogLab log-in ID and password. If you do not have a log-in ID and password, see your instructor for information on how to get one for your class.
2. Click the Submit information button.
3. If the information is correct, the Start experiment button will become activated. Click the button to begin the experiment.

Start a trial by clicking the Next trial button. You will see a question involving a math problem, such as:

Is $10/2 + 2 = 7$?

Read the math problem out loud (i.e., say "Is ten divided by two plus two equal to seven?") and then decide whether the given answer is correct or incorrect. If the problem is correct, click once on the Yes button; if the problem is incorrect, click once on the No button.

You will then see a word. Read the word out loud. You will then see another math problem.

At some point, you will be asked to recall all the words from the series. Simply click on the buttons that are labeled with words you have just seen in the order in which you saw the words.

Your operation-span score is valid only if you were more than 85% accurate in evaluating the math problems.

At the end of the experiment, you will be asked if you want to save your data to a set of global data. After you answer the question, a new Web page window will appear that lists your class averages for this experiment. On that page is also a link to your personal data.

Additional References

Conway, A., Kane, M., Bunting, M., Hambrick, D., Wilhelm, O., & Engle, R. (2005). Working memory span tasks: A methodological review and user's guide. *Psychonomic Bulletin & Review, 12*, 769-786.

Hitch, G., Towse, J., & Hutton, U. (2001). What limits children's working memory span? Theoretical accounts and applications for scholastic development. *Journal of Experimental Psychology: General, 130*, 184-198.

Towse, J., Hitch, G., & Hutton, U. (2000) On the interpretation of working memory span in adults. *Memory & Cognition, 28*, 341-348.

Basic Questions

1. Operation span correlates with other tasks involving working memory. What does in mean if two variables have a positive correlation? What does in mean if they have a negative correlation?

2. How is operation span calculated in this demonstration?

3. How is operation span different from what is typically described as memory span?

Advanced Questions

1. Operation-span experiments provide evidence that we have a general pool of resources for working memory. What implications does this have for multi-tasking?

2. While you are driving, your roommate reads you a list of items you need to get at the store. Why might it be difficult for you to effectively remember these items?

3. Name a job that would require someone with a high operation span. Explain your answer.

Discussion Question

1. In this demonstration, the math problems typically impair one's ability to remember the list words. Why do you think this is the case?

Position Error

Minimum time to complete this experiment: 20 minutes

Background

Many tasks require people to remember not only a set of items but also the order of the items. For example, a telephone number is meaningful only if the items are recalled in the correct order. When people do not recall an item in its correct order, the errors they make are systematic.

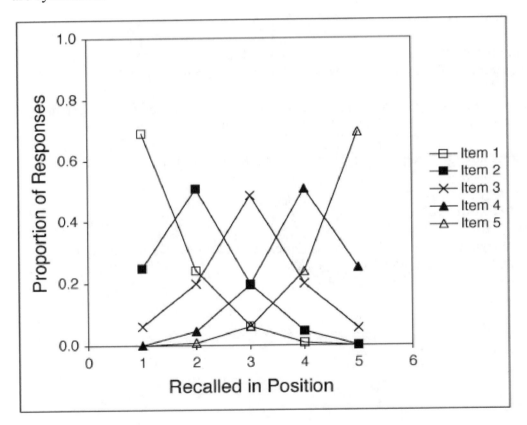

The graph above shows what these systematic errors would look like when people try to recall a five-item list in order. Most of the time, the items are recalled in the correct position. So, the line marked Item 1 has its largest value at position 1; the line marked

Item 2 has its largest value at position 2; and so on. When an order error is made, the graph shows that the item is most likely to be recalled either 1 position too soon or 1 position too late. So, when Item 3 is not recalled in position 3, it is most likely to be recalled in position 2 or position 4. Results like these have important implications for theories of memory. If all you look at is percent correct, then you might think that forgetting means that the information is lost from the memory system. However, you are still remembering something about the item: You usually recall the item in a position adjacent to the correct position.

Instructions

1. In the text fields below, enter your CogLab log-in ID and password. If you do not have a log-in ID and password, see your instructor for information on how to get one for your class.
2. Click the Submit information button.
3. If the information is correct, the Start experiment button will become activated. Click the button to begin the experiment.

Start a trial by clicking on the Next trial button. On the left of the window, a sequence of 7 letters will appear, with each letter presented for one second. After the full sequence has been presented, the buttons on the right will show labels for items just shown. Your task is to click on the buttons in the same order that the letters were presented. If you think the first letter was M, click on the button labeled M first. If you think the sixth letter was F, click on the button labeled F sixth.

After you have finished clicking on all the buttons to recreate the list, click on Next trial to start the next sequence. There are 20 trials.

At the end of the experiment, you will be asked if you want to save your data to a set of global data. After you answer the question, a new Web page window will appear that lists your class averages for this experiment. On that page is also a link to your personal data.

Additional References

Smyth, M., Hay, D., Hitch, G., & Horton, N. (2005). Serial position memory in the visual-spatial domain: Reconstructing sequences of unfamiliar faces. *Quarterly Journal of Experimental Psychology A: Human Experimental Psychology, 58*, 909-930.

Davis, C. & Bowers, J. (2004). What do letter migration errors reveal about letter position coding in visual word recognition? *Journal of Experimental Psychology: Human Perception and Performance, 30*, 923-941.

Maylor, E. (2002). Serial position effects in semantic memory: Reconstructing the order of verses of hymns. *Psychonomic Bulletin & Review, 9*, 816-820.

Basic Questions

1. When trying to recall a list of items in order, what are the two most common position errors?

2. What does a position error analysis tell about memory as compared to an overall performance analysis?

3. What target position did you most accurately recall? What target position did you have the most trouble with at recall?

Advanced Questions

1. Look at your data as well as the global data. What items in the list seem to have related response patterns?

2. If you plotted item number on the x-axis and percent correct on the y-axis, what would the graph look like (assuming the errors follow the predicted pattern)?

3. Imagine you're completing a history assignment and one of the questions asks you to complete a timeline for the prominent historical events discussed in class. You know you have all the important events down, but your instructor tells you you've made one error. The good news is your instructor allows you to correct your error if you can find it. Where is the best place to look for your error? What type of errors should you keep an eye out for?

Discussion Question

1. Many people report that it is easier to recall the number sequences for the early trials of the experiment as compared to the trials that occur toward the end of the experiment. Why do you think this might be the case?

Sternberg Search

Minimum time to complete this experiment: 20 minutes

Background

Many researchers of memory believe that there exists a short-term memory (STM) system that holds information for a few seconds. If the information in STM is not transferred to long term memory (LTM) for more-permanent storage, it vanishes. As evidence of the existence of STM grew, researchers started to explore its properties. In a series of articles starting in 1966, Saul Sternberg developed an experimental approach to explore how information was retrieved from STM.

The basic approach is simple. Subjects were shown a short (one to six items) list of numbers and asked to memorize them. After putting them to memory, a probe number was shown. The probe number was either one of the numbers in the list or a new number. The subject was to respond as quickly as possible, indicating whether the probe number was in the list or not. The reaction-time of the subject should reflect the time spent searching STM to determine whether the probe number is part of the list. By varying the number of items in the list, Sternberg hypothesized that he could test several theories of STM search.

For example, some neural-network theories of memory suggest that every item in memory can be accessed simultaneously due to the parallel nature of search in these networks. If such a search took place in STM, one would expect the reaction-times not to vary as the number of items (memory set size) increased.

On the other hand, if memory search required consideration of each item in succession, the reaction-times should increase with memory set size because the subject will, on average, have to search through more items. Sternberg's data was consistent with the successive (or serial) search.

Sternberg found two additional properties that were interesting. First, reaction-times grew linearly with increases in memory set size. For each additional item in the memory set, subjects took (on average) an additional 38 milliseconds to make their responses. Thus, it seems the probe item is compared one-by-one with each item in STM, and each comparison takes approximately 38 milliseconds.

Second, when he compared reaction-times for probe Present and Absent trials (probe item was in the memory set or not, respectively), Sternberg found no differences in reaction-times. This finding is notable because an Absent response can only be made after all items in STM have been searched and found not to match the probe item. At first glance, it might seem that a Present trial could terminate as soon as the probe item is matched with the appropriate item in STM. As a result, with a self-terminating search, one would expect Present trials to be faster, but the data contradict this hypothesis.

The counterintuitive finding from Sternberg's study is that search of STM is always exhaustive. That is, the cognitive processes responsible for searching STM for a particular item search through all items in STM before reporting whether or not the probe item is in memory.

Sternberg's study and his analysis of the data had a major influence on models of memory and cognitive psychology in general. While more-recent modeling approaches have shown that the implications of the data on theories of memory search are not as straightforward as once believed, the experimental approach and theorizing is classic. [For a review of the field, see Van Zandt & Townsend (1993).] This experiment allows you to participate in a variation of the Sternberg memory search task.

Instructions

1. In the text fields below, enter your CogLab log-in ID and password. If you do not have a log-in ID and password, see your instructor for information on how to get one for your class.
2. Click the Submit information button.
3. If the information is correct, the Start experiment button will become activated. Click the button to begin the experiment.

Start a trial by pressing the space bar. A fixation point will appear in the middle of the screen. After a second, a memory set consisting of 1, 3, or 5 numbers will appear on the screen for 1.2, 3.6, or 6 seconds, respectively. Study the numbers and commit them to memory. The memory set will disappear and then a probe item will appear 1 to 3 seconds later. Your task is to determine whether the probe item was in the list of just presented numbers. Respond as quickly as possible by pressing the / key (for Present) or z key (for Absent). You will receive feedback on whether you were correct. When you are ready for the next trial, press the space bar again.

There are a minimum of 60 trials in the experimental session. For each Present and Absent condition, 10 trials are presented for each memory set size. If you make a mistake (e.g., say the item was present when it was not), the trial will be repeated (with different numbers) later in the experiment. In this way, only reaction-times for trials in which you were correct are used. If you find you are often making mistakes, you should try slowing down your responses and/or try harder.

If you are distracted during a trial (e.g., you sneezed, attention drifted, you zoned out,...), press the *t* key instead of *z* or /. This will discard the trial. Press the space bar to start the next trial. The discarded trial will be rerun later in the experiment.

At the end of the experiment, you will be asked if you want to save your data to a set of global data. After you answer the question, a new Web page window will appear that lists your class averages for this experiment. On that page is also a link to your personal data.

Additional References

Houlihan, M., Pritchard, W., & Robinson, J. (2001). Effects of smoking/nicotine on performance and event-related potentials during a short-term memory scanning task. *Psychopharmacology, 156*, 388-396.

Scheffers, M., Humphrey, D., Stanny, R., Kramer, A., & Coles, M. (1999). Error-related processing during a period of extended wakefulness. *Psychophysiology, 36*, 149-157.

Kotchoubey, B., Jordan, J., Grozinger, B., Westphal, K., & Kornhuber, H. (1996). Event-related brain potentials in a varied-set memory search task: A reconsideration. *Psychophysiology, 33*, 530-540.

Basic Questions

1. What is the relationship between memory set size and reaction-time in a typical Sternberg Search task?

2. What is a self-terminating search? What is an exhaustive search?

3. Is your personal data consistent with Sternberg's findings? Explain.

Advanced Questions

1. Does your data support an exhaustive STM memory search or a self-terminating STM search? Why?

2. Use your data to predict your reaction-time for a memory set of seven items for a probe present and a probe absent response.

3. What does it mean to say there is a linear relationship between two variables? Would you classify the relationship between memory set and reaction-time from your personal data as linear?

Discussion Question

1. Do you think it is to our advantage that we use an exhaustive search of short-term memory as opposed to a self-terminating search? Why or why not?

Implicit Learning

Minimum time to complete this experiment: 25 minutes

Background

The term implicit learning refers to "the process by which knowledge about the rule-governed complexities of the stimulus environment is acquired independently of conscious attempts to do so" (Reber, 1989, p. 219).

One form of implicit learning involves serial-pattern learning. In this task, subjects are asked to press one of four keys as quickly as they can whenever they see a stimulus, such as an asterisk, appear in any of four locations (labeled A, B, C, and D). If the asterisk appears in location A, the subject is asked to press (for example) the z key. If the asterisk appears in location B, the subject is asked to press the x key. There is an underlying pattern that defines the order of locations. It is this pattern that the subject will learn. As the sequence is repeated, subjects press the keys more quickly. This indicates that learning has taken place. More evidence comes from a transfer test, in which the pattern is changed (again, without telling the subject). Now the subjects press the keys much more slowly.

The key evidence to support the idea that learning is implicit, not conscious, comes from tests in which subjects are asked what the pattern was. The typical finding is that subjects are unaware of the pattern, but their behavior shows that they have nonetheless learned it (see Stadler & Frensch, 1998).

This demonstration is based on a study reported by Destrebecqz and Cleeremans (2001). There will be a long series of trials in which you will be asked to indicate the location of a circle. Please try to respond as quickly as you possibly can. At the end of the experiment, you will be asked what the rule was that determined the location of the circle.

Instructions

1. In the text fields below, enter your CogLab log-in ID and password. If you do not have a log-in ID and password, see your instructor for information on how to get one for your class.
2. Click the Submit information button.

3. If the information is correct, the Start experiment button will become activated. Click the button to begin the experiment.

After clicking on the Start experiment button, a window will appear that is about the same size as your computer screen. Start a trial by pressing the space bar. A short time later, a circle will appear in one of the four locations listed below. Your task is to indicate the location of the circle by pressing the appropriate key as quickly as you can.

If the circle appears in the left-most location, press the *z* key as quickly as you can.
If the circle appears in the second location, press the *x* key as quickly as you can.
If the circle appears in the third location, press the . key as quickly as you can.
If the circle appears in the right-most location, press the / key as quickly as you can.

If the . and / keys are not the right-most keys on your keyboard, please use the Instructions menu (that will appear once you start the demonstration) to change the response keys so that you are using the right-most keys. There are 288 trials (each trial takes only a few seconds) and you can take a rest every 24 trials. Press the space bar to start each trial.

Click on the Next trial button to start a trial.

At the end of the experiment, you will be asked if you want to save your data to a set of global data. After you answer the question, a new Web page window will appear that lists your class averages for this experiment. On that page is also a link to your personal data.

Additional References

Kuhn, G., & Dienes, Z. (2005). Implicit learning of nonlocal musical rules: Implicitly learning more than chunks. *Journal of Experimental Psychology: Learning, Memory, and Cognition, 31*, 1417-1432.

Jiang, Y., & Leung, A. (2005). Implicit learning of ignored visual context. *Psychonomic Bulletin & Review, 12*, 100-106.

Karpicke, J., & Pisoni, D. (2004). Using immediate memory span to measure implicit learning. *Memory & Cognition, 32*, 956-964

Degel, J., Piper, D., & Koster, E. (2001). Implicit learning and implicit memory for odors: The influence of odor identification and retention time. *Chemical Senses, 26*, 267-280.

Basic Questions

1. What is the main difference between explicit and implicit learning?

2. While doing this demonstration did you feel as though you were learning a pattern of responses? Were you surprised to find out you participated in the version (random/pattern) of the experiment you did?

3. Using the graph from the demonstration's global data, determine if implicit learning is taking place? Explain why you drew the conclusion that you did.

Advanced Questions

1. You have just received you driver's license and the first place you drive to on your own is to your music lesson. When you get to your lesson, your instructor asks you what driving route you took to get there. You have a great deal of trouble describing your driving route to your instructor, but obviously you had no problem getting there. Explain how this could happen.

2. You just finished taking a mid-term exam in your hardest class of the semester. Despite it being a multiple-choice test (there were only four options to choose from for each question), you know you did not do very well. You can honestly say that you did not know the answer to one question; in fact, you could not even eliminate any of the multiple-choice options. When you get your test back, you are pleasantly surprised to see you received a 60%. How could you have thought you did so much worse than you did?

3. Name three activities that are typically learned implicitly.

Discussion Question

1. In a complex implicit-learning task, sometimes people are better off just paying attention to the task instead of trying to figure out the underlying pattern or structure. Why do you think this is the case?

Levels of Processing

Minimum time to complete this experiment: 30 minutes

Background

In the 1960s, the most common view of memory was that it consisted of a series of memory stores, including sensory memory, short-term memory, and long-term memory. Beginning in the 1970s, a different perspective was developed that said that the type of processing might be more important than the hypothetical store that retained the information.

Craik and Lockhart (1972) stressed four points in the development of their Levels of Processing framework. First, they said that memory was the result of a successive series of analyses, each at a deeper level than the previous one. A shallow level of processing could be focusing on how a word sounds; a deeper level of processing could be focusing on the meaning of a word. Second, Craik and Lockhart assumed that the deeper the level of processing, the more durable the resulting memory. Third, the levels of processing view assumes that rehearsal can be relatively unimportant. A lot of rehearsal using a shallow level of processing will lead to worse memory than much less rehearsal using a deep level of processing. The final point had to do with how memory should be studied: Because the emphasis is on processing rather than on structure, Craik and Lockhart suggested that researchers should use incidental learning rather than intentional learning. The reason is that the experimenter wants to study the effects of a particular type of processing. If the subject knows that there will be a memory test and tries to learn the material, the subject might use a different type of processing. If the subject is unaware that there will be a memory test, there is no reason to use a different type of processing.

	Sensory Register	Short-Term Store	Long-Term Store
Format	Literal Copy	Acoustic	Semantic
Capacity	Small	Very Small	Infinite
Duration	Up to 500 ms	Up to 30 sec	Years

There are two ways of accounting for basic memory phenomena. Reading down the table shows the structural view: If an item is in short-term store, its format will be acoustic, the capacity will be very small, and you'll be able to remember it for 20 to 30 seconds. Omitting the top row shows the processing view: If an item is encoded acoustically, the capacity is very small and the duration is around 30 seconds. According to the processing view, the first row becomes irrelevant.

Adapted from Table 5.1 of Neath & Surprenant (2003).

The typical levels-of-processing experiment uses incidental learning. A subject is asked to rate words based on the number of letters or consonants, or on the words' pleasantness. Because the subject is unaware that there will be a memory test later, the experimenter can assume that, once the rating task is over, the subject will not process the item further. After all of the ratings are done, the subject receives a surprise recall or recognition test. The usual finding is that the deeper the level of processing, the better the performance on the test.

This demonstration is adapted from one reported by Craik and Tulving (1975). Ideally, you would be unaware that there will be a memory test at the end and unaware that the three tasks are designed to induce different levels of processing.

Instructions

1. In the text fields below, enter your CogLab log-in ID and password. If you do not have a log-in ID and password, see your instructor for information on how to get one for your class.

2. Click the Submit information button.

3. If the information is correct, the Start experiment button will become activated. Click the button to begin the experiment.

Press the space bar to start each trial. There are two phases. In Phase I, you will see a word and a judgment task. There are three types of judgment tasks. For all judgments, you should press the z key to indicate a NO response and the / key to indicate a YES response.

Judgment 1 The first type of judgment is to decide if the word has a particular pattern of consonants and vowels. If it has the same pattern, press the / key. If it does not, press the z key. For example, you might see the word dog followed by cvc. You should press the / key because dog is spelled with a consonant, then a vowel, and then a consonant.

Judgment 2 The second type of judgment is to decide if two words rhyme. If they do, press the / key. If they don't, press the *z* key. For example, you might see the word fish followed by boat. You should press the *z* key because they do not rhyme.

Judgment 3 The third type of judgment is to decide if one word has a similar meaning to another. If they do, press the / key. If they don't, press the *z* key. For example, you might see the word angry followed by mad. You should press the / key because both angry and mad have similar meanings.

After you have completed the judgment, press the space bar for the next trial.

After you have completed all 60 judgments, you'll enter Phase II. Again, you'll press the space bar to start each trial. You will be shown a series of words, half of which were shown in Phase I, and half of which are new words. Please answer the question, "Was this word in Phase I?" If it was, press the / key to indicate that YES, the word was in Phase I. It is was not, press the *z* key to indicate that NO, the word was not in Phase I. There are 60 judgments in Phase I, and 120 trials in Phase II.

At the end of the experiment, you will be asked if you want to save your data to a set of global data. After you answer the question, a new Web page window will appear that lists your class averages for this experiment. On that page is also a link to your personal data.

Additional Resources

Kronlund, A. & Whittlesea, B. (2005). Seeing double: Levels of processing can cause false memory. *Canadian Journal of Experimental Psychology, 59*, 11-16.

Royet, J., Koenig, O., Paugam-Moisy, H., Puzenat, D., & Chasse, J. (2004). Levels-of-processing effects on a task of olfactory naming. *Perceptual and Motor Skills, 98*, 197-213.

Eich, J. (1985). Levels of processing, encoding specificity, elaboration, and CHARM. *Psychological Review, 92*, 1-38.

Basic Questions

1. In this demonstration, how are you asked to evaluate words to induce a shallow level of processing? How are you asked to evaluate words to induce a deep level of processing?

2. What is incidental learning? How do researchers typically study incidental learning?

3. Was your recall performance affected by your level of processing at study? Explain.

Advanced Questions

1. A friend reads you a phone number to put in your cell phone's phonebook. Approximately how long do you have to put this number into your phonebook before you forget it?

2. Suppose you slept in on Saturday, read a book, drove to your parents' house, made your parents dinner, ate, drove home, and went to bed. On Monday, according to levels of processing theory, are you more likely to remember if you were stopped by a traffic light on your way to your parents' house or what you had for dinner? Why?

3. What methods, other than the one used in this demonstration, could be used to induce a deep level of processing for a given word?

Discussion Question

1. Describe a situation in which a shallow level of processing might be preferred over a deeper level of processing.

Encoding Specificity

Minimum time to complete this experiment: 30 minutes

Background

According to the encoding specificity principle (Tulving, 1983), the recollection of an event depends on the interaction between the properties of the encoded event and the properties of the encoded retrieval information. In other words, whether an item will be remembered at a particular time depends on the interaction between the processing that occurred during encoding and the processing that occurred at retrieval.

This principle has important implications for what you can say about memory. Because it is the interaction of both encoding and retrieval that is important, it means that you cannot make any statement about the mnemonic properties of an item or a type of processing or a cue unless you specify both the encoding and the retrieval conditions (Tulving, 1983). Thus, you cannot say things like:

Recognition is easier than recall.
Deep processing is better than shallow processing.
Pictures are recalled better than words.

These statements are all meaningless because the encoding and retrieval conditions are not mentioned. It is easy to create situations in which recall is easier than recognition, shallow processing leads to better memory than deep processing, and words are recalled better than pictures.

This demonstration is loosely based on Thomson and Tulving (1970). Some target words will be presented alone at study and some will be presented along with a cue. At test, there are three cue conditions: no cue, same cue, or different cue. What determines your ability to recall a particular target is the interaction between how you process it at encoding and how you process it at test. If the cue changes, it is likely that you will process the item in a slightly different way than when the same cue is presented again.

Instructions

1. In the text fields below, enter your CogLab log-in ID and password. If you do not have a log-in ID and password, see your instructor for information on how to get one for your class.
2. Click the Submit information button.
3. If the information is correct, the Start experiment button will become activated. Click the button to begin the experiment.

There are two phases to this demonstration. Phase I. Start a trial by pressing the space bar. You will see a series of word pairs, such as cup-DESK. Each pair is shown for about 3 seconds. Sometimes there won't be a cue, and instead you'll see something like ????-DESK. There are 45 pairs of words.

In Phase II, you will be asked to recall the words that were shown in uppercase in Phase I. Sometimes you will be given a cue, and sometimes you won't. For example, you might see: cup-D--K. To respond, type in the two missing letters. If you can't remember the target, just type in any two letters. Press the space bar for the next test item.

There are 45 word pairs in Phase I, and 45 trials in Phase II.

At the end of the experiment, you will be asked if you want to save your data to a set of global data. After you answer the question, a new Web page window will appear that lists your class averages for this experiment. On that page is also a link to your personal data.

Additional References

Hannon, B., & Craik, F. (2001). Encoding specificity revisited: The role of semantics. *Canadian Journal of Experimental Psychology, 55*, 231-243.

Reddy, B., & Bellezza, F. (1983). Encoding specificity in free recall. *Journal of Experimental Psychology: Learning, Memory, and Cognition, 9*, 167-174.

Krane, R., & Hatton, L. (1980). Encoding specificity and modality effects in episodic memory. *Psychological Research, 42*, 353-362.

Basic Questions

1. When you were given no cue at study, in what test condition (strong cue, weak cue, or no cue) did you have the best recall? When given a weak cue at study, in what test condition did you have the best recall?

2. According to the encoding specificity principle, what is the most important factor for recall?

3. Are strong memory cues always better than weak memory cues? Explain your answer.

Advanced Questions

1. To get a driver's license, one usually must pass a written exam as well as an in-car driving test. From what you know about encoding specificity, why is the in-car test so important?

2. You have a friend who is taking a physics course at 8am and is performing poorly on the exams. He/she tells you that he/she has been studying for the class almost every evening, but still is not performing well. Using the information your friend has given you and what you know about encoding specificity, what advice would you give your friend?

3. On Sunday morning you see someone at brunch when you recognize but you can't think of his/her name or where you know him/her from. The next day at work you see the same person again, but this time you know his/her name right away. Why might this be?

Discussion Questions

1. Using the findings surrounding encoding specificity, what suggestions about study habits would you give someone who wanted to improve his/her performance on tests?

2. You have lost your keys. What can you do to help yourself remember where you might have left them?

Serial Position

Minimum time to complete this experiment: 20 minutes

Background

This demonstration explores the effect of list position on free recall. In many instances, we are presented with a list of items and must remember each of the items (e.g., grocery lists). If the order of the items is not required for accurate recall, the task is said to be unordered or free.

A general finding of free-recall tasks is that recall of an item is strongly influenced by its position in a list. A common finding is that the last few items in the list are remembered best (called a recency effect), the first few items are remembered fairly well (called a primacy effect), but items in the middle of the list are not recalled very well at all. Surprisingly, this property holds true for many types of items and for a wide variety of durations (seconds to years). The effect of serial position has played a major role in the development of memory theories.

Instructions

1. In the text fields below, enter your CogLab log-in ID and password. If you do not have a log-in ID and password, see your instructor for information on how to get one for your class.
2. Click the Submit information button.
3. If the information is correct, the Start experiment button will become activated. Click the button to begin the experiment.

Start a trial by clicking the Next trial button. The empty space on the left of the window will show a sequence of ten letters, each presented for one second. After the full sequence has been presented, the buttons on the right will become activated. Your task is to click on the buttons that correspond to the letters in the sequence just shown in any order. You cannot click on more than ten buttons, and each button can be clicked only once for a given sequence. After you have finished clicking on all of the buttons, click on Next trial to start the next sequence. The experiment includes fifteen sequences, with different letters making up the sequence each time.

Feel free to use whatever mental tricks you find helpful for recalling the consonants. Some people mentally (or verbally) rehearse items to themselves. Some people also click on the buttons for the last few items in the list before they fade from memory.

You can also create variations of this experiment by changing what you do during presentation of the sequence, or how you report back items. For example, if you try to recall the letters in the sequence in the order they were presented, you will likely find that the recency effect disappears. If you repeat a phrase to yourself during presentation of the sequence, you will likely find that your overall performance drops.

At the end of the experiment, you will be asked if you want to save your data to a set of global data. After you answer the question, a new Web page window will appear that lists your class averages for this experiment. On that page is also a link to your personal data.

Additional References

Smyth, M., Hay, D., Hitch, G., & Horton, N. (2005). Serial position memory in the visual-spatial domain: Reconstructing sequences of unfamiliar faces. *Quarterly Journal of Experimental Psychology A: Human Experimental Psychology, 58*, 909-930.

Haberlandt, K., Lawrence, H., Krohn, T., Bower, K., & Thomas, J. (2005). Pauses and durations exhibit a serial position effect. *Psychonomic Bulletin & Review, 12*, 152-158.

Surprenant, A. (2001). Distinctiveness and serial position effects in tonal sequences. *Perception & Psychophysics, 63*, 737-745.

Reed, P. (2000). Serial position effects in recognition memory for odors. *Journal of Experimental Psychology: Learning, Memory, and Cognition, 26*, 411-422.

Basic Questions

1. What is the primacy effect? Does your data show a primacy effect? Why or why not?

2. What is the recency effect? Does your data show a recency effect? Why or why not?

3. Serial position experiments typically have subjects use free recall during the test phase. What is free recall in this context?

Advanced Questions

1. If this demonstration added two items at the end of the ten item list, based on the typical serial position effects, how would the longer list change your recall of the early list items (positions 1, 2, and 3), the middle list items (positions 4, 5, 6, and 7) and the late list items (positions 8, 9, and 10)?

2. A technology company is holding open interviews from 8am to 2pm this Friday. You are very interested in the job and want to make sure you are remembered by your interviewer. Using what you have learned in this demonstration, what can you do to make this happen?

3. You are putting together a presentation for your psychology class and you notice that parts of your presentation are better than others. How should you organize your presentation to leave the class with the best impression possible?

Discussion Question

1. What types of professions could utilize what we know about serial recall? For each profession you come up with, describe specifically what they could do.

Suffix Effect

Minimum time to complete this experiment: 20 minutes

Background

People often have to recall a series of items in order, such as a phone number. When the list of items is heard (as opposed to read silently), people usually are very good at remembering the final list item. However, if the list is followed by an irrelevant item (the suffix), recall of the final item is substantially impaired.

The suffix has to be perceived as speech in order for it to have a large effect. If the suffix is a pure tone, there is no impairment. Although the suffix has to be speech, it does not have to be a word. In general, the suffix will have a larger effect the more acoustically similar it is to the list items. One reason that the suffix effect has attracted a lot of attention is that recall is impaired even when the suffix is expected and even when the suffix is the same item (usually the digit 0) on every trial.

The best explanation is that when the suffix is perceptually grouped with the list items, it functionally increases the list length. So, rather than trying to recall a 9-item list, you are in effect recalling a 10-item list (Neath & Surprenant, 2003).

Instructions

1. In the text fields below, enter your CogLab log-in ID and password. If you do not have a log-in ID and password, see your instructor for information on how to get one for your class.
2. Click the Submit information button.
3. If the information is correct, the Start experiment button will become activated. Click the button to begin the experiment.

This experiment requires a computer that can play sounds. We recommend using headphones so that you do not disturb other people. Please make sure the volume is not too loud before you put the headphones on.

A window will appear, and a second smaller window will appear with abbreviated instructions. Close the instructions window. You can open it again later from the CogLab Info. menu.

Click on the Next trial button to start a trial.

On each trial, you will hear the digits 1 through 9 in random order, followed by either a tone or the digit zero. Then you will see the response buttons become active. Your task is to click on the buttons in the same order that the digits were presented. After you have finished clicking on all the buttons to recreate the list, click on Next trial to start the next sequence.

Being correct means that you click on the buttons in the same order the items appeared in the sequence. There is no way to correct mistakes in button presses, so be careful in your selections. There are 30 trials.

At the end of the experiment, you will be asked if you want to save your data to a set of global data. After you answer the question, a new Web page window will appear that lists your class averages for this experiment. On that page is also a link to your personal data.

Additional References

Parmentier, F., Tremblay, S., & Jones, D. (2004). Exploring the suffix effect in serial visuospatial short-term memory. *Bulletin & Review, 11*, 289-295.

Penney, C. (1985). Elimination of the suffix effect on preterminal list items with unpredictable list length: Evidence for a dual model of suffix effects. *Journal of Experimental Psychology: Learning, Memory, and Cognition, 11*, 229-247.

Watkins, M., & Watkins, O. (1974). A tactile suffix effect. *Memory & Cognition, 2*, 176-180.

Basic Questions

1. What is the current explanation of the suffix effect that was given in the text?

2. Did your recall performance vary based on whether the target list was followed by the tone or the digit? Did you show the suffix effect? Explain.

3. What property of the suffix determines the magnitude of its effect in recall performance?

Advanced Questions

1. One of your parents has just listed some items for your brother to get at the grocery store. What could you do to make his recall of these items difficult?

2. Using your personal data, calculate your suffix effect. Using the global data, calculate the group suffix effect.

3. You have forgotten your password (a sequence of numbers and letters) for your home security system, so you call your security provider to get it. They read you the password over the phone and then ask you if there is anything else they can do for you. You say no,

thank them, and hang up. Assuming you try to remember the password instead of writing it down, what was problematic about this phone call regarding your future recall performance for your password?

Discussion Question

1. If you are orally given information that you want to remember later, discuss some things you can do to maximize your recall performance.

Remember/Know

Minimum time to complete this experiment: 30 minutes

Background

In a typical test of recognition memory, a subject might be shown a test item and asked if it was one that was presented on a particular list. The target might be either old (it was on the list) or new (it was not on the list). If the subject decides that an old test item was on the list, it is called a hit. If the subject decides that a new test item was on the list, it is called a false alarm.

A relatively recent change in testing recognition memory has been the introduction of the Remember/Know paradigm (Tulving, 1985). When subjects judge an item to be old, they are asked to make a further distinction. If they are consciously aware of some aspects of the original episode, they should indicate that they remember the item. For example, they can remember a particular thought that the word triggered, or they can remember thinking it was a coincidence that this particular word followed the previous one. If they have no conscious awareness of the learning episode, they should respond that they just know that the item was on the list.

The distinction can be explained in another way. If you were asked, "Who was the first president of the United States?", you most likely would name George Washington. However, you probably do not consciously recollect the original episode during which you learned this information. Rather, you just know the answer. In contrast, consider the following statement: Abraham Lincoln's first vice-president was Hannibal Hamlin, who was born in Paris, Maine. If, later on, someone asks you, "Who was Abraham Lincoln's first vice-president?", you might answer with Hannibal Hamlin. If you were consciously aware that you first learned this fact while reading a Web page on CogLab, you would remember this information in the remember/know sense. Note that it is not the type of information that makes a difference. Rather, it is the presence or absence of conscious awareness of aspects of the prior experience that are important.

This demonstration replicates studies reported by Gardiner (1988) and Rajaram (1993). You will be shown a series of words and asked to generate either a synonym or a word that rhymes. Then you will be given a recognition test in which you will be asked to indicate whether you recognize the word.

Instructions

1. In the text fields below, enter your CogLab log-in ID and password. If you do not have a log-in ID and password, see your instructor for information on how to get one for your class.
2. Click the Submit information button.
3. If the information is correct, the Start experiment button will become activated. Click the button to begin the experiment.

Press the space bar to start each trial. There are two phases. You will need a blank sheet of paper and a pen for the first phase. In Phase I, you will see a word and an instruction. If the instruction says Synonym for, write down a word that has the same meaning as the word shown. If the instruction says Rhymes with, write down a word that sounds the same as the target word. When you are done, press the space bar for the next item. You will need to write down your work quickly. Each item is shown for only 5 seconds.

After this, you'll enter Phase II. Press the space bar to start each trial. You will be shown a series of words, half of which were shown in Phase I and half of which are new words. Please answer the question, "Was this word in Phase I?" If it was, decide whether you remember the word or simply know it was on the list. Press r to indicate remember, and k to indicate know. If the word was not on the list, press the n key.

The judgment *remember* means that you are consciously aware of the learning episode. You can recollect some aspect of the experience, such as the word you provided as a synonym or rhyme, or the word that came before, or your thoughts about the word. If can't recollect such information, you should choose *know*.

There are 80 words shown in Phase I and 160 trials in Phase II.

At the end of the experiment, you will be asked if you want to save your data to a set of global data. After you answer the question, a new Web page window will appear that lists your class averages for this experiment. On that page is also a link to your personal data.

Additional References

Crawley, S. & French, C. (2005). Field and observer viewpoint in remember-know memories of personal childhood events. *Memory, 13*, 673-681.

Konstantinou, I. & Gardiner, J. (2005). Conscious control and memory awareness when recognizing famous faces. *Memory, 13*, 449-457.

Gardiner, J. & Java, R. (1990). Recollective experience in word and nonword recognition. *Memory & Cognition, 18*, 23-30.

Gardiner, J. (1988). Functional aspects of recollective experience. *Memory & Cognition, 16*, 309-313.

Basic Questions

1. In the context of this demonstration what does it mean to know something? Give an example of something that you know.

2. In the context of this demonstration, what does it mean to remember something? Give an example of something that you remember.

3. Did you show a levels-of-processing effect for your remember judgments? Explain your answer.

4. Did you show a levels-of-processing effect for your know judgments? Explain your answer.

Advanced Questions

1. You are putting together a school project on NASA, and you want to include personal accounts (how they felt, where they were, what they were thinking, who they were with) of people who watched the first moon landing on live television. In your search for people who can give you these accounts, do you want to look for people who know about this historic event or remember it? Why?

2. You are at the movie theatre and you see someone you recognize. Later you find out it was your 7th grade English teacher. Would you categorize your initial recognition of your teacher as knowing or remembering? Why?

3. Your little sister starts talking about a family vacation that you had gone on quite some time ago when she was only 3 years old. She swears she remembers the trip but you are skeptical. How would you go about trying to figure out if she actually remembers the trip or just knows about the trip?

Discussion Question

1. Do you think people are more confident about things they know or things they remember? Explain your answer.

False Memory

Minimum time to complete this experiment: 15 minutes

Background

An important issue for theories of cognition is how well we remember things. It is important because nearly every aspect of cognition depends on memory to some degree. To understand problem solving, decision making, attention, and perception, you need to know the abilities and limits of memory. The quality of memory is important for practical reasons as well. Many significant events depend on reports from human observers. From eyewitness testimony in murder trials to arguments with a spouse about who said what, memory and memory accuracy is critical. A surprising finding is that there is no way to assess memory accuracy without objective evidence (such as a tape recording or a photograph). The vividness or confidence of the person recalling the memory is not an accurate indication of the truth of the memory. This is not to say that most memories are inaccurate. We must be pretty accurate much of the time or else living would be quite difficult. However, for those situations in which accuracy of detail is important, memories cannot be trusted, no matter how adamant the recaller is about the vividness of the memory.

This experiment demonstrates one methodology that biases people to recall things that did not occur. The memories associated with experiments of this type are often called false memories. The method was first used by Deese (1959) and has been extended more recently by Roediger and McDermott (1995). The task is like many other memory experiments. A sequence of words is presented (verbally or visually) and the observer must subsequently classify a set of words as either in the sequence (old) or not in the sequence (new).

What differentiates this experiment from other memory experiments is that the sequences are specially designed to bias observers to report a particular word that was not included in the list. When people report that one of these words was in the sequence but it really was not, they are having a false memory. In some cases, people will report that they vividly recall seeing (or hearing) the word, so their memories are very strong, despite their inaccuracy.

Instructions

1. In the text fields below, enter your CogLab log-in ID and password. If you do not have a log-in ID and password, see your instructor for information on how to get one for your class.
2. Click the Submit information button.
3. If the information is correct, the Start experiment button will become activated. Click the button to begin the experiment.

After clicking on the Start experiment button, a window will appear with a blank area on the left and a number of buttons on the right. Start a trial by pressing the Next trial button. A sequence of words will appear on the left of the window, with each word presented for one and a half seconds. After the full sequence has been presented, the buttons on the right will show labels for words, including some of those just shown. The other buttons will contain distractor words. You must distinguish the old words from the new distractor words. Your task is to click on the buttons for the words that were just shown. Not all of the words in the sequence will be listed on the buttons. After you have finished clicking on all of the buttons that you remember being in the sequence, click on Next trial to start the next sequence.

The experiment includes only six trials. For each trial, click on the word buttons that were in the sequence just presented.

At the end of the experiment, you will be asked if you want to save your data to a set of global data. After you answer the question, a new Web page window will appear that lists your class averages for this experiment. On that page is also a link to your personal data.

Additional References

Lampinen, J., Meier, C., Arnal, J., & Leding, J. (2005). Compelling untruths: Content borrowing and vivid false memories. *Journal of Experimental Psychology: Learning, Memory, and Cognition, 31*, 954-963.

Garry, M., & Wade, K. (2005). Actually, a picture is worth less than 45 words: Narratives produce more false memories than photographs do. *Psychonomic Bulletin & Review, 12*, 359-366.

Slotnick, S., & Schacter, D. (2004). A sensory signature that distinguishes true from false memories. *Nature Neuroscience, 7*, 664-672.

Dehon, H., & Bredart, S. (2004). False memories: Young and older adults think of semantic associates at the same rate, but young adults are more successful at source monitoring. *Psychology and Aging, 19*, 191-197.

Basic Questions

1. In regard to false-memory experiments, what are special distractors?

2. Did you report seeing words that were not on the original list? If so, were these inaccurately remembered words mostly normal distractors or special distractors?

3. How can one access the accuracy of someone's memory?

Advanced Questions

1. Come up with a list of 10 words that you think could create a false memory. Using this list, what particular word/words do you think could be falsely remembered?

2. You are driving your brother and sister to your aunt's house for dinner. You haven't been to her house in a while, so you ask your siblings if either of them knows the way. Your sister says she believes she knows the way. Your brother is much more confident that he knows the way and says he can visualize the last time he went to your aunt's house. The problem is they disagree on how to get there. Whom should you believe?

3. Last time you went to see your doctor, you remembered him/her wearing a stethoscope, but later found out that, because of his/her hearing impairment, your doctor does not use a stethoscope. Why might you have been mistaken?

Discussion Question

1. What kind of implications do experiments on false memory have for evaluating the validity of eyewitness accounts?

114

Forgot-It-All-Along Effect

Minimum time to complete this experiment: 30 minutes

Background

There has been much controversy over the issue of recovered memories. (For an excellent overview, see Conway, 1997.) This is the apparent finding that people who enter psychotherapy suddenly recover memories of events that happened to them years ago, usually memories of sexual abuse. Schooler, Bendiksen, & Ambadar (1997) use the term discovered rather than recovered memories because the latter implies that the memories are of real events whereas the former is neutral on whether the memory is of a real event or not.

Schooler et al. (1997) note that there are three independent claims being made when a person in therapy discovers a memory:

The event that is remembered is a real event.
The event was forgotten for a period of time.
The event is suddenly remembered.

Schooler et al. point out that these three elements are independent. For example, the event could be real and the memory could be accurate, but there might not have been a period during which the person was unaware of the event. Each of these claims can in principle be empirically evaluated.

Schooler et al. (1997) found 4 cases in which they can demonstrate objectively that (1) the original event occurred, (2) there was a period of time during which the person did not remember the event, and (3) the memory was suddenly discovered. What this demonstrates is not that all discovered memories are of real events but rather that, in at least some cases, a person can experience an event, can fail to remember that event, and then later can recall the event.

For the memory theorist, what is most interesting is the finding that, at the time of discovery, the person has the experience of currently remembering the event but also believing they had not previously remembered the event. One explanation of this failure by people to remember what they had remembered has been termed the forgot-it-all-along effect (Schooler et al., 1997). (The name is based on the knew-it-all-along effect in which subjects who were told of a particular outcome overestimated what they would have known.) The basic idea is that during the discovered-memory experience, the person thinks about the episode in a different way.

This demonstration is a laboratory analog of this forgot-it-all-along effect that was devised by Arnold & Lindsay (2002). No one is claiming that this is exactly the same effect as when people say they had not remembered being abused earlier but now they do. Rather, it is a demonstration that people can forget what they had remembered.

There are three phases. In Phase I, you will see a list of word pairs, a cue, and a target. In Phase II, you will receive a cued-recall test. Sometimes the cue will be the same as in Phase I and sometimes it will be different. In Phase III, you will be given a memory judgment task: You will be asked if you recall a target in the Phase II test. You should remember that you recall an item better when the context is the same and you should forget that you recall an item when the context is different.

Instructions

1. In the text fields below, enter your CogLab log-in ID and password. If you do not have a log-in ID and password, see your instructor for information on how to get one for your class.
2. Click the Submit information button.
3. If the information is correct, the Start experiment button will become activated. Click the button to begin the experiment.

There are three phases to this demonstration. Phase I. Start a trial by pressing the space bar. You will see a series of word pairs, such as cup-DESK. Each pair is shown for about 3 seconds. There are 44 pairs of words.

In Phase II, you will be given a cued-recall test. You will be shown a cue and will be asked to recall the word that was presented with it. For example, you might see: cup-D--K. To respond, type in the two missing letters. If you can't remember the target, just type in any two letters. Press the space bar for the next test item.

In Phase III, you will be shown a cue and target pair again, but this time you will be asked if you recall the target in Phase II. Press *y* to indicate YES, you do remember it;

press *n* to indicate that NO, you do not remember it. Press the space bar for the next test item.

There are 44 word pairs in Phase I, and 44 trials in Phase II and III.

At the end of the experiment, you will be asked if you want to save your data to a set of global data. After you answer the question, a new Web page window will appear that lists your class averages for this experiment. On that page is also a link to your personal data.

Additional References

Padilla-Walker, L., & Poole, D. (2002). Memory for previous recall: A comparison of free and cued recall. *Applied Cognitive Psychology, 16*, 515-524.

Joslyn, S., Loftus, E., McNoughton, A., & Powers, J. (2001). Memory for memory. *Memory & Cognition, 29*, 789–797.

Bouton, M., Nelson, J., & Rosas, J. (1999). Stimulus generation, context change, and forgetting. *Psychological Bulletin, 125*, 171–186.

Basic Questions

1. Why did Schooler, Bendiken, & Ambadar (1997) use the term discovered memories as opposed to recovered memories?

2. Did you forget (in Phase III) that you had correctly remembered items during the test phase (Phase II)? How do you know?

3. Were your individual experimental results similar to the predicted results of this experiment? Why or why not?

Advanced Questions

1. A friend tells you he/she does not remember telling you about his/her senior prom, but you remember him/her telling you about it very clearly. What could you do to make it more likely that he/she will remember?

2. Everyone in your Latin class did poorly on the exam last week, but the instructor tells all of you that he/she would be willing to give everyone a replacement test that would cover exactly the same material if everyone thinks they can do better. One of the other students in the class comments that they could not possibly do worse the second time around. What do you think about that statement? Why?

3. Taking into account the predicted results of this experiment, what effect does context have in memory?

Discussion Question

1. Many people have discovered memories while in therapy and sometimes these memories are of a sensitive nature (i.e., abuse, violence). How do you think these memories should be handled?

Prototypes

Minimum time to complete this experiment: 20 minutes

Background

Part of cognitive psychology explores the concept of concepts. What cognitive events happen when you think about a chair? How is the concept of chair represented in the cognitive system? This is a subtle issue. For example, surely a seat at a formal dining table is chair, but what about a recliner, a stool, a couch, or a tree stump? The issue is important because the representation of concepts is the basis of everything else we can do mentally with concepts. In a very real sense, how we think and what we can learn is largely determined by how we represent concepts.

An efficient way to represent concepts would be to keep only the critical properties of a concept. This set of critical properties is sometimes called a prototype or schema. The idea of prototypes is that a person has a mental construct that identifies typical characteristics of various categories. When a person encounters a new object, he/she compares it to the prototypes in memory. If it matches the prototype for a chair well enough, the new object will be classified and treated as a chair. This approach allows new objects to be interpreted on the basis of previously learned information. It is a powerful approach because you do not need to store all previously seen chairs in long-term memory. Instead, only the prototype needs to be kept.

This experiment allows you to participate in a type of experiment that is often used to investigate the creation and storage of concepts. It is a variation of a method used by Posner & Keele (1968), which is one of the earliest studies to systematically explore concept representation in a controlled way. Rather than using an already well-known concept such as a chair, Posner and Keele had participants learn patterns of dots. The patterns were variations of a few prototypes, but the prototypes themselves were not seen during a training phase. During the training phase, participants learned to classify the variations, with the underlying prototype being the basis for correct classifications.

After learning to classify the variants, participants were shown a variety of dot patterns. In particular, they were shown patterns that were shown during the training phase, new variant patterns, and the patterns corresponding to the prototypes. Classification and reaction-time performance were nearly equal for the previously seen variants and the prototypes. Performance was slightly worse for the new variants. This is significant because both the new variants and the prototypes were never seen during testing. To classify dot patterns that were not previously seen, the participants must be using a mental concept of what corresponds to the different categories. Since performance is better for the prototype patterns than for the new variants, the mental concept is similar to the prototype patterns. The conclusion seemed to be that people created a mental representation that was a mixture of the variant patterns used during training (that is, a prototype).

Posner and Keele's experiment led to an intense investigation of concept formation and representation. Much of that research is consistent with prototype theories. However, there are aspects of the experimental data (even in Posner and Keele's experiment) that suggest that the prototype theories cannot be the sole basis for concept representation. For example, our behavior is often influenced by the properties of individual experiences, and some theories of concept formation suggest that this alone can account for the data purported to imply prototypes. Nevertheless, prototypes are a part of many theories of cognition in a variety of forms. This demonstration is a variation of Posner and Keele's experiment.

Instructions

1. In the text fields below, enter your CogLab log-in ID and password. If you do not have a log-in ID and password, see your instructor for information on how to get one for your class.
2. Click the Submit information button.
3. If the information is correct, the Start experiment button will become activated. Click the button to begin the experiment.

After clicking on the Start experiment button, a window will appear that fills the screen. Press the space bar to start a trial. A fixation point will appear for a second and then will be replaced by randomly placed dots. Your task is to classify the dot pattern as A (press the z key) or as B (press the / key). On the first few trials, you will not be able to properly classify the patterns, but you will receive feedback on each trial and so can learn which pattern corresponds to which keypress. You should make your responses as quickly as possible, but try to be accurate.

The experiment consists of separate training and testing phases. The training phase includes at least 60 trials (trials in which a mistake is made are repeated later in the experiment) and the testing phase contains at least 30 trials. Each dot pattern in the training phase is a variation of one of two fixed prototype random dot patterns. The variations are made by randomly taking ten of the twenty-five dots in a prototype and moving them to a new position.

After completing the training phase, a new set of dot patterns is presented. The transition from training to testing is fairly seamless, and you may not notice when it happens. The dot patterns in the testing phase are of six types. One is the prototype that corresponds to the A category. Another is the prototype that corresponds to the B category. The other four patterns are new variations of these prototypes (two variations for each prototype). Each dot pattern is presented five times in random order.

Throughout this experiment your task is always the same. As quickly as possible classify the pattern as A or B. Press the space bar to start the next trial.

At the end of the experiment, you will be asked if you want to save your data to a set of global data. After you answer the question, a new Web page window will appear that lists your class averages for this experiment. On that page is also a link to your personal data.

Additional References

Nosofsky, R., & Stanton, R. (2005). Speeded classification in a probabilistic category structure: Contrasting exemplar-retrieval, decision-boundary, and prototype models. *Journal of Experimental Psychology: Human Perception and Performance, 31*, 608-629.

Zaki, S., & Nosofsky, R. (2004). False prototype enhancement effects in dot pattern categorization. *Memory & Cognition, 32*, 390-398.

Smith, J., & Minda, J. (2002). Distinguishing prototype-based and exemplar-based processes in dot-pattern category learning. *Journal of Experimental Psychology: Learning, Memory, and Cognition, 28*, 800-811.

Dopkins, S., & Gleason, T. (1997). Comparing exemplar and prototype models of categorization. *Canadian Journal of Experimental Psychology, 51*, 212-230.

Basic Questions

1. Describe what someone's prototype for a dog might be like.

2. Looking at your experimental results, did you show the prototype effect in this demonstration? How do you know?

3. How does a prototype model explain the prototype effect?

Advanced Questions

1. What is the typicality effect? How does the prototype model account for typicality effects?

2. On a school trip to the zoo, a grade school child sees a penguin and a cardinal for the first time. According to the prototype model, which bird will the child classify as a bird more quickly? Why?

3. You are taking a botany course and you are doing some field work. You come across three trees that you identify as conifer trees. You have seen two of the trees before but not the third. You are surprised because, despite not having seen the third tree before, you identify it as a conifer tree before identifying the other two trees you have seen before. Why might this be the case?

Discussion Question

1. A competing model to the prototype model is the exemplar model. Describe the exemplar model and explain how it accounts for prototype effects.

Lexical Decision

Minimum time to complete this experiment: 15 minutes

Background

Theories of human language propose that a mental dictionary exists, a lexicon, that contains a variety of information about words. This lexicon contains information about a word's meaning (its semantic content), its part of language (noun, verb, adjective, etc.), and its relationship to other words (What can it follow? What can follow it? How can it be modified?). Psychologists are interested in the organization of this lexicon.

The lexicon is similar to a dictionary in that it holds information about words and other components of language. Physical dictionaries generally organize words alphabetically. This arrangement makes it easy to find any word, provided the spelling is known or can be guessed. Because dictionaries usually are used to find the meanings of known words or to check if a word is spelled properly, this organization is useful.

In the mental lexicon, though, the most useful feature of a word may not be its spelling, but its meaning and its relationship to other words. If words are arranged in the lexicon by semantic relationships, words that are related to each other (e.g., chair, seat, table) would be close together in the lexicon, whereas words that are unrelated to each other (e.g., chair, dinosaur, broccoli) would be far apart.

In this demonstration, you will be asked to determine if a series of letters is a word or a nonword. The computer will record your reaction-time, that is, how fast you are able to make your decision about each letter string. Remember to make your decision as quickly and accurately as you can.

Instructions

1. In the text fields below, enter your CogLab log-in ID and password. If you do not have a log-in ID and password, see your instructor for information on how to get one for your class.
2. Click the Submit information button.
3. If the information is correct, the Start experiment button will become activated. Click the button to begin the experiment.

Press the space bar to start a trial. A small fixation square will appear in the middle of the screen. Fix on this square. One to four seconds later, a word or nonword will appear above the fixation square. Decide if the item is a word or a nonword as quickly as possible. Press the / key if the item is a word. Press the *z* key if the item is not a word. The item will disappear when you press either of these keys, so you will know your response has been recorded.

Two to three seconds later, the next word or nonword will appear. Again, decide if the item is a word or nonword by pressing the / key or *z* key as quickly as possible. You will receive feedback when you respond too quickly (before the item appears), too slowly, or incorrectly.

There are at least 70 total trials. You must classify the items correctly for the trial to count, so if you find that you are making many classification mistakes, slow down.

At the end of the experiment, you will be asked if you want to save your data to a set of global data. After you answer the question, a new Web page window will appear that lists your class averages for this experiment. On that page is also a link to your personal data.

Additional References

Ratcliff, R., Thapar, A., Gomez, P., & McKoon, G. (2004). A diffusion model analysis of the effects of aging in the lexical-decision task. *Psychology and Aging, 19*, 278-289.

Ratcliff, R., Gomez, P., & McKoon, G. (2004). A diffusion model account of the lexical decision task. *Psychological Review, 111*, 159-182.

Chwilla, D., & Kolk, H. (2002). Three-step priming in lexical decision. *Memory & Cognition, 30*, 217-225.

Wentura, D. (2000). Dissociative affective and associative priming effects in the lexical decision task: Yes versus no responses to word targets reveal evaluative judgment tendencies. *Journal of Experimental Psychology: Learning, Memory, and Cognition, 26*, 456-469.

124

Basic Questions

1. What types of information are held in one's mental lexicon?

2. Were your results consistent with the demonstration predictions? Explain your answer.

3. Demonstrations like the one you just completed typically show semantic priming. What is semantic priming?

Advanced Questions

1. You enjoy watching game shows and one of your favorites is Jeopardy. Jeopardy is a quiz show in which contestants answer questions from a set of identified categories. When you watch the show, you notice that if you did not see the question category before the question was asked you are never able to come up with the correct answer before the question timer runs out. Using what you have learned from this demonstration, why might this be the case?

2. Identify words that would prime each of the following words: cold, angry, and soft.

3. You are writing a test and you want to make it as challenging as possible. Using what you have learned in this demonstration, how can you organize the test questions to achieve this goal?

Discussion Question

1. This demonstration showed semantic priming. What other types of word priming are there? Describe each one you come up with.

Absolute Identification

Minimum time to complete this experiment: 15 minutes

Background

Lots of research in cognitive psychology has focused on whether there is a fundamental limit on people's capacity to process information and, if so, what that limit is. It might often seem that we have almost unlimited potential, especially when it comes to identifying and recognizing different items. Think of all the different people you can identify, or cars, or animals, or buildings, or pieces of furniture. Given the ease with which all of these items can be identified, it comes as a surprise to most people to find that when items vary in just one dimension, they cannot identify even seven items. The research that demonstrates this limitation is often done using a procedure known as absolute identification.

In a typical absolute-identification experiment, people are exposed to a set of stimuli that vary systematically along only one dimension (e.g., nine tones of different frequencies, or eight lines of different lengths). A label, often a digit, is associated with each stimulus. The task is simply to produce the correct label in response to the presentation of an item from the set.

In the memory task, the participant viewed a trigram of consonants (e.g., GKT, WCH,...) and then performed a number of algebraic computations (e.g., counting backward by 3s) for less than 20 seconds. The data showed that recall of the trigram was less likely as the participant worked on the algebraic computations for longer durations.

When the items are evenly spaced, the first and last items in the series are identified most easily. In contrast, identification of the middle items is usually quite poor. Such effects are found for many dimensions, such as frequency, loudness, weight, area, line length, and semantic continua.

One curious aspect is that performance seems fundamentally limited: No matter how many trials, you are never perfect at this task as long as the stimuli vary along only one dimension (Shiffrin & Nosofsky, 1994). If the stimuli vary along two or more dimensions, the task becomes trivially easy. For example, you probably have no trouble identifying the letters in the alphabet. This is because the letters vary on multiple dimensions including height (the letter t is taller than the letter e), curvature (the letter i is straight, the letter s is all curves), and others.

Instructions

1. In the text fields below, enter your CogLab log-in ID and password. If you do not have a log-in ID and password, see your instructor for information on how to get one for your class.
2. Click the Submit information button.
3. If the information is correct, the Start experiment button will become activated. Click the button to begin the experiment.

This experiment requires a computer that can play sounds. We recommend using headphones so that you do not disturb other people. Please make sure the volume is not too loud before you put the headphones on.

A window will appear that fills nearly the entire screen, and a smaller window will appear with abbreviated instructions. Close the instructions window. You can open it again later from the CogLab Info. menu.

Click on the space bar to start a trial. You will first hear all 9 tones. Tone 1 is the lowest in pitch, Tone 9 is the highest in pitch. Press the space bar to start the demonstration.

On each trial, you will hear one of the 9 tones. Your task is to press a key that indicates which tone you think it is. For example, if you think it is Tone 2, press the 2 key. If you think it is Tone 6, press the 6 key. The computer will tell if you were correct. If you were not correct, the computer will also tell you which tone it was. You start each trial by pressing the space bar. There are 90 trials. This sounds like a lot, but it takes only a couple of seconds per trial.

At the end of the experiment, you will be asked if you want to save your data to a set of global data. After you answer the question, a new Web page window will appear that lists your class averages for this experiment. On that page is also a link to your personal data.

Additional References

Stewart, N., Brown, G., & Chater, N. (2005). Absolute identification by relative judgment. *Psychological Review, 112,* 881-911.

Rouder, J., Morey, R., Cowan, N., & Pfaltz, M. (2004). Learning in a unidimensional absolute identification task. *Psychonomic Bulletin & Review, 11*, 938-944.

McCormack, T., Brown, G., Maylor, E., Richardson, L., & Darby, R. (2002). Effects of aging on absolute identification of duration. *Psychology and Aging, 17*, 363-378.

Lacouture, Y., & Lacerte, D. (1997). Stimulus modality and stimulus-response compatibility in absolute identification. *Canadian Journal of Experimental Psychology, 51*, 165-170.

Basic Questions

1. In what dimension did the tones in this demonstration vary?

2. If you were given extensive training on this task, how would your results change?

3. Which tones were you most accurately able to identify? Which tones did you have the most difficulty identifying?

Advanced Questions

1. Using the global data, graph the results of this demonstration by plotting the tones presented (1-9) on the x-axis and the average number of times each tone was correctly identified on the y-axis. What is the general shape of the curve you just plotted?

2. Identify a category of items for which you are good at distinguishing among its members. Why is your identification performance of items within this category so good?

3. You are designing an interface for a control room at a factory. One of the factory employees shows you the interface they currently use. One of the features of the old interface is a light indicator that goes off multiple times a day. Its flashing rate indicates one of 7 responses that the control-room operator needs to make. Why is this aspect of the current interface design problematic? What could you do to make it better?

Discussion Question

1. In what ways are the predicted results of this demonstration similar to the typical results from an ordered serial recall task?

Link Word

Minimum time to complete this experiment: 30 minutes

Background

The link word method (e.g., Atkinson & Raugh, 1975) is a way of associating or linking two words together. It is based on the finding that when people form an interactive image between two concepts, one item becomes an excellent cue for retrieving the second item. As applied to foreign vocabulary learning, the purpose of the link word method is to learn a working vocabulary and basic grammar of a foreign language as quickly as possible. Conversational fluency in a foreign language will be achieved only by extended study and practice in the foreign country. The link word method will get you going faster than rote learning and will complement formal instruction.

Gruneberg (1994) describes a system for learning French. (There are systems for other languages also; see unforgettablelanguages.com.) The key is to form an interactive image made up of one object that corresponds to the English word and one that corresponds to the French. For example, the French for goat is chèvre (SHEVR). Imagine a goat sleeping on your Chevy truck. Carefully study the image you have formed for about 10 seconds or so. After studying about 10 words, a quick test is given. This ensures practice in generating the French word.

Then a bit of grammar is introduced. French words are either masculine (le) or feminine (la). To remember the gender of a word, you create an interactive image with either a boxer (to convey masculine) or a bottle of French perfume (to convey feminine). For example, imagine pouring a bottle of perfume over a goat to stop the bad smell. Then imagine a boxer punching a rabbit. You learn the gender of the words you previously learned, and then are tested again (e.g., you are asked to come up with la chèvre and le lapin).

The next stage is to learn about a dozen useful words, such as adjectives (which are then tested), followed by learning the French present tense of to be. Finally, you put all of this together and produce sentences such as "Le lapin est petit." You can go through an entire book in about twelve hours or so, and end up with a vocabulary of 500 or more words. More importantly, you can easily remember the words that you have learned.

This demonstration illustrates the use of the link word technique to learn words. (It won't cover grammar, etc.) The words and descriptions come from Gruneberg (1994) and are used with permission of the author, Dr. Michael Gruneberg.

Instructions

1. In the text fields below, enter your CogLab log-in ID and password. If you do not have a log-in ID and password, see your instructor for information on how to get one for your class.
2. Click the Submit information button.
3. If the information is correct, the Start experiment button will become activated. Click the button to begin the experiment.

When the demonstration begins, you will see a new window appear. Click once on the Next trial button to start a trial. You will see a French word (with a guide to pronunciation) and the word's meaning in English. You also will be given a suggestion of an image to form. Try to form as vivid an image as you can, and make sure the two objects in your image interact. Try to spend 10 seconds examining your image.

After you have seen 50 words, you will be given a vocabulary test. For the test, you will be shown a French word and asked to type in the English meaning. When you have entered the word, click once on the Next trial button.

There are 50 words, and 50 test questions for a total of 100 trials.

At the end of the experiment, you will be asked if you want to save your data to a set of global data. After you answer the question, a new Web page window will appear that lists your class averages for this experiment. On that page is also a link to your personal data.

Additional References

Beaton, A., Gruneberg, M., Hyde, C., Shufflebottom, A., & Sykes, R. (2005). Facilitation of receptive and productive foreign vocabulary learning using the keyword method: The role of image quality. *Memory, 13*, 458-471.

Campos, A., Amor, A., & Gonzalez, M. (2004). The importance of the keyword-generation method in keyword mnemonics. *Experimental Psychology, 51*, 125-131

Campos, A., Gonzalez, M., & Amor, A. (2003). Limitations of the mnemonic-keyword method. *Journal of General Psychology, 130*, 399-413.

Wieczynski, D., & Blick, K. (1996). Self-referencing versus the keyword method in learning vocabulary words. *Psychological Reports, 79*, 1391-1394.

Basic Questions

1. Look at your individual data. How many words did you correctly translate? For the words you correctly translated, did you use the image you visualized during the study phase?

2. There was no control condition in this experiment. What could have been done to add a control condition?

3. How does forming an interactive image between a concept you are not familiar with and a concept you are familiar with help with recall of the unfamiliar item?

Advanced Questions

1. Using the link word method, what types of images are most effective in helping people remember?

2. The Spanish word for dog is perro and the Spanish word for cat is gato. Use the link word method to help yourself remember how to translate perro and gato from Spanish to English. Describe your process.

3. In what other situations could one use the link word method besides learning a foreign language? For each situation you come up with, give an example of one of the images you might use.

Discussion Question

1. What problems do you foresee in using the link word method for learning a foreign language?

Word Superiority

Minimum time to complete this experiment: 30 minutes

Background

Humans are extremely good at recognizing visual patterns. Even the fastest of modern computers are nowhere near as efficient or thorough at identifying visual targets. How we acquired this level of sophistication is not fully understood. What is clear is that context plays an important role in interpreting a physical stimulus. We are not simply detectors of patterns of light; instead, we infer interpretations of the physical stimulus.

The effect of context is made clear in a phenomenon called the word superiority effect (Reicher, 1969). In the experiment, an isolated letter such as K or a word such as WORK is briefly flashed on the screen and then immediately replaced by a mask of Xs and Os. The observer is then forced to choose between whether a D or a K was presented. A key component of the experiment is that either of the choices at the end of WOR would create a valid word. Thus, the observer's knowledge that the presentation contained a word does not automatically tell him/her which letter was presented. Even with this control, the experimental finding is that detection of K is better when it is part of a word than when it is presented in isolation. This is the word superiority effect.

This result seems paradoxical. In detecting an isolated letter, there is only one item to focus on. When a word is presented, more letters must be processed before the word can be detected. Thus, it would seem, detecting a letter in a word should be more difficult than detecting a letter in isolation. The data, however, demonstrate exactly the opposite effect.

This finding has been of significant interest to researchers who explore the processes involved in recognizing patterns. Although the word superiority effect has been a motivating result for a variety of theories, the effect has not been completely explained by any current theory. This demonstration allows you to participate in a version of the word superiority experiment.

Instructions

1. In the text fields below, enter your CogLab log-in ID and password. If you do not have a log-in ID and password, see your instructor for information on how to get one for your class.
2. Click the Submit information button.
3. If the information is correct, the Start experiment button will become activated. Click the button to begin the experiment.

After clicking on the Start experiment button, a window will appear to start the experiment. Start a trial by pressing the space bar. A fixation dot will appear in the middle of the window. Stare at it. One second later, a word or an isolated letter will briefly flash on the screen. The duration of this word or letter is very brief (approximately 40 milliseconds). Then the word/letter is replaced with a mask of Xs and Os. Half a second later, instructions will appear about which position you are to report on. These instructions are of the form *--- S or M? This indicates that you are to report on whether the letter in the first position is an S or an M. An instruction such as --*- E or L? indicates that you are to report on whether the letter in the third position is an E or a L. Simply type in the letter that you saw at the indicated position. You will not receive any feedback on whether your guess was correct. The letter you type, however, will be shown in red on the bottom half of the screen. This indicates that the computer has registered the key you pressed.

Additional References

Grainger, J., Bouttevin, S., Truc, C., Bastien, M., & Ziegler, J. (2003). Word superiority, pseudoword superiority, and learning to read: A comparison of dyslexic and normal readers. *Brain and Language, 87*, 432-440.

Salvemini, A., Stewart, A., Purcell, D., & Pinkham, R. (1998). A word-superiority effect in the presence of foveal load. *Perceptual and Motor Skills, 86*, 1311-1319.

Krueger, L. (1992). The word-superiority effect and phonological recoding. *Memory & Cognition, 20*, 685-694.

Estes, W., & Brunn, J. (1987). Discriminability and bias in the word-superiority effect. *Perception & Psychophysics, 42*, 411-422.

Basic Questions

1. What is the word superiority effect?

2. Does your data show the word superiority effect? Explain why or why not.

3. Why could one argue that the typical word superiority effect findings are counter intuitive?

Advanced Questions

1. What is bottom-up information? What is top-down information?

2. Using the definitions from your answer to Advanced Question one, which type of information is likely to be the cause of the differences in letter detection performance typically seen in the word superiority effect? Explain your answer.

3. You walk by the same art gallery everyday on your way home from work. Sometimes when walking by the gallery, you glance through the store window, but all you are able to see is that there is something painted on the back wall. You see it clearly enough to describe it very well yet you have no idea what it is. One day you decide to go inside the gallery. You find out that what you were seeing was the nose from a wall mural of a woman's face. Why were you unable to identify what you had seen until you went inside the gallery?

Discussion Question

1. We often encounter ambiguous stimuli in our environment. Describe a situation in which contextual information could be used to help identify an ambiguous stimulus. Be sure to identify the various possibilities of the stimulus, the context, and what one might conclude about the stimulus based on the contextual information.

Categorical Perception—Identification

Minimum time to complete this experiment: 20 minutes

Background

People perceive most stimuli continuously. For example, when you look at a rainbow, you see a smooth transition from red to yellow (like the image below):

You usually do not perceive stimuli categorically. Categorical perception means that you see either pure red or pure yellow and nothing in between (like the image below):

This is called categorical perception because, instead of getting a percept that is ambiguous, you get a percept that perfectly matches an ideal example of a particular category. One thing that people seem to perceive categorically is speech (Harnard, 1987). What is interesting about this is that even when the physical stimuli change continuously (like the upper image), people perceive them categorically (like the lower image).

For example, both /b/ and /p/ are stop consonants: To produce these, you close your lips, then open them, release some air, and the vocal chords begin vibrating. Hold your hand in front of your mouth and say /ba/ and then /pa/. The difference between /ba/ and /pa/ is the time between the release of the air and the beginning of the vibration. This is referred to as voice onset time or VOT. For /b/, VOT is very short. Voicing begins at almost the same time as the air is released. For /p/, the voicing is delayed.

Researchers can construct a series of stimuli in which the VOT changes in small steps. When people are asked to identify these stimuli, they generally have no difficulty: The first few are identified as /b/ and the second few are identified as /p/. What is most interesting is how the middle items are identified. Unlike most other stimuli, people do not report hearing something that is a bit like /b/ and a bit like /p/. Rather, they report hearing either /b/ or /p/.

To demonstrate categorical perception of speech stimuli, you really need two different measures. This lab provides one of those measures: It lets you find the point at which your percept changes from ba to pa through an identification task. The second (which is provided in the Categorical Perception - Discrimination experiment) examines your ability to tell whether two tokens are the same or different.

Instructions

1. In the text fields below, enter your CogLab log-in ID and password. If you do not have a log-in ID and password, see your instructor for information on how to get one for your class.
2. Click the Submit information button.
3. If the information is correct, the Start experiment button will become activated. Click the button to begin the experiment.

This experiment requires a computer that can play sounds. We recommend using headphones so that you do not disturb other people. Please make sure the volume is not too loud before you put the headphones on.

Click once on the Next trial button to hear a sound. Your task is to report what it most sounds like. Click once on the BA button if you think the sound was most like BA or click once on the PA button if you think the sound was most like PA.

Occasionally, the sound that is played may be distorted. If you did not hear the sound clearly, click once on the Redo button instead of on the BA or PA buttons. The trial will be repeated later on in the session. There are 10 trials for each stimulus, for a total of 90 trials.

At the end of the experiment, you will be asked if you want to save your data to a set of global data. After you answer the question, a new Web page window will appear that lists your class averages for this experiment. On that page is also a link to your personal data.

Additional References

Baker, S., Idsardi, W., Golinkoff, R., & Petitto, I. (2005). The perception of handshapes in American sign language. *Memory & Cognition, 33*, 887-904.

Quinn, P. (2004). Visual perception of orientation is categorical near vertical and continuous near horizontal. *Perception, 33*, 897-906.

Damper, R., & Harnad, S. (2000). Neural network models of categorical perception. *Perception & Psychophysics, 62*, 843-867.

Basic Questions

1. What is an identification task? Give an example of an identification task.

2. What aspect of speech sound is the primary factor in determining if one perceives the /ba/ sound or the /pa/ sound?

3. Did your personal data show you had a strong tendency for categorical perception? Explain your answer.

Advanced Questions

1. In this demonstration, there were nine speech sound stimulus conditions (Ba1, Ba2, … Ba9). Each stimulus condition, as displayed on the experimental results page, had a VOT that was delayed 5ms from the condition before it. Let's pretend that we also did another experiment similar to this one, except that we used 45 speech sound stimulus conditions and each condition was delayed 1ms from the condition before it. Would you predict the pattern of results to be similar to or different from those of this demonstration? Explain your answer.

2. In many situations we are forced to make categorical judgments. Name a job in which someone has to categorize people/things that actually fall on a continuum. Describe the categorization this person has to make.

3. Why is it useful for us to have categorical speech perception?

Discussion Question

1. Other than its own auditory properties, what do we use to help us identify a given speech sound?

Categorical Perception—Discrimination

Minimum time to complete this experiment: 20 minutes

Background

People perceive most stimuli continuously. For example, when you look at a rainbow, you see a smooth transition from red to yellow (like the image below):

You usually do not perceive stimuli categorically. Categorical perception means that you see either pure red or pure yellow and nothing in between (like the image below):

This is called categorical perception because, instead of getting a percept that is ambiguous, you get a percept that perfectly matches an ideal example of a particular category. One thing that people seem to perceive categorically is speech (Harnard, 1987). What is interesting about this is that even when the physical stimuli change continuously (like the upper image), people perceive them categorically (like the lower image).

For example, both /b/ and /p/ are stop consonants: To produce these, you close your lips, then open them, release some air, and the vocal chords begin vibrating. Hold your hand in front of your mouth and say /ba/ and then /pa/. The difference between /ba/ and /pa/ is the time between the release of the air and the beginning of the vibration. This is referred to as voice onset time or VOT. For /b/, VOT is very short. Voicing begins at almost the same time as the air is released. For /p/, the voicing is delayed.

Researchers can construct a series of stimuli in which the VOT changes in small steps. When people are asked to identify these stimuli, they generally have no difficulty: The first few are identified as /b/ and the second few are identified as /p/. What is most interesting is how the middle items are identified. Unlike most other stimuli, people do not report hearing something that is a bit like /b/ and a bit like /p/. Rather, they report hearing either /b/ or /p/.

To demonstrate categorical perception of speech stimuli, you really need two different measures. The first examines your ability to identify which sound you are hearing (and is provided in the Categorical Perception - Identification experiment). The second examines your ability to tell whether two tokens are the same or different. If you are perceiving the stimuli categorically, it should be easy for you to correctly say that the tokens are different if they come from opposite sides of the category boundary. It should be very difficult for you to decide they are different if they come from the same side of the category boundary. In this lab, you will hear two sounds and your task is to say whether they are the same or different.

Instructions

1. In the text fields below, enter your CogLab log-in ID and password. If you do not have a log-in ID and password, see your instructor for information on how to get one for your class.
2. Click the Submit information button.
3. If the information is correct, the Start experiment button will become activated. Click the button to begin the experiment.

This experiment requires a computer that can play sounds. We recommend using headphones so that you do not disturb other people. Please make sure the volume is not too loud before you put the headphones on.

Click once on the Next trial button to hear two sounds. Your task is to report if they are the same or different. If you think they are the same, click once on the Same button. If you think they are different, click once on the Different button.

Occasionally, the sound that is played may be distorted. If you did not hear the sound clearly, click once on the Redo button; the trial will be repeated later on in the session. There are 140 trials.

At the end of the experiment, you will be asked if you want to save your data to a set of global data. After you answer the question, a new Web page window will appear that lists your class averages for this experiment. On that page is also a link to your personal data.

Additional References

Serniclaes, W., Ventura, P., Morais, J., & Kolinsky, R. (2005). Categorical perception of speech sounds in illiterate adults. *Cognition, 98*, B35-B44.

Laukka, P. (2005). Categorical perception of vocal emotion expressions. *Emotion, 5*, 277-295.

Gerrits, E., & Schouten, M. (2004). Categorical perception depends on the discrimination task. *Perception & Psychophysics, 66*, 363-376.

Basic Questions

1. What is a discrimination task? Give an example.

2. Did your personal experimental results follow a pattern similar to the predicted experimental results? Why or why not?

3. Define VOT (voice onset time).

Advanced Questions

1. List some other properties of speech sounds.

2. Why is it often more useful to look at the global data rather than an individual's data when trying to understand the effects of an experiment's independent variables?

3. Variations caused by mispronunciation, environmental auditory noise, and a variety of other factors could cause one to categorize a speech sound incorrectly. Similar speech sounds are susceptible to erroneous categorization. For example, we have learned that the consonant sounds of /b/ and /p/ are similar. List some word pairs that may be confused with each other because of an incorrectly categorized /b/ or /p/ speech sound.

Discussion Question

1. Can experience and/or training affect one's ability to make perceptual discriminations? Give support for your answer.

Wason Selection

Minimum time to complete this experiment: 10 minutes

Background

Research has shown that people find it very difficult to decide what information is necessary in order to test the truth of an abstract logical-reasoning problem. The Wason Selection Task is often used to examine this issue.

A typical experiment using the Wason Selection Task will present some rule and ask subjects to see if the rule is being violated. Consider the rule: If a card has a D on one side, it has a 3 on the other side. Subjects are aware that on the particular set of cards, each one has a letter on one side and a number on the other side. Four cards are shown, such as those below:

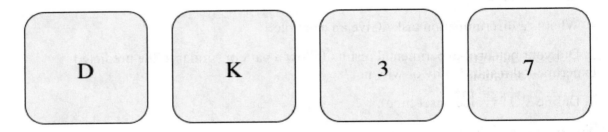

Very few people can correctly pick the two cards to turn over to verify the rule. The correct cards are D and 7; most likely, you picked D and 3. Seeing what is on the reverse of the 7 card can lead to falsifying the rule if a D shows up. Seeing what is on the reverse of the 3 card cannot falsify the rule. It can confirm the rule, but not falsify it.

Consider another rule: If you borrow my car, you must fill up the gas tank. Four cards are shown below:

Borrowed Car	Did Not Borrow Car	Empty Gas Tank	Full Gas Tank

Which cards do you turn over to see if the rule is being followed? You should find that now the answer is more obvious: You want to know what's on the reverse of "Borrowed Car" and "Empty Gas Tank."

This lab is based on a series of experiments reported by Wason & Shapiro (1971). You will be given a series of rules to verify. Half of them are abstract and half are thematic (the same kind of rule shown above about borrowing a car). The basic idea is that you can test rules when you have some knowledge or experience that is appropriate, but not when you lack this experience. In the thematic case, then, you are not really using logic per se but rather your experience. In the abstract case, you cannot use your experience and have to rely solely on logic.

Instructions

1. In the text fields below, enter your CogLab log-in ID and password. If you do not have a log-in ID and password, see your instructor for information on how to get one for your class.
2. Click the Submit information button.
3. If the information is correct, the Start experiment button will become activated. Click the button to begin the experiment.

Start a trial by clicking on the Next trial button. You will see a rule and four buttons. The rule will ask about two kinds of events. Your task is to select two cards to see what is on the other side so that you can see if the rule is true or false. To select a card, simply click on the appropriate button. Once you have clicked on a card, you cannot change your response.

There are 6 trials, 3 with abstract rules and 3 with thematic rules.

At the end of the experiment, you will be asked if you want to save your data to a set of global data. After you answer the question, a new Web page window will appear that lists your class averages for this experiment. On that page is also a link to your personal data.

Additional References

Wada, K., & Nittono, H. (2004). Cancel and rethink in the Wason selection task: Further evidence for the heuristic-analytic dual process theory. *Perceptual and Motor Skills, 98,* 1315-1325.

Almor, A., & Sloman, S. (2000). Reasoning versus text processing in the Wason selection task: A nondeontic perspective on perspective effects. *Memory & Cognition, 28,* 1060-1070.

Oaksford, M., & Chater, N. (1995). Information gain explains relevance which explains the selection task. *Cognition, 57,* 97-108.

Sperber, D., Cara, F., & Girotto, V. (1995). Relevance theory explains the selection task. *Cognition, 57,* 31-95.

Basic Questions

1. What are subjects asked to do in a typical Wason Selection Task?

2. Give an example of an abstract rule. Give an example of a thematic rule.

3. Why do participants typically perform better with thematic rules as opposed to abstract rules?

Advanced Questions

1. You and your family have just finished Thanksgiving dinner and some of your family members are starting to get sick. Your sister thinks that the Jello salad is what made everyone sick. During dinner, you noticed that your brother ate some of the Jello salad but your aunt did not. You also know that your grandpa got sick, but your mother did not. Which two people should you talk with to test your sister's hypothesis and what do you need to ask them?

2. Logic can be broken down into deductive reasoning and inductive reasoning. Give an example of each type of reasoning.

3. You have an instructor who told your class that anyone who did not have perfect attendance could not receive an A in the course. At the end of the semester, you want to know if your instructor stuck with this attendance policy. You have a friend who was also in the class and he/she received a B. Would it be helpful to find out if your friend had perfect attendance or not? Explain your answer.

Discussion Question

1. Using what you have learned from this demonstration, what advice would you give a student who is struggling with the concepts being used in his/her algebra class?

144

Typical Reasoning

Minimum time to complete this experiment: 10 minutes

Background

Tversky and Kahneman (1983) are well known for their research showing that people's estimates of probability are often very different from the objective probabilities. The reason, they argue, is that people often use heuristics to help them estimate the answer. Heuristics can be seen as sacrificing some accuracy for an increase in speed. By using heuristics, people can very quickly come up with an answer that is usually good enough for day-to-day purposes. These heuristics, however, can lead to incorrect judgments.

One of the most striking errors is known as the conjunction fallacy. In its most simple form, it says that people think that having both A and B occur is more likely than having just A occur or just B occur. According to objective probabilities, the probability of two events occurring has to be less than the probabilities of either of the events happening by itself. In some circumstances, however, people are more likely to say the conjunction (having both events occur) is more likely.

In particular, the conjunction fallacy is more likely when the items are typical than when they are atypical. For example, read the following:

Julie is 26 years old, has a degree in physical education, has been physically fit since childhood, and loves the outdoors.

People think it is more likely that Julie is a ski instructor who also teaches aerobics (a conjunction involving an activity thought to be more typical of ski instructors) than that Julie is a librarian who also teaches aerobics (a conjunction involving an activity thought to be less typical of librarians). When the activity is particularly typical, the conjunction can be thought more likely than the single events (e.g., that Julie is a ski instructor).

This demonstration is based on an experiment by Shafir, Smith, and Osherson (1990). You will read short descriptions about several people and you will be asked to rate the probability that these people have certain professions and/or engage in certain activities.

Instructions

1. In the text fields below, enter your CogLab log-in ID and password. If you do not have a log-in ID and password, see your instructor for information on how to get one for your class.
2. Click the Submit information button.
3. If the information is correct, the Start experiment button will become activated. Click the button to begin the experiment.

After clicking on the Start experiment button, a window will appear. Start a trial by clicking once on the Next trial button. You will be shown a short description of a person. Read the description carefully. After each description, you will be asked to judge how likely it is, on a scale from 0 to 7, that the person has a particular profession or engages in a particular activity. For example, you might be asked the following:

How likely is it that Bob bets on horse racing?

If you are absolutely certain, based on the description of him that you have just read, that Bob would never bet on horse racing, click on the 0 = Impossible button. If you are absolutely certain that Bob bets on horse racing, click on the 7 = Certain button.

There are no correct or incorrect answers. Please respond based on the assumption that the person described is a real person. There are only 12 trials, so please read each description carefully before responding.

At the end of the experiment, you will be asked if you want to save your data to a set of global data. After you answer the question, a new Web page window will appear that lists your class averages for this experiment. On that page is also a link to your personal data.

Additional References

Fisk, J., & Slattery, R. (2005). Reasoning about conjunctive probabilistic concepts in childhood. *Canadian Journal of Experimental Psychology, 59*, 168-178.

Fisk, J., & Pidgeon, N. (1998). Conditional probabilities, potential surprise, and the conjunction fallacy. *Quarterly Journal of Experimental Psychology A: Human Experimental Psychology, 51*, 655-681.

Fantino, E., Kulik, J., Stolarz-Fantino, S., & Wright, W. (1997). The conjunction fallacy: A test of averaging hypotheses. *Psychonomic Bulletin & Review, 4*, 96-101.

Basic Questions

1. What is an advantage of using heuristics? What is a disadvantage of using heuristics?

2. Describe the conjunction fallacy.

3. For this demonstration, on average did participants give higher ratings for single events or conjunctions of events? Based on the demonstration results, are participants making their judgments by using objective probabilities? Why or why not?

Advanced Questions

1. You and two of your co-workers have just interviewed a candidate for a job opening at your law firm. Your boss asks you what inferences you drew about the job candidate during the interview. What can you do to maximize your likelihood of making a correct inference?

2. John is a young, energetic, muscular, and outgoing individual. Estimate the likelihood that he a) is tall and likes sports. and b) is tall, likes sports, and has lots of friends.

3. You and a friend are taking a walk. While on your walk, you pass a middle-aged woman. You tell your friend that she seems like someone who is very intelligent. Your friend agrees but adds that she seems to be very confident as well. Who is more likely to be correct? Why?

Discussion Question

1. What is a stereotype? How do stereotypes relate to the findings of this demonstration?

Risky Decisions

Minimum time to complete this experiment: 10 minutes

Background

Our lives are full of decisions. We must choose which books to read, movies to see, courses to take, person to date, routes to drive, and thousands of other decisions every day. You would hope that people weigh their options carefully and make the best decision possible. Studies in cognitive psychology, however, tell us that the way people make decisions is influenced by a variety of factors. In fact, it is fairly easy to create contexts in which people choose certain options. Many of these tendencies are called framing effects, because the perceived context or way the choices are framed make a big difference, even for situations that are otherwise equivalent. Framing effects have been noted for centuries and many were summarized by Kahneman & Tversky (1982).

To understand some of these framing effects, we need to distinguish between two types of decision-making choices: risky and riskless. A risky choice is one for which there is a probability or chance of different possibilities occurring. For example, if you decide to spend money on a lottery, there is an unknown outcome. You may win a lot of money or you may not. The final outcome is not made by your decision. Your decision simply enters you into a probabilistic situation. A riskless choice is one for which the ultimate outcome is decided by the choice. For example, if you decide to invest your money in a bank account and earn interest, you have made a riskless choice.

Different people are comfortable with different amounts of risk. Some people tend to be risk-seeking and look for situations for which the ultimate outcome is unknown. Other people tend to be risk-avoiding and look for the sure bets. Regardless of your comfort level with risk, your tendency to be risk-avoiding or risk-seeking can be influenced by the context within which the options are presented to you. A common finding in the experimental literature on decision making is that people tend to be risk-seeking when the options available to them seem to involve losses. People tend to be risk-avoiding when the options available to them seem to involve gains. Interestingly, as long as you are honest in your responses, this effect does not disappear, even when you know of its influence on you.

This demonstration shows how the framing of the options to look like gains or losses changes your willingness to deal with risk. Decision-making experiments tend to be done by asking participants to imagine themselves in a particular situation and then to choose between two or more possibilities. This approach depends on the honesty of the participants. You can easily get invalid results by refusing to answer honestly.

This demonstration also shows another common finding in studies of decision making: Changes tend to be more important than final states. All of the questions in the experiment involve sums of money (U.S. dollars). There are pairs of questions that are equivalent in the sense that you will reach the same absolute amount of money, or possible amount of money in a risky option, for either question in a pair. If your decision making were based solely on the final amount of money you would have, you would make the same decision for either member of the pair. Odds are, however, that you will behave quite differently across the pair members, choosing the risky option for one question but the riskless option for the other. Many aspects of economics and business pertain to properties of decision making. The old business adage of focusing on the bottom line is an effort to avoid the tendency among people to focus on changes instead of absolute effects. Characteristics of decision-making tendencies are also well known by advertisers and politicians, who will sometimes influence people's decisions by framing options in certain ways. You can also learn to make better decisions (in the sense of making decisions that are more in line with your beliefs) by taking a more objective approach in your daily life and by learning some details about statistical reasoning.

Instructions

1. In the text fields below, enter your CogLab log-in ID and password. If you do not have a log-in ID and password, see your instructor for information on how to get one for your class.
2. Click the Submit information button.
3. If the information is correct, the Start experiment button will become activated. Click the button to begin the experiment.

A window will appear where the experimental questions and choices will be presented, and a smaller window will appear with abbreviated instructions. Close the instructions window. You can open it again later from the CogLab Info. menu.

On each trial you will be asked to imagine that you have just received a salary of a certain amount of money. This amount will vary across questions. You will see two options and you will be asked which one you would prefer. For example, you might see:

Imagine that you get a bonus of $350 from your job. You are now faced with a situation in which you must choose one of the following options. Which would you choose?

A: A sure loss of $60

OR

B: A 0.4 probability of losing $0 and 0.6 probability of losing $100

If you pick Option A, you will have a final total of $290 because you are guaranteed to lose $60. If you pick Option B, you might lose nothing (and keep all $350) but you might lose $100 and end up with only $250. For this example, if you picked Option B you would lose $100 six times out of ten.

To indicate your preference, click on the button that corresponds to the option that you think is best. If you prefer Option A, click on the A button. If you prefer Option B, click on the B button. You may change your choice before starting the next trial. In making your decision, try to imagine what the money would actually be worth to you. For example, if you owe a threatening loan shark $290, perhaps it is better to pick the riskless situation (Option A) so that you are certain to be able to completely pay off the debt. On the other hand, if you really need $350 and having $290 will not suffice, perhaps it is better to take the risky option (Option B) and hope you keep all of the money. You should make the decision relative to your real-world situation (which is hopefully not so stressful). Some people will like Option A best and some will like Option B best; there are no absolutely correct answers.

Other trials include options with gains of money instead of losses. The starting amounts of money, the loss or gain amounts, and the probabilities vary across trials. After you are satisfied with your choice, press the space bar to start the next trial. There are a total of 12 trials.

At the end of the experiment, you will be asked if you want to save your data to a set of global data. After you answer the question, a new Web page window will appear that lists your class averages for this experiment. On that page is also a link to your personal data.

Additional References

Schlottmann, A., & Tring, J. (2005). How children reason about gains and losses: Framing effects in judgment and choice. *Swiss Journal of Psychology, 64*, 153-171.

Kuhberger, A., Schulte-Mecklenbeck, M., & Perner, J. (1999). The effects of framing, reflection, probability, and payoff on risk preference in choice tasks. *Organizational Behavior and Human Decision Processes, 78*, 204-231.

Kuhberger, A. (1998). The influence of framing on risky decisions: A meta-analysis. *Organizational Behavior and Human Decision Processes, 75*, 23-55

Chien, Y., Lin, C., & Worthley, J. (1996). Effect of framing on adolescents' decision making. *Perceptual and Motor Skills, 83*, 811-819.

Basic Questions

1. What distinguishes a risky choice from a riskless choice?

2. In relation to decision making, what is risk-seeking behavior? When are people likely to be risk-seekers?

3. In relation to decision making, what is risk-avoiding behavior? When are people likely to be risk-avoiders?

Advanced Questions

1. The city council has a difficult decision to make. For the sale of 3 acres of land, a developer has offered them a lump sum of $10,000 or a percentage of the profits from the land development, which they have been told has a 50% chance of being $15,000 and a 50% chance of being $5000. Which option do you think they will choose? Why?

2. Describe a situation (not involving money) in which one would likely be a risk-avoider?

3. For all of the decisions in this demonstration, the expected value for each of the two choice options was equal. Define expected value and explain why it was important for the expected value of the risky choice to be equal to the expected value of the riskless choice.

Discussion Question

1. Identify some factors, not mentioned in this demonstration, that might affect a person's likelihood of engaging in risk-seeking or risk-avoiding behavior. Describe how each of these factors might influence one's behavior.

Decision Making

Minimum time to complete this experiment: 10 minutes

Background

Our lives are full of decisions. We must choose which books to read, movies to see, courses to take, person to date, routes to drive, and thousands of other decisions every day. You would hope that people weigh their options carefully and make the best decision possible. Studies in cognitive psychology, however, tell us that the way people make decisions is influenced by a variety of factors. In fact, it is fairly easy to create contexts in which people choose certain options. Many of these tendencies are called framing effects, because the perceived context or way the choices are framed make a big difference, even for situations that are otherwise equivalent. Framing effects have been noted for centuries and many were summarized by Kahneman & Tversky (1982).

This demonstration asks a series of questions. There are two sets of questions. The different sets ask essentially the same questions, but they are presented differently.

Decision-making experiments tend to be done by asking participants to imagine themselves in a particular situation and then to choose between two or more possibilities. This approach depends on the honesty of the participants. You can easily get invalid results by refusing to answer honestly.

Instructions

1. In the text fields below, enter your CogLab log-in ID and password. If you do not have a log-in ID and password, see your instructor for information on how to get one for your class.
2. Click the Submit information button.
3. If the information is correct, the Start experiment button will become activated. Click the button to begin the experiment.

A window will appear with three buttons and an area that will show the questions. A smaller window will appear with abbreviated instructions. Close the instructions window. You can open it again later from the CogLab Info. menu.

On each trial you are given a description of a situation and then two options from which you chose one. Make your choice and then click on the Next trial button to continue.

At the end of the experiment, you will be asked if you want to save your data to a set of global data. After you answer the question, a new Web page window will appear that lists your class averages for this experiment. On that page is also a link to your personal data.

Additional References

Gonzalez, C., Dana, J., Koshino, H., & Just, M. (2005). The framing effect and risky decisions: Examining cognitive functions with fMRI. *Journal of Economic Psychology, 26*, 1-20.

Ronnlund, M., Karlsson, E., Laggnas, E., Larsson, L., & Lindstrom, T. (2005). Risky decision making across three arenas of choice: Are younger and older adults differently susceptible to framing effects? *Journal of General Psychology, 132*, 81-92.

McKenzie, C. (2004). Framing effects in inference tasks--and why they are normatively defensible. *Memory & Cognition, 32*, 874-885.

Levin, I., Johnson, R., Deldin, P., Carstens, L., Cressey, L., & Davis, C. (1986). Framing effects in decisions with completely and incompletely described alternatives. *Organizational Behavior and Human Decision Processes, 38*, 48-64.

Basic Questions

1. What is the main difference between a rational and an irrational decision maker?

2. In relation to decision making, what is a framing effect?

3. Does your class data show evidence for rational or irrational decision making? Explain your answer.

Advanced Questions

1. Last week you and a friend went to an electronics store. You purchased a television for $600 and your friend bought a video game for $40. Today you saw in the newspaper that

the electronics store was having a huge sale and your television is now $580 and your friend's game is $20. You decide it is not worth it for you to go and get a price change, but you call your friend because you can not think of a reason why he/she would not want to go and get a price adjustment. The potential savings for you and your friend is exactly the same so why might you assume your friend would want a price adjustment when you did not?

2. You are a factory manager and, unfortunately, today there was a systems failure. Despite the quick work of your employees, 400 out of the 500 units that your factory produced today were lost. How could you frame the day's productivity (number of units produced) in order to keep up your employees morale?

3. You own a restaurant and decide that all your meals will cost $7 before 5pm and $8 after 5pm. You can advertise this by saying that there will be a discount on meals served before 5pm or you can say there will be a surcharge on meals served after 5pm. How should you advertise your prices? Explain your answer.

Discussion Question

1. Making decisions can be taxing, so people often rely on heuristics. What is a heuristic? Identify and describe one heuristic. Identify a situation when the heuristic you identified would lead you to an erroneous decision.

Monty Hall

Minimum time to complete this experiment: 15 minutes

Background

Most people have a poor understanding of probability. One common problem occurs when evaluating combinations of events. The Monty Hall 3-Door problem is a classic example. Based on the TV game show, Let's Make A Deal, the problem involves 3 doors. Behind one of the doors is a prize. The contestant picks one door. Monty Hall, the eminent emcee, picks one of the remaining two doors to open and shows that the prize is not there. The question is: Do you stay with your original pick or do you change your pick? (We'll assume Monty Hall is playing fair and always does this.)

You originally begin with a 1 in 3 chance (0.333 probability) of picking the correct door. Many people think that it doesn't matter whether you stay with your original pick or switch after Monty reveals his door.

This interpretation is incorrect. You are better off always switching; over the long term, you will average 66% correct. If you always stay, you will average 33% correct over the long term. If you randomly switch or stay, you will average 50% over the long term.

Here's how to think of it. You pick a door randomly, let's say it is Door 1. You have a 1 out of 3 chance of being correct. This means there is a 2 out of 3 chance that the prize is behind Door 2 or Door 3. If you do nothing, you will be correct approximately 1/3 of the time. However, when Monty Hall shows you that one of the other doors (let's say Door 2) is incorrect, that means that there is now a 2 out of 3 chance that the remaining door is correct. This means that if you pick Door 3, you will be correct approximately 2/3 of the time.

Instructions

1. In the text fields below, enter your CogLab log-in ID and password. If you do not have a log-in ID and password, see your instructor for information on how to get one for your class.
2. Click the Submit information button.

3. If the information is correct, the Start experiment button will become activated. Click the button to begin the experiment.

This lab simulates the Monty Hall 3-Door Problem. It lets you try out the various options and see how often you would win. Start a trial by clicking on the Next trial button. Then select a door. One of the doors will have its contents changed from ? to - to indicate there is no prize. Now, you decide whether to pick your original door again or whether to switch. Once you either confirm your original choice or pick a new door, the winning door will be shown (with a +) and the other losing door will be shown (with a -).

To maximize the number of wins, make your first selection randomly and then always change to the other door. To minimize the number of wins, make your first selection randomly, then always stick with your first choice.

At the end of the experiment, you will be asked if you want to save your data to a set of global data. After you answer the question, a new Web page window will appear that lists your class averages for this experiment. On that page is also a link to your personal data.

Additional References

Burns, B., & Wieth, M. (2004). The collider principle in causal reasoning: Why the Monty Hall dilemma is so hard. *Journal of Experimental Psychology: General, 133,* 434-449.

Tubau, E., & Alonso, D. (2003). Overcoming illusory inferences in a probabilistic counterintuitive problem: The role of explicit representations. *Memory & Cognition, 31,* 596-607.

Krauss, S., & Wang, X. (2003). The psychology of the Monty Hall problem: Discovering psychological mechanisms for solving a tenacious brain teaser. *Journal of Experimental Psychology: General, 132,* 3-22.

Basic Questions

1. For this demonstration, did you try to maximize your wins or maximize your losses? What strategy did you use to accomplish your goal?

2. What is the probability of a coin landing heads up in a fair coin toss? What is the probability of a randomly selected day of the week starting with the letter S?

3. What is the joint probability of rolling a four on a six-sided die and correctly guessing a randomly picked number as being odd or even?

Advanced Questions

1. Imagine a Monty Hall situation with four doors instead of three (there is still only one correct door). After selecting door number one, you are shown that door number two is incorrect. Should you stay with door number one or switch to one of the remaining doors? What are your chances of choosing the right door if you stay with your original door? What are your chances of choosing correctly if you switch?

2. What is the probability of a coin landing heads up on the next coin toss, assuming you had just seen three consecutive coin tosses in which the coin landed heads up?

3. You go to your refrigerator to find something to eat and see three types of leftovers from meals earlier in the week. One of the meals made you sick the last time you ate it but you do not remember which one. You pick one at random and hope for the best. A moment later your roommate comes in and grabs one of the two remaining dishes and indicates that the dish he/she chose was one of the dishes that were okay to eat. At this point, should you stay with your original food choice or switch? Why?

4. If you have a glass jar with five blue marbles, three red marbles, and two green marbles, what is the joint probability of randomly choosing a blue marble (you keep the marble in your hand) and then choosing a red marble?

Discussion Question

1. What is the main difference between an independent event and a dependent event? Give an example of each type of event.

GLOSSARY

ABSOLUTE IDENTIFICATION helps to explain why it is difficult to identify objects when they differ from other objects to be identified by only one dimension (for example, length). Identification improves if the items vary by more than one dimension.

APPARENT MOTION The perceived motion of a single light that results when stationary lights are flashed on and off in rapid succession.

ATTENTION The ability to selectively choose some stimuli for processing and ignore others.

ATTENTIONAL BLINK The brief time after paying attention to a stimulus during which attention cannot be focused on a subsequent stimulus.

AUTOMATIZED BEHAVIOR A behavior that proceeds without conscious direction once the series of movements is initiated.

BLIND SPOT The functionally blind area in each eye, located at the optic disk. If light falls on this area, we can't see it.

BRAIN ASYMMETRY The two distinct hemispheres of the brain have different capabilities. The left hemisphere is said to deal with language and analytical thought, while the right hemisphere is said to deal with spatial relations and creativity.

BROWN-PETERSON EFFECT showed that there is a separate short-term memory (STM) system that holds information for several seconds. Without an active effort by the participant, information in STM fades away.

C is a measure of response bias in a signal-detection experiment; a value greater than zero indicates a conservative bias and a value less than zero indicates a liberal bias.

CATEGORICAL PERCEPTION-DISCRIMINATION refers to the ability to detect whether two stimuli are the same or different.

CATEGORICAL PERCEPTION-IDENTIFICATION refers to the point at which one's categorical perception changes from one distinct category to another.

CHANGE BLINDNESS it is the inability to detect changes in the environment or on a cognitive task.

CHANGE DETECTION it is the ability to detect changes in the environment or on a cognitive task.

CLASSICAL CONDITIONING is a type of learning in which a stimulus acquires the capacity to stimulate a response that was originally brought about by another stimulus, that is, learning by association.

CONJUNCTIVE SEARCH is the type of search performed in a visual-search task when identifying the target requires distinguishing it from distractors on more than one dimension.

CORRECT REJECTION is a trial in a signal-detection experiment in which a participant correctly reports that a target was not present.

DISTRACTOR TASK is a task (such as mental arithmetic) designed to prevent active rehearsal of information in short-term memory.

D-prime (d′) is a measure of participant sensitivity in a signal detection experiment; the larger the d′ the greater the sensitivity.

ENCODING SPECIFICITY The memory of an event is related to the interaction between the properties of the encoded event and the properties of the encoded retrieval information.

ENDOGENEOUS CUE is a cue that must be identified and intentionally acted upon by the participant.

EXHAUSTIVE SEARCH is a search of memory that ends only after all items have been accessed.

EXOGENOUS CUE is a cue that automatically draws one's attention to the location of its presentation.

EXPLICIT LEARNING occurs when one consciously or intentionally acquires knowledge about a stimulus or a task.

FALSE ALARM is a trial in a signal-detection experiment in which a participant incorrectly reports that a target is present.

FALSE MEMORY is a memory that a person recalls about things that did not occur. It is seen in therapeutic settings.

FORGOT-IT-ALL-ALONG is a memory phenomenon in which an individual experiences an event, correctly recalls the event when tested, but later forgets that they accurately remembered the event during the recall test.

FOVEA is the central area on the retina of each eye that is densely packed with light sensitive receptors. We turn our fovea toward whatever we are looking at to see the details of that object better.

FRAMING EFFECTS refer to the influence of context on the way people make decisions.

GARNER TASK The Garner task is a speeded classification test of the influence of irrelevant information on a perceptual task.

GARNER TASK – INTEGRAL When dimensions in a Garner task are integral, they are often processed as one dimension and interference occurs, hence processing speeds decrease. One example is hue and brightness.

GARNER TASK – SEPARABLE When dimensions in a Garner task are separable, they are often processed as separate dimensions and there is no interference effect. One example is hue and size.

GESTALT PSYCHOLOGY is an area of psychology that follows the premise that people organize their perceptions according to certain patterns, so that what you see as a whole is not equal to the sum of its parts.

HEURISTICS are quickly produced problem solving short cuts that may not always lead to a correct answer.

HIT is a trial in a signal-detection experiment in which a participant correctly identifies a target.

ICONIC STORE is a visual sensory storage system lasting a few hundred milliseconds.

IMPLICIT LEARNING occurs when one unconsciously or unintentionally acquires knowledge about a stimulus or a task.

INTERSTIMULUS INTERVAL (ISI) is the period of time between the offset of a first stimulus and the onset of a second stimulus.

IRRELEVANT SPEECH EFFECT The memory for a list of items may be impaired when an irrelevant speech (auditory) stimulus follows the presentation of the list, even when the list is visually presented.

KORTE'S LAWS are statements describing aspects of apparent motion, such as the relation between the ISI and the spatial separation required for motion to be perceived.

LEVELS OF PROCESSING In general, memory is better when it is processed at a deep level compared to a shallow level. Structural decisions are shallow, while semantics require deeper processing.

LEXICAL DECISION is a test of the mental lexicon.

LEXICON is a mental dictionary containing information about a word's meaning, its part of language, and its relationship to other words.

LINK WORD is a mnemonic technique that uses interactive imagery to associate a familiar word with a novel or new word. It is often used to learn a new language.

Log(alpha) is a measure of participant sensitivity in a signal-detection experiment.

MASKING is the impaired performance on the judgment of a target stimulus due to the presentation of another stimulus (the mask).

MEMORY SPAN is the capacity of short-term or working memory. It is measured in how many list items a participant can recall in their correct order.

MENTAL ROTATION is a technique used to study the nature of mental images. The greater the degree of rotation, the slower the reaction-time.

MENTAL SCANNING is the active process of exploring cognitive representations.

METACONSTRAST MASKING is a special case of masking in which the target and mask have no overlapping contours and the mask is presented after the target.

METHOD OF CONSTANT STIMULI is a psychophysical method that requires the observer to make judgments about stimuli in terms of whether they are perceived to be greater or less than a standard stimulus.

MISS is a trial in a signal-detection experiment in which a participant fails to detect a target.

MNEMONIC DEVICE is a technique used to increase one's memory.

MODALITY EFFECTS can help to explain why the memory for the last item in a list of items improves when it is presented in specific modalities, for example when a list is read out loud or is silently mouthed.

MONTY HALL is a classic problem of understanding probability. You are given 3 choices to pick from and only one of these choices is correct. After making your selection, you are shown that 1 of the 2 remaining choices was incorrect. You are then asked if you wish to stay with your original choice or switch to the remaining choice. According to the Monty Hall logic, you increase your probability of winning over the long term if you always switch. Probability increases from 1/3 (0.33) to 2/3 (0.66).

MULLER-LYER ILLUSION is the arrow illusion in which the shank with the outward wings appears longer than the shank with the inward wings even though the shanks are the same objective length.

OPERATION SPAN refers to the number of sequential operation-word strings that a participant can attend to. The greater your operation span, the greater the attention span.

OPTIC DISK is the region in each eye where the optic nerve exits; it contains no light-sensitive receptors and produces the blind spot.

PARALLEL SEARCH is a search of memory in which every item is accessed simultaneously.

PARTIAL REPORT is the technique George Sperling used in his early studies of the sensory memory. It is called partial because participants were asked to recall only one row of the presented matrices. (Also see whole report.)

PERCEPTUAL SPAN is the amount of information that can be gathered in a single precept.

PHONOLOGICAL SIMILARITY Performance tends to decrease when the items of a list sound similar than when the items sound different.

POSITION ERROR GRADIENTS help to explain the systematic errors that an individual may make when recalling a list of items. Generally, adjacent items are mixed up.

PRIMACY EFFECT The first few items in a list are remembered particularly well in a free recall task.

PROTOTYPE is a mental construct that has the critical properties of a concept. It is used to identify new objects.

PSYCHOMETRIC FUNCTION is a graph that relates the probability of a certain response to variations in a physical characteristic of a stimulus.

PSYCHOPHYSICS is a sub-discipline of psychology that attempts to relate reported characteristics of perception to physical properties of stimuli that give rise to those reports.

RECENCY EFFECT The last few items in a list are remembered particularly well in a free recall task.

RECEPTIVE FIELD is any stimulus that changes a neuron's firing rate.

REMEMBER/KNOW is a recognition memory phenomenon that tries to distinguish between memories that one *remembers*, consciously aware of some aspect of the original learning situation, or *knows*, having no conscious awareness of the learning situation.

RISKY DECISIONS In decision-making, the choice of taking a risk or not taking a risk is strongly influenced by how the situation is framed. A risky choice is one in which there is a probability or chance of different possibilities occurring. A riskless choice is one in which the ultimate outcome is decided by the choice.

SELF-REFERENT EXAMPLES are examples that are personally relevant. They tend to improve one's memory.

SELF-TERMINATING SEARCH is a search of memory that ends as soon as a match has been found.

SERIAL POSITION Memory of an item depends on where it is positioned within a list. The items at the beginning and the end tend to be remembered more often than the items in the middle. (Also see recency and primacy effects.)

SERIAL SEARCH is a search of memory in which items are accessed successively.

SIGNAL DETECTION is a procedure that provides a separate measure of sensitivity and response bias for situations in which observers are required to detect the presence of a faint target.

SIGNAL-DETECTION THEORY proposes that the detection of a stimulus involves sensory processes as well as decision processes.

SIMON EFFECT Response time may be reduced and accuracy may increase when a stimulus is presented in the same relative location as the response required.

SPATIAL CUEING A participant's responses may be faster at locating a target that is previously cued but slower when the target's location is not previously cued.

STERNBERG SEARCH Saul Sternberg developed this technique of exploring how information is retrieved from short-term memory.

STROOP EFFECT refers to the difficulty participants have in naming ink colors of color words when the ink colors and the color words do not agree.

SUFFIX EFFECT The recall of the last item in a list that is read aloud may be impaired if the list is followed by an irrelevant suffix.

TYPICAL REASONING When estimating likelihoods, individuals tend to make reasoning errors based on time-saving heuristics and generalizations. One reasoning error we make is the *conjunction fallacy*, in which two typical events seem more probable that one typical event.

VISUAL SCOTOMA is a damaged part of the retina that causes a blind spot.

VISUAL SEARCH is a task in which the participant searches a visual image for the presence of a particular item. The participant responds as quickly as possible once the item is found or once he/she is certain that the item is not present.

VON RESTORFF EFFECT is a recall-memory phenomenon that helps to explain why the memory of an item in a list improves if it is distinctive from the surrounding items.

WASON SELECTION TASK is a task that is used to test the truth of an abstract logical rule. Four cards with information on both sides are displayed and participants are asked which 2 cards must be turned over in order to verify the given rule.

WHOLE REPORT Early memory studies used this technique in which participants recall a whole matrix of letters. This technique showed a recall ability of 4.5 items.

WORD SUPERIORITY A letter that is part of a word is recognized more easily than a letter in isolation.

CONTENTS

This book belongs to - - -
BradLanghorst

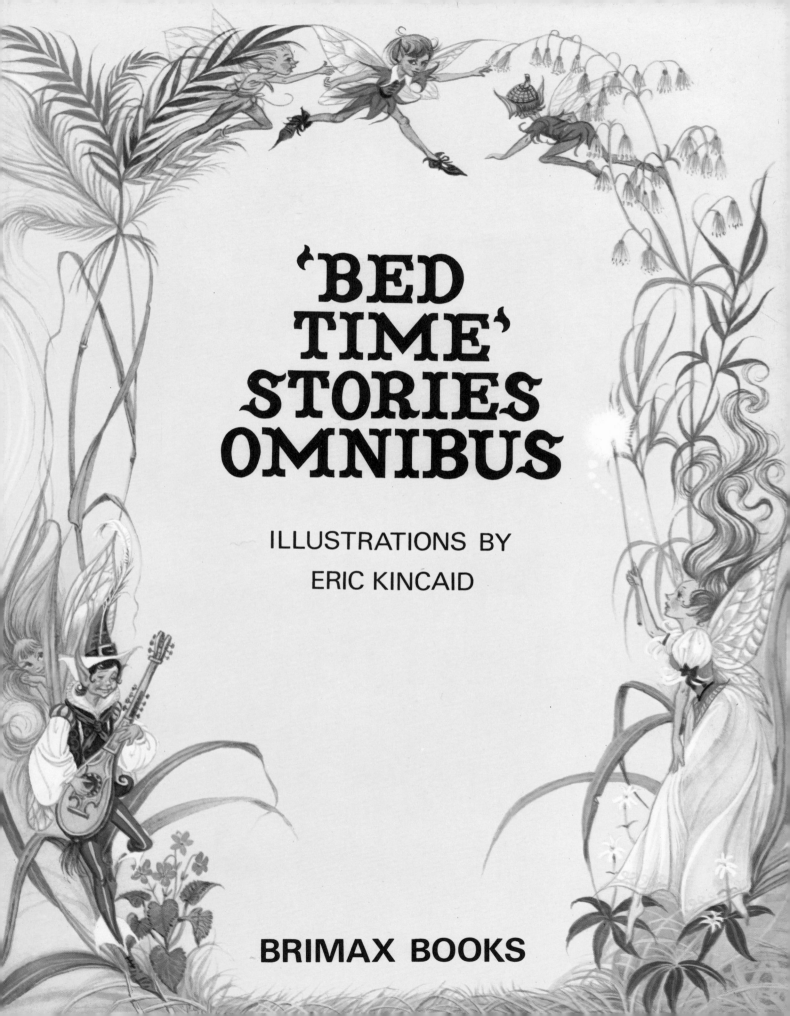

'BED TIME' STORIES OMNIBUS

ILLUSTRATIONS BY

ERIC KINCAID

BRIMAX BOOKS

This omnibus comprises stories from
Four volumes READ AGAIN SERIES
© Brimax Rights Ltd. 1979. All rights reserved.
First published in Great Britain 1979 by BRIMAX BOOKS.
Third printing 1981. Printed in Hong Kong.
ISBN 0 86112 004 3

JOE THE DREAMER

Joe Dreamer fished for whales
Beside a tiny brook;
He dreamt of all the tales
That filled his story book.

He dreamt of Merry Megs,
A witch with many a trick,
Who saved her weary legs
By riding on a stick.

And then of little Jim,
A goblin brisk and sprightly,
Before you speak to him
Bow low three times politely.

And next of Merlin Wise,
Older than time can tell;
Don't look into his eyes
Or he might work a spell.

And when he'd done his dream
Of wizard, witch and elf,
Joe sat beside the stream
And dreamt about himself.

PERVIE THE PIGLET

Priscilla was a fine pig. Whenever Farmer Biggs entered her and her piglets in a show she was awarded the first prize. She always had ten piglets in a litter and they were always pink and perfect.

Her last family, though, was of eleven and that extra one really was the odd one out. Instead of doing what his brothers and sisters did he went his own way and found his own amusements. His most noticeable trick was running round and round the pigsty. The farmer's little daughter, Kate, called him 'Pervie' because he was so perverse – always doing the opposite to what he should be doing. Even Priscilla used the name.

"Pervie," she grunted. "Could you possibly put yourself in a more pleasing position?"

She always talked like that – very fond of using words beginning with 'p' for 'pig'.

"Pervie, Pervie. . . .You are the most perplexing piglet. . . . My poor head is pounding with your prancing performances!"

Pervie didn't understand half she said but he loved to hear all her strange expressions. In fact, he thought up more tricks to see if she knew more words.

Kate had named him well – very well indeed.

One day, he made a discovery; he noticed that their sty was not the only world. Outside the bars of the iron gate there stretched another; a much wider one. Out there animals and birds were free; they roamed about doing exactly as they pleased.

That was the life for him. . . .But how could he get to that fine free world?

He pushed his little snout through the railings and wriggled. It wasn't going to be easy. Almost immediately, a sharp pain struck at the middle of his curly tail. He edged himself back into the sty. Priscilla was holding on tight and she didn't let go until he was safely down on all four trotters.

She fixed him with a disapproving eye.

"Pervie," she began in a stern voice. "Put that particular pastime right out of your mind. We are prize pigs. We are preserved and perfected here in this clean sty. This is our special place and you must be satisfied."

But Pervie wasn't satisfied.

Next time he squeezed his rear end through first; this way he could keep watch on his mother. It was a clever idea, but it didn't work.

Priscilla spotted what he was up to and pulled him back by his ear.

Kate heard Pervie squeal and saw his mother holding on. She called to her father.

"I think Priscilla has turned against Pervie, Dad. She was biting him!"

Farmer Biggs examined the piglet.

"You're right, Kate. She's split his ear!"

Poor Pervie. . . .He was no longer perfect. . . .He couldn't be entered for the show.

"May I have him, Dad?" Kate asked.

So, Pervie left the sty and joined the outside world. He was Kate's pet and although he missed his mother at first, he soon put Kate in her place and followed her everywhere.

A few days before the Agricultural Show, a new item was added as an attraction for the children. 'Odd and unusual pets' it said. 'Bring them along and win a prize!'

"I'll take Pervie," said Kate.

So Pervie went to the show after all.

He had to endure a good clean up and being enclosed in a makeshift sty. This didn't please him at all. The judging was about to begin when Pervie decided he'd had enough. Rooting under the insecure hurdles, he dislodged them and was off!

"What perfect, peautiful pleasure!" he whispered to himself, trying to talk like Priscilla. Some faint scent in the air reminded him of her. He was reminded also of his old tricks and he started to race round and round and round!

In no time at all there was chaos!

Children screamed; old people were knocked off balance and show officials ran about shouting and looking ridiculous.

Pervie was the star turn of the afternoon.

When the crowds saw how funny it was they let out a roar of laughter. This grew and spread across the field as Pervie widened his racing circles.

Suddenly, he altered course; turned completely and made a bee-line in the opposite direction. It was even more hilarious – chasers scattered as the pink object dived between their legs.

Far out, across the show ground, he came up sharp against some strong, well-staked fencing. A ticket 'First Prize' hung on a spoke. There lay Priscilla and ten perfect piglets.

Oh, how delighted he was to see her. His ears flapped and trembled with joy – even the torn one. He pushed and pushed his nose into her pen and she met him with tender little grunting noises. While she kissed him on his tender little snout, Pervie stood quite still – but his tail went round faster and faster.

Kate was the first to catch up with him; she grabbed him firmly and popped him in with his mother.

The people cheered. Then, many asked how it was that a pig with a family would accept another – a strange piglet. Kate had to tell the story over and over: that Pervie *was* her piglet and that he had been clever enough to find her.

When it came to the choosing of the most unusual pet; well, Pervie's name was shouted by all the onlookers.

"Pervie! Pervie. . . .He's the one. . . .Pervie!"

The crowd joined in the chant. The judge agreed.

"For entertaining us so well," he said, "I present Pervie with the prize. Piglet of the famous, well-known Priscilla, he has this afternoon, proved himself to be the most pleasing and most peculiar pet of the show."

Pervie was listening. 'Hallo,' he thought, 'my mother is not the only one who talks like that. . . .And who's peculiar anyway?'

He straightened his tail, curled it up again and gave a little grunt – his very first!

He'd added to his mother's reputation. Her perverse piglet had won a prize! Things were pretty good.

"Yes," he said. "Everything is positively perfect!"

NO BUTTER FOR HIS BREAD

It was breakfast time and the Master wanted butter for his bread.

"Molly!" he called to the dairy maid, "Bring me butter for my bread."

"I can't sir," said Molly.

"Can't!" said the Master. "No such word as can't," and then he added, "Why can't you?"

"Because there is no butter," said Molly.

"No butter!" The Master jumped from his chair and knocked it with a clatter to the floor. "No butter. . . .what do you mean NO BUTTER!!!!"

"There is no butter in the dairy. There is no butter in the kitchen," said Molly.

She righted the Master's chair. He sat down again and glared. He didn't frighten Molly. She knew he was gentle as butter himself underneath his crusty outside. And she knew how much he liked butter on his bread.

"Why isn't there any butter?" he stormed.

"Because. . . ." said Molly. "Because. . . ."

"You're the milk maid. . . ." roared the Master, "Go to the dairy and make me some." He was getting hungry and he couldn't eat bread without butter. He knew he was getting bad tempered. He didn't like being bad tempered.

"Sir," said Molly as though he wasn't shouting at all. "I've been in the dairy since six. The cream in the churn will not turn into butter."

"Don't be ridiculous!" shouted the Master. And jumping from his chair, again knocking it to the floor with a clatter, he marched to the dairy with his napkin caught on his waistcoat button, and with Molly running after him not in the least flustered.

The dairy was cool and airy, and it cooled the Master's temper. "I'm sorry I shouted Molly," he said, "But you know how I like my butter. . .and you really mustn't say there isn't any butter when all you have to do is churn it. Now be a good girl and start churning. . ."

"Very well," said Molly. If the Master wouldn't believe her then he would have to see for himself. "Surely it's ready now," said the Master who was pacing backwards and forwards in front of Daisy the cow so quickly that she was beginning to wonder if she should toss him over the moon. "Here. . .let me look." Molly took the lid off the churn. The cream from Daisy's milk was pale as the palest primrose and as fluid as the water in the pond. "What's the matter with it?" demanded the Master.

"What's the matter with your milk?" he demanded of Daisy the cow.

Daisy looked at him with her large brown eyes and mooed. Her moo could have meant anything.

"What's to be done?" demanded the Master.

"Well it seems to me as though it has had a spell put on it," said Molly.

"Spell. . .rubbish!" said the Master.

"Then why won't it turn?" asked Molly.

"Well, what are you waiting for? How do you break a spell?" asked the Master impatiently. He was getting so hungry for bread and butter he was prepared to believe anything and try anything.

"We could try holding it over running water?" said Molly.

That's how it was that the Master's wife found the Master standing in the middle of the stream in the middle of the meadow holding a milk churn over his head.

"Come out of there at once, your feet are getting wet," she scolded.

The Master did as he was told and water and fishes poured from his shoes.

"Drat," he said, as he shook the churn. "It's still sloshing about."

He thought he had better explain to his wife who was dropping the stranded fish back into the stream.

"There's a spell on the milk. It won't churn. I haven't had breakfast. I'm hungry. I want my bread and butter. What shall I do?"

"Tie a rowan sprig to it, dear," said his wife sweetly. "Everyone knows that's how a spell is broken."

There just happened to be a rowan tree close by the dairy. But a sprig tied to the churn made not the slightest difference to the milk.

"So that always works, does it?" said the Master huffily. "What else always works?"

"Horseshoes over the dairy door," said the Master's wife.

There were so many horseshoes over the dairy door there wasn't room for another one.

The Master's wife wanted her husband to buy her a new dress, so she just had to think of something. She thought and thought and could think of nothing. Molly sat beside her and thought and thought and also thought of nothing. The Master churned and churned till his arms ached and his hair was wet with perspiration.

"Who would want to put a spell on a churn of milk?" he panted as he stopped to catch his breath. "It's no one who likes butter that's for sure!"

Molly and the Master's wife looked at one another. Both knew exactly what the other was thinking.

"Molly," said the Master's wife. "Get your bonnet."

"Where are you going?" asked the Master.

"To visit the witch who lives at the mill," said his wife.

"Don't be silly. She likes butter. I've heard she likes butter as much as I do."

"Liking has nothing to do with it," said his wife. "Having, has. . .and I've heard that her butter churn fell over and broke into a hundred pieces."

"Stuff and nonsense," muttered the Master, and went back to his own churning.

Molly and the Master's wife went straight to the mill before their courage failed them. Neither of them would have dared to go alone.

"Yes," said the witch when they questioned her, very politely and very carefully, of course. It doesn't do to upset a witch. "My butter churn IS broken and I can't find the right spell to mend it. I have put a spell on all the unbroken churns. I have no butter so no one else shall."

"Yes," said the witch. "I will take off the spell if you promise to bring me a large pat of freshly made butter every other day."

When Molly and the Master's wife got home, the Master was dancing a jig in the dairy and Daisy was mooing.

"I did it. . .I found the answer. . .it's turned to butter."

"No, you didn't," said the Master's wife. "Now you go straight this minute and take some of that butter to the witch at the mill."

"Why? Why should I?" demanded the Master. But of course, as soon as his wife told him why he should he scooped some into a bowl. He ran all the way to the mill and left it on the witch's doorstep and then he ran all the way home again and had a late breakfast, while his wife went to town and bought a new dress and Molly swept out the dairy and crooned to Daisy the cow.

PEAS

A gardener kneeling on his knees
Planted several rows of peas.
The sunshine shone, the breezes blew,
And all the little peapods grew.

Then, in the night, from a nearby hole,
A family of mice to the garden stole.
They climbed the stems with the greatest ease,
And that was the end of the garden of peas!

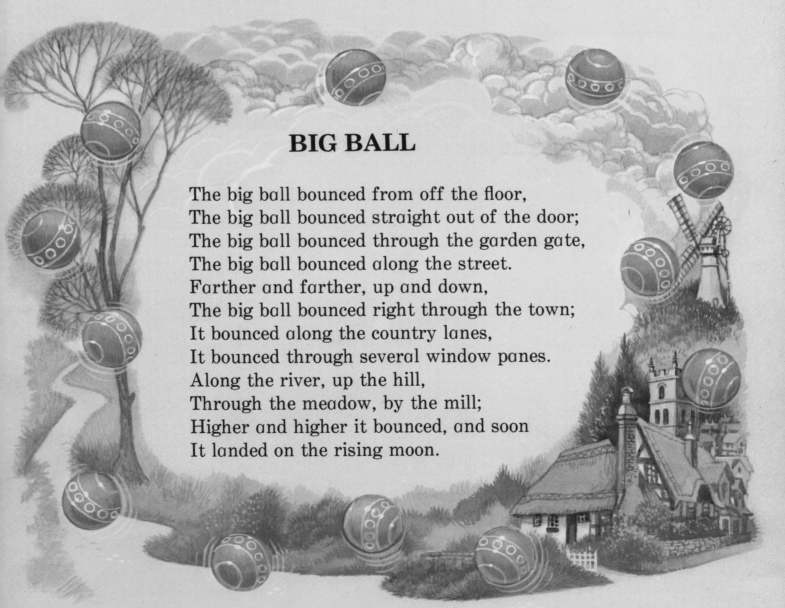

BIG BALL

The big ball bounced from off the floor,
The big ball bounced straight out of the door;
The big ball bounced through the garden gate,
The big ball bounced along the street.
Farther and farther, up and down,
The big ball bounced right through the town;
It bounced along the country lanes,
It bounced through several window panes.
Along the river, up the hill,
Through the meadow, by the mill;
Higher and higher it bounced, and soon
It landed on the rising moon.

JUST IN TIME

Squire George was a part-time wizard. Sometimes he was mostly squire and went about his business in the village. Sometimes he was mostly wizard and practised spells from his spell book and did a little bit of magic here and there. And sometimes he was neither squire, nor wizard, but was himself and rode out on his horse just to feel the sun on his face and the wind blowing through his hair.

One day, he had been sitting at his magic spell book for so long his head began to ache.

"I think I'll go for a gallop on my horse," he said and he pushed the spell book to one side.

It didn't take long to put on his riding boots and saddle up his horse.

"Take it steady," he said to his horse as they trotted up the steep hill behind the village. Once at the top it was a different story. The hill stretched for miles with bouncy grass underfoot and clouds racing overhead.

"Gee up there," cried the Squire. With a glad whinny the horse kicked up his heels and they were off.

Down in the village little Billy was bent on mischief. He could see the tiny silhouette of the Squire and his galloping horse up on the hill.

"He'll be up there for hours," he said. "Now is my chance to steal his book of spells." And first making sure that there was no one to observe him he crept along the lane and up the path towards the Squire's big house. He pushed open the door and crept inside. It was still, and very quiet, with not even a ticking clock to break the silence.

He pushed open the study door. There was a book with its pages lying open on the desk. Was that it?

He paused, and waited and listened. He didn't want to be caught in the act of taking it.

Up on the hill, something made the Squire feel prickly behind his ears and down the back of his spine. There was something wrong. . .somewhere.

"Whoa!" he cried to his horse. They pulled up sharply at a point where they could see the rooftops of the village and the roof of the Squire's own house.

He remembered he had left his book of spells open on his desk. Suppose. . .just suppose someone got hold of it. Someone who didn't understand how careful you had to be with magic spells. The damage might be so awful it could never be repaired. He couldn't remember locking the front door either. Perhaps there was someone stealing his book at this very moment.

He had to get home quickly. He whispered to his horse and they took the quickest way down, which happened to be straight over the rooftops. They nearly fell and broke all their bones when the horse's hoof caught one of the pinnacles on the church tower, but by a firm strong pull on the reins on the part of the Squire and a frantic kick by the horse they managed to land bumpily, but safely.

The Squire ran to his house. He was only just in time. Little Billy was just sneaking out of the front door with the spell book under his arm.

"Mine, I believe," said the Squire. And Billy found himself without the spell book and sitting in the fish pond with a waterlily tucked over his ear and a toad croaking at his elbow. . .

"Oh..oh.." he moaned. "He'll turn *me* into a toad. . . I know he will. . ." The Squire didn't say he would and he didn't say he wouldn't. Instead he looked at Billy sternly and said, "Go home, boy." Which Billy did, trailing water weed and waterlilies from his breeches.

As for the Squire, he was so relieved to have saved the village from disaster, that he resolved from that day onwards always to keep his book of spells under lock and key, and that is just what he did.

A PIECE OF ROPE

I've slung a rope up in a tree,
It's hanging from a branch;
But when I mount and swing away
It's my stallion on the ranch.

He's swift and strong, a champion;
My friend, so sure and true;
We'll track down all the 'baddies'
Like cowboys in Westerns do.

We help to drive the cattle,
We cross the scorching plain;
We outshoot any ambush
Set up to kill for gain.

Then when we've made our journey,
And arrive 'all-in' – work done,
I tether up my splendid steed
And put away my gun.

If the 'baddies' ever get me
I'll be very brave – I hope;
But of course it's only a lovely game;
And my horse – just a piece of rope!

NED OF THE TODDIN

Once upon a time, there was a little tortoiseshell kitten with pointed ears and a twitchy tail. His name was Ned of the Toddin, which was rather a strange name, but it was the only one he had, and he soon got used to it. His mother's name was Waowhler, and his father's name was Skaratch, and they all lived together on an emerald green bank between an old stone farmhouse and a brambly wood.

Now you could tell that Ned of the Toddin was not an ordinary kitten, because he began to look out for mice when he was only two hours old. When he was only two days old, he could skip about and talk better than most grown-up cats. When he was only three days old he was a full-size furry kitten, and when he was four days old he began to go out on his adventures.

First of all he trotted daintily up to the old stone farmhouse when nobody was about, just to see what it was like. There on the grey stone step were three bottles of snow-white milk with shiny silver tops.

"Give me some milk," cried Ned, "or I'll knock your tops off with my twitchy tail."

But the milk bottles just stood there, as deaf as three white posts, and didn't do anything at all. So Ned went up to the first milk bottle and carefully pressed its silver top with his twitchy tail. Then he took it between his furry paws and drank all the milk out of it. GULP. GULP. GULP. Just like that. Then he went up to the second milk bottle and pressed its silver top carefully with his twitchy tail. Then he took it between his furry paws and drank all the milk out of that too. But when he came to the third, he had really had enough, so he drank no more than the smooth cream off the top. LAP. LAP. LAP. Just like that. It was delicious. When the farmer came to look for his milk he was very surprised indeed to find most of it gone.

"Well I don't know," he said.

In the meantime, Ned of the Toddin went skipping gaily over the emerald green grass towards the sparkling river that ran along behind the farmhouse. Now an ordinary kitten is very frightened indeed of water, but Ned didn't mind it a bit. There he stood, on the riverside, and as he looked down into the sparkling water he could see a lot of little fish swimming lazily about in the sunshine, for all the world as if it was a Sunday, with nothing to do.

"Come up and be eaten, little fish," cried Ned, "or I'll splash all of the water out of the river with my twitchy tail."

But the little fish were far too busy doing nothing to listen to Ned, and they just went on swimming lazily about in the sunshine.

"Come up and be eaten, little fish," cried Ned again, "or I'll knock all your scales off with my twitchy tail."

But the little fish could not hear what Ned was saying. They just went on swimming round and round in the sparkling water. So Ned jumped straight into the river and gobbled up all the lazy fish. GOBBLE. GOBBLE. GOBBLE. Just like that.

Then he sprang merrily out of the water onto the river side. He shook himself so hard that the little water drops made a rainbow in the sunshine.

"That's better," he said.

Then he went on his way for all the world like an ordinary kitten who is simply out for a stroll among the daisies and dandelions.

He hadn't gone very far when he came upon a rather muddy pigsty. Inside the pigsty was a very large pig indeed. He had pink flapping ears, and pink trotters, and a curly pink tail. His name was Groanergut Swilltrough, and he was the most bad-tempered pig in the neighbourhood. As soon as he saw Ned he gave an unfriendly little grunt. GHHHH. Just like that.

"Go away, little kitten," he said. "I haven't got time for you today." Groanergut kicked several pieces of mud at Ned as he stood in the entrance to the pigsty.

"If you do that again," said Ned. "I'll knock your ears flat with my twitchy tail."

Groanergut Swilltrough gave a horrid little squeal. EEEEE. Just like that. Then he kicked some much larger pieces of mud at Ned. Any ordinary kitten would have run away, but Ned was not an ordinary kitten by a long way. All he did was hit Groanergut's piggy nose with his twitchy tail. WOP. Just like that.

"SQUEEEEEAL!" said Groanergut, looking very shocked indeed.
He got as much mud as he could, and tried to kick it over Ned,
but Ned skipped cleverly out of the way, and it all missed. Then
Groanergut ran up to Ned, and tried to squash him into the mud, but
Ned pulled his flapping ears over his eyes with his twitchy tail, so
that he couldn't see where he was going. He bumped into the side of
the pigsty with a terrible THUD. Just like that.

"EEEEEE," said Groanergut. He lay there exhausted.

In the meantime, Ned of the Toddin went happily on his way across
the emerald green grass, all sprinkled on with snow-white daisies.
He went past the old stone farmhouse, and he was just on his way home
when he smelled a delicious smell. He sniffed, and sniffed again,
but he didn't know what it was because he was only four days old, and
you couldn't expect him to know *everything*. SNIFF. SNIFF. SNIFF.
He followed the smell all the way back to the old farmhouse. It led
him over the grey stone step, and into the spotless white kitchen.

There, on the wooden table, was a beautiful piece of yellow cheese.
Ned sniffed carefully. No doubt about it. The smell led right up
to the cheese. Quick as a flash Ned jumped onto the table and ate up
the cheese. SWILLOWSWALLOW. Just like that.

"That was delicious," he said.

Just then he heard someone coming, so he jumped straight down off the wooden table and went quietly out through the door. When the farmer's wife saw that her cheese had gone she was very surprised indeed.

"Well I don't know," she said.

As soon as he got home, Ned the Toddin told his mummy and daddy all he had done during the day. Skaratch and Waowhler raised their furry eyebrows, because they had never heard of such an extraordinary kitten before.

"Well," said Skaratch.

"Well," said Waowhler.

So Ned curled up on a patch of soft moss and went to sleep, because he really was a bit tired after his adventures. There he lay, in a little tortoiseshell bundle, for all the world like a quiet well-behaved kitten of whom any mother could be proud.

"PRRRRRR," he said. "PRRRRRR."

BESSIE THE ELEPHANT

Bessie the elephant blushed with shame;
She had forgotten her name, her name.
She asked the stork, but he would not tell,
The parrot he merely said "Well well."
She asked the lion, who roared with laughter,
And ten little monkeys came giggling after.
She asked the hippo, who yawned aloud,
The stately peacock was much too proud.
The donkey he merely gave a bray,
The dormouse was shy, and couldn't say.
Bess blew her trumpet: "Oh tell me do."
Then all of them answered: "You are you!"

35

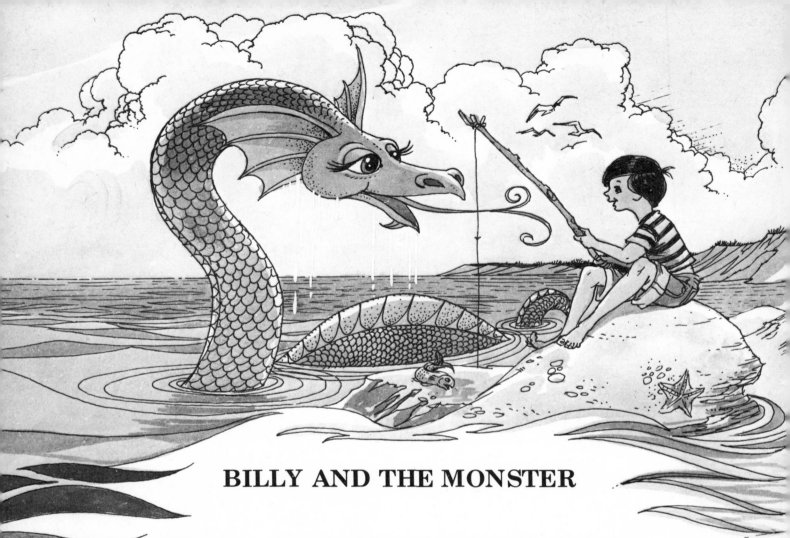

BILLY AND THE MONSTER

Billy sat on the rocks fishing. It was nearly supper time and he'd caught nothing. Suddenly a voice said:

"Will this one do?"

Billy turned to see a monster's head raised up out of the water and a fish flapping on the rocks.

"I'm Jessica," said the monster.

"OH. . .Thank you!. . .I'm Billy. . .Can I do anything for *you*?" Jessica wanted some different food.

"I'm tired of fish," she said.

Billy raced home. He ate his supper and was back at the rock with his pockets bulging. Jessica waited.

"Come for a ride," she said, humping her back. Away they went, Billy singing at the top of his voice and Jessica beating time with her tail.

It was fun. Billy went up and down riding the monster like a rocking horse.

"I'll take you to my island," said Jessica.

Billy could see it in the distance; it looked a wonderful place. When Jessica slid up on to the beach, she lowered her back for Billy to get off. Then she surrounded him with her coiled body.

"Now Billy," she said, "what have you brought me?"

For the first time Billy noticed how beautiful she was. Her big dark eyes with thick lashes, the coloured markings on her silky skin and her gentle voice; they made her someone quite special.

"Oh, yes. . .I have. . ." he stammered. He felt he should say, 'Your Royal Highness', or 'Your Majesty!' He pulled a packet from his pocket almost ashamed of his simple gift.

"I could only bring bread. I hope you like it."

He broke a piece off and held it for her. She took it carefully, eating slowly, tasting it well.

"More, please," she asked.

Billy fed her until the last crust had gone.

"That's all, Jessica. Were you disappointed?"

She smiled: "Not at all, Billy. It was delicious!. . .What did you call it?"

Billy was delighted to have pleased her.

"Bread," he answered.

"Mmm. . .bread," she repeated. The word was new to her. Then she made him a pillow with her tail.

"There, lie down, Billy. You must be tired."

He was soon fast asleep.

Billy awoke to see eyes peeping at him over the wall of
Jessica's body. These eyes belonged to crabs, lobsters, an
octopus waving her arms about and a smiling dolphin. He
liked the dolphin.

"They found crumbs from your bread," said Jessica.
"They're hoping for some more."

Billy wished he did have more; but his pockets were empty.

"They want you to make some," went on Jessica. "In fact,
they demand it."

Billy could see they were excited and quarrelsome.

"I can't!" he said. "Mother makes it!"

"Shall I bring your mother here?" Jessica whispered.

Billy shook his head. "No, she wouldn't come! Besides, she couldn't make bread here!"

Jessica was thinking.

"Would your mother make bread for me to bring back?" she asked.

"Well. . .Yes," Billy began, "if she had enough flour."

Jessica smiled. "Then my plan will work. I'll promise them bread and leave to get it. You must wait here. I'll turn back and come close in under the water. When you see my tail, jump on and we'll be away." It sounded a good idea.

"Won't they be angry and swim after us?" asked Billy.

Jessica's eyes twinkled.

"They might – but they're slow – except the dolphin and he's a friend."

She raised herself up, looked at them all and made a speech. Some clapped their claws, pleased; others grumbled. The dolphin came to stand by Billy. Jessica pushed out to sea.

"Keep them happy," advised the dolphin. "You were singing last night – start singing now."

Billy was glad to have something to do.

"I'll try," he said. His voice wouldn't come at first but soon he was braver and louder. The dolphin swayed to the music. Before long all the creatures were clapping, tapping and stamping – a real percussion band!

While they were all enjoying themselves, Jessica's tail appeared, slithering towards Billy, from the waves.

"Keep singing," muttered the dolphin, "and go – Now!"

Billy jumped – but stopped singing!

The creatures looked round.

"We've been tricked!" they cried. "You promised us bread! You promised!"

They scuttled down the beach and dived in after Jessica and Billy. Jessica outswam them all. Billy saw his mother out looking for him. He waved and shouted. How amazed she was to see him riding on the back of a monster!

He ran to her and brought her to the water's edge to meet his friend Jessica. They sat talking and Billy's mother said she would be glad to make lots of bread so that Jessica could keep her promise to the sea creatures.

Just then, who should come to join them but the dolphin. He was smiling, looking very happy. He'd persuaded the disappointed crabs, lobsters and the octopus that if only they'd be patient instead of bad tempered, everyone would be satisfied.

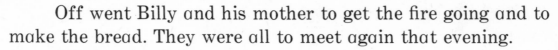

Off went Billy and his mother to get the fire going and to make the bread. They were all to meet again that evening.

What a party they had!

Jessica caught fish which Billy cooked on the beach. When his mother brought the crisp, crusty loaves there was a loud cheer. On the rocks, sat all the creatures, waiting for their share. They clapped and praised the excellent food called 'bread'. After supper they entertained one another. The dolphin gave acrobatic leaps out of the water; Billy sang and his mother told them a story.

Jessica had never enjoyed herself so much.

"Please, Billy's mother, may we come again?" she asked.

Everyone laughed and waved. "Yes, yes. . .Do please come again!"

The dolphin whispered, "She's our queen, you know."

Billy's heart bounced! "I knew it!" he muttered. . ."I just knew it!"

SPROGGET

Whenever I feel lonely and the day is dull or sad,
I whisper to my special friend – the best I ever had.
He comes at once – from nowhere; he's ready for a game;
"Hi, Sprogget!" I call out to him, for Sprogget is his name.

He loves to hide up in a tree – he's dressed in shades of green;
With dainty shoes and fitting cap – the smartest to be seen;
And just to add a final touch to clothes of softest leather
There, above a pointed ear, he wears an orange feather.

No one ever sees him: I'm the only one who can;
Because my friend called Sprogget is a magic sort of man.
There's nothing, really, he can't do – at any time of day;
At night he'd fly me to the moon; I've only got to say.

At meal times he's most useful; he helps me eat things up
And when there's milk I have to drink – he shares it from my cup.
I phone him and he rings me back; I know which calls are mine;
But Mummy says, "Wrong number!" when it's Sprogget on the line!

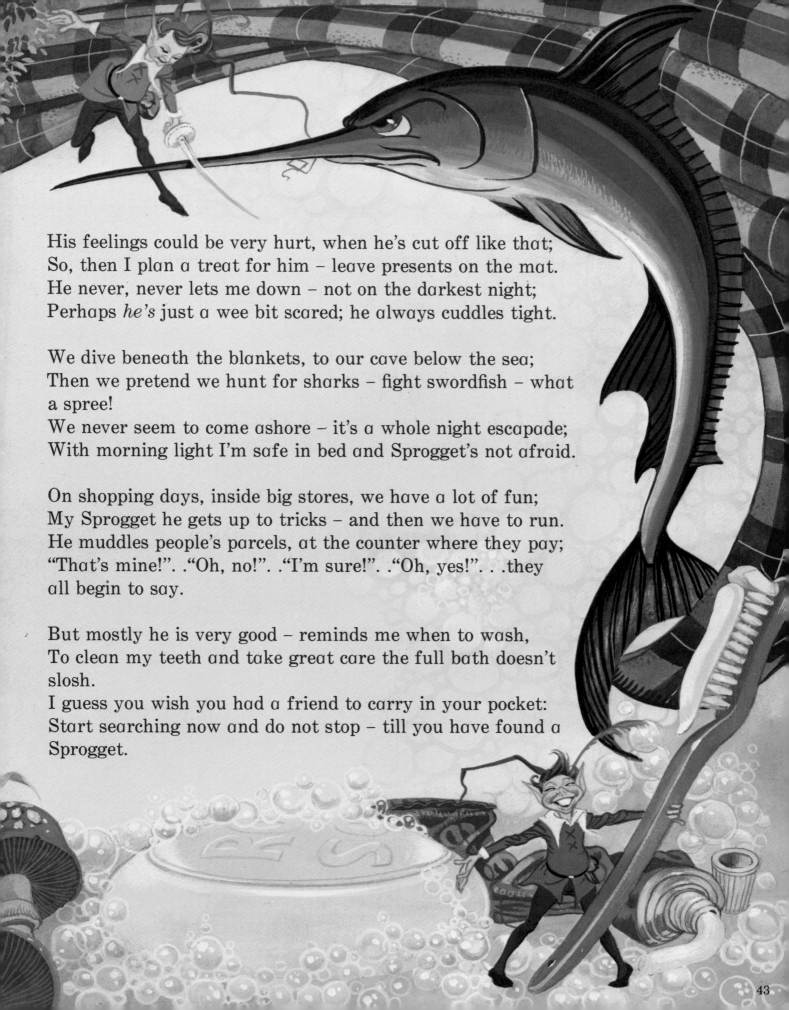

His feelings could be very hurt, when he's cut off like that;
So, then I plan a treat for him – leave presents on the mat.
He never, never lets me down – not on the darkest night;
Perhaps *he's* just a wee bit scared; he always cuddles tight.

We dive beneath the blankets, to our cave below the sea;
Then we pretend we hunt for sharks – fight swordfish – what
a spree!
We never seem to come ashore – it's a whole night escapade;
With morning light I'm safe in bed and Sprogget's not afraid.

On shopping days, inside big stores, we have a lot of fun;
My Sprogget he gets up to tricks – and then we have to run.
He muddles people's parcels, at the counter where they pay;
"That's mine!". ."Oh, no!". ."I'm sure!". ."Oh, yes!". . .they
all begin to say.

But mostly he is very good – reminds me when to wash,
To clean my teeth and take great care the full bath doesn't
slosh.
I guess you wish you had a friend to carry in your pocket:
Start searching now and do not stop – till you have found a
Sprogget.

THE UNEXPECTED RAINBOW

High above the earth in the land of clouds there were two kingdoms, the kingdom of Sol, and the kingdom of Splash. Both of these were ruled by powerful kings.

Now the king of Splash lived in a tall, proud castle on top of a big black rain cloud. While not many miles away, on a big, fluffy sun cloud lived the king of Sol.

You would think that living so close to one another, the two kingdoms would be friendly, but this was not so. In fact they were always quarrelling because the king of Splash always wanted it to rain, and the king of Sol always wanted it to be sunny.

So in order to make things fair, the two kingdoms agreed that one day it would be nice and sunny so that people could go for picnics, and the next, it would rain so as to give the trees and flowers a good drink.

For a time this plan worked very well, until one day things went very wrong.

The king of Splash was getting rather old, and at times he was apt to be very forgetful. His memory was getting so bad, that sometimes he even forgot to eat his breakfast.

On this particular morning, the king woke up even more forgetful than usual. He not only forgot to eat his breakfast, but he also forgot which day it was.

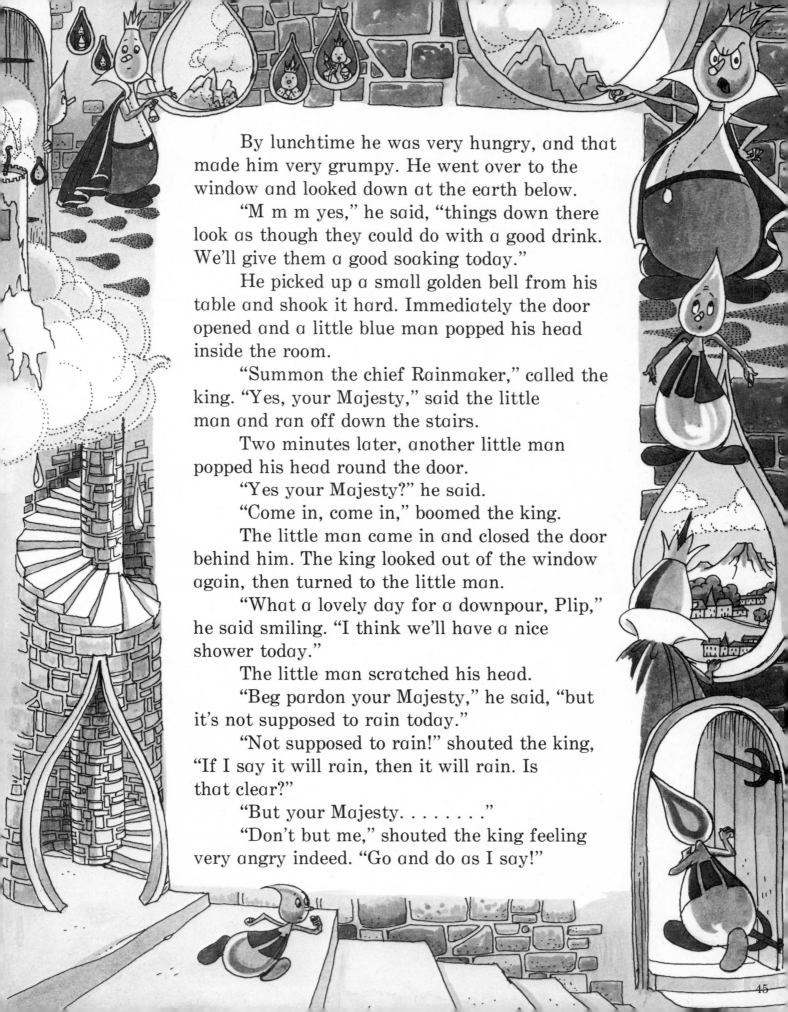

By lunchtime he was very hungry, and that made him very grumpy. He went over to the window and looked down at the earth below.

"M m m yes," he said, "things down there look as though they could do with a good drink. We'll give them a good soaking today."

He picked up a small golden bell from his table and shook it hard. Immediately the door opened and a little blue man popped his head inside the room.

"Summon the chief Rainmaker," called the king. "Yes, your Majesty," said the little man and ran off down the stairs.

Two minutes later, another little man popped his head round the door.

"Yes your Majesty?" he said.

"Come in, come in," boomed the king.

The little man came in and closed the door behind him. The king looked out of the window again, then turned to the little man.

"What a lovely day for a downpour, Plip," he said smiling. "I think we'll have a nice shower today."

The little man scratched his head.

"Beg pardon your Majesty," he said, "but it's not supposed to rain today."

"Not supposed to rain!" shouted the king, "If I say it will rain, then it will rain. Is that clear?"

"But your Majesty. . . . ."

"Don't but me," shouted the king feeling very angry indeed. "Go and do as I say!"

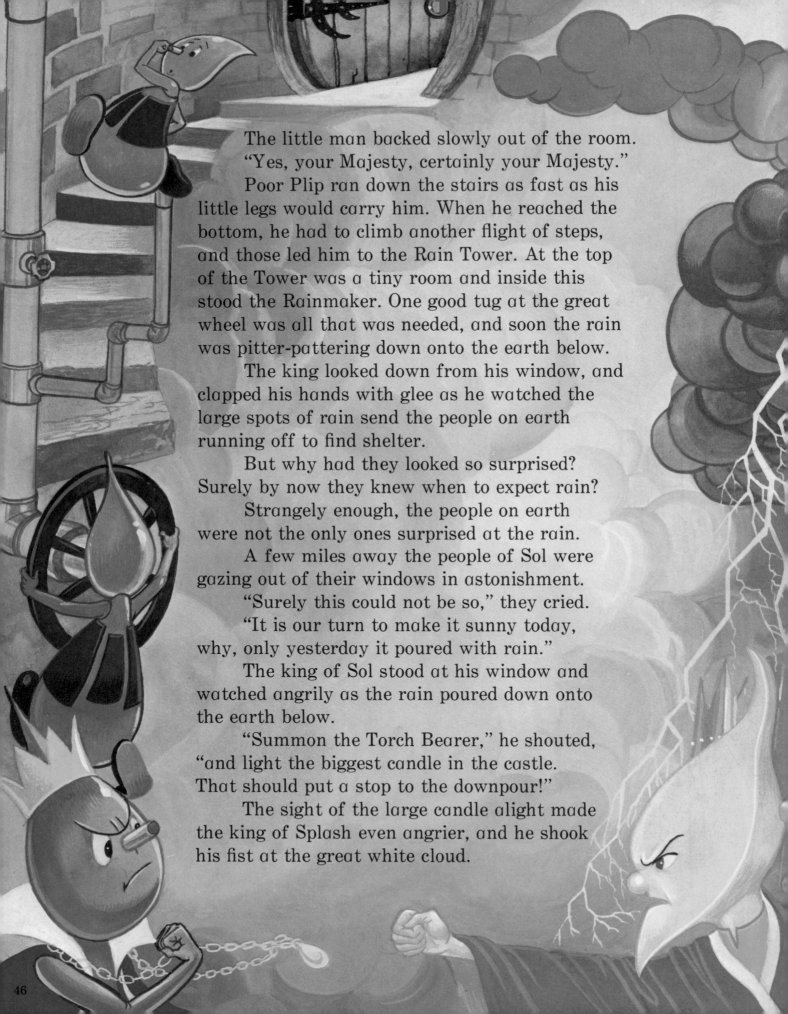

The little man backed slowly out of the room. "Yes, your Majesty, certainly your Majesty."

Poor Plip ran down the stairs as fast as his little legs would carry him. When he reached the bottom, he had to climb another flight of steps, and those led him to the Rain Tower. At the top of the Tower was a tiny room and inside this stood the Rainmaker. One good tug at the great wheel was all that was needed, and soon the rain was pitter-pattering down onto the earth below.

The king looked down from his window, and clapped his hands with glee as he watched the large spots of rain send the people on earth running off to find shelter.

But why had they looked so surprised? Surely by now they knew when to expect rain?

Strangely enough, the people on earth were not the only ones surprised at the rain.

A few miles away the people of Sol were gazing out of their windows in astonishment.

"Surely this could not be so," they cried.

"It is our turn to make it sunny today, why, only yesterday it poured with rain."

The king of Sol stood at his window and watched angrily as the rain poured down onto the earth below.

"Summon the Torch Bearer," he shouted, "and light the biggest candle in the castle. That should put a stop to the downpour!"

The sight of the large candle alight made the king of Splash even angrier, and he shook his fist at the great white cloud.

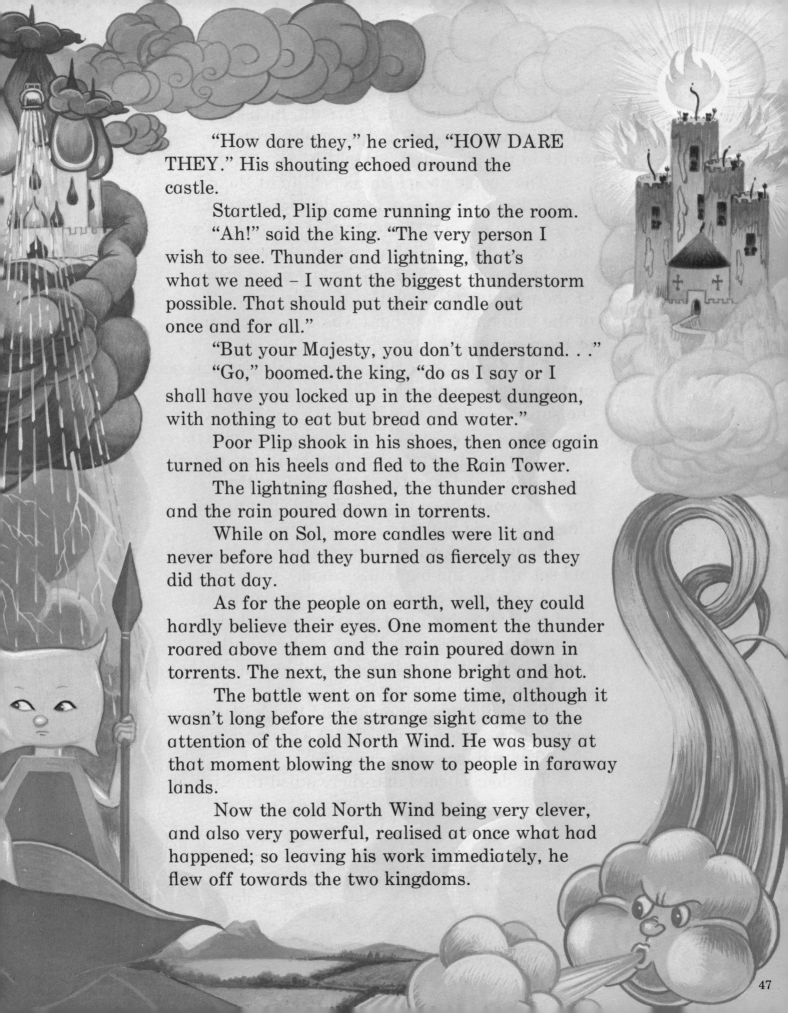

"How dare they," he cried, "HOW DARE THEY." His shouting echoed around the castle.

Startled, Plip came running into the room.

"Ah!" said the king. "The very person I wish to see. Thunder and lightning, that's what we need – I want the biggest thunderstorm possible. That should put their candle out once and for all."

"But your Majesty, you don't understand. . ."

"Go," boomed the king, "do as I say or I shall have you locked up in the deepest dungeon, with nothing to eat but bread and water."

Poor Plip shook in his shoes, then once again turned on his heels and fled to the Rain Tower.

The lightning flashed, the thunder crashed and the rain poured down in torrents.

While on Sol, more candles were lit and never before had they burned as fiercely as they did that day.

As for the people on earth, well, they could hardly believe their eyes. One moment the thunder roared above them and the rain poured down in torrents. The next, the sun shone bright and hot.

The battle went on for some time, although it wasn't long before the strange sight came to the attention of the cold North Wind. He was busy at that moment blowing the snow to people in faraway lands.

Now the cold North Wind being very clever, and also very powerful, realised at once what had happened; so leaving his work immediately, he flew off towards the two kingdoms.

"I'll teach the pair of them," he said angrily. Taking one mighty breath, he blew out all the candles on Sol, and promptly froze the water in the giant Tap on Splash.

The people of Splash looked up at their Rainmaker in horror. A large drop of water had frozen solid around the bottom of the great Tap, and try as they might they could not make it rain.

On Sol too, the people looked up in dismay at the proud golden candles. All that was left of the brilliant yellow light was now just a puff of black smoke.

The people on earth came out of their houses and looked up at the sky. What had happened to the sun, and where was the rain?

These were very strange goings on indeed.

By now, the king of Splash had been told of his mistake, and was feeling very silly. He knew he would have to go and apologise to the king of Sol and make friends with him again.

So he ordered his carriage to be made ready and set off for the big white cloud.

The king of Sol sat on his throne with his head resting on his hand. What was he to do? Perhaps he had been too hasty. After all, the king of Splash was getting old and he had heard that he was rather forgetful at times.

Suddenly there came a loud knock at the door. . .Rap. . .Rap. . .Rap. . .RAAP!

"Humph, come in," he called.

The door opened and there stood the king of Splash.

The king got up from his throne and held out his hands.

"My dear fellow," he cried.

The king of Splash walked up to him and took his hands.

"I've been an old fool," said the king of Splash.

"And I have been too hasty," said the king of Sol.

Suddenly, without warning, came a loud BANG and all the doors of the palace flew open.

"So, I see you have made friends again." It was the North Wind.

"Yes, we have," said the two kings together.

"I see," said the North Wind. Then he thought for a moment.

"Well, do you both solemnly promise never to quarrel again?"

Both kings nodded their heads.

"Very well, in that case I shall send for my brother the warm South Wind, to undo the work I have done."

The North Wind kept his promise and sent for his brother.

One great puff of his warm breath and immediately the water in the giant Tap unfroze, and once again the golden candles of Sol burned bright and hot.

So everything turned out happily in the end and just to show the people on earth that the two kingdoms had made friends, the people of Sol and Splash joined together and painted a giant rainbow across the sky.

LONG AGO

When Granny was a little girl
She bought things in the street;
Muffins from the Muffin Man
And chestnuts for a treat;
Crispy, hot, delicious;
Burning in her hand;
The smell as nuts were roasting
She remembers – it was grand.

Then, there was the Organ Man;
The children gathered round
Laughing at his monkey,
Dancing to the sound;
Tossing him a penny
As the hurdy-gurdy played;
While pennies kept on tinkling
The Organ Man, he stayed.

But Granny liked the man the best
With windmills on his barrow;
Reds and yellows, bright and gay
Whirring in the breeze.
"Oh Mother, Mother!" she would say,
"A jam jar, quickly please!"
Then out to change it for the toy:
To think a jar could buy such joy!

And while she played and chased about
In other streets she'd hear him shout:
"Windmills for jam jars. . .jam jars. . .
jam jars!"
Fading as he went;
And Granny was so happy
With the jam jar she had spent.

CHEESE AND BEES

"Haste away and lock the doors," shouted Martha McGimble as she ran through the village street, her hair falling from its net and the vegetables falling from her basket so great was her hurry. "Haste you away. . .the tinkers are on the road."

At the mention of tinkers everyone in the sleepy village street woke with a start.

"Quick Mary. . .lock up the chickens," shouted Mary's mother.

"Take the pig into the barn and bolt the door," shouted Daniel's father.

The women ran to take in their washing. The men gathered up their rakes and hammers. The children picked up their balls and called to their dogs.

"The tinkers are coming. . .hurry. . .hurry. . ."

Normally the village folk welcomed tinkers. The kind of tinker, that is, who sold pots and pans and stewed his dinner in an old iron pot over a kindling fire. These tinkers, the tinkers they ran from, were tinkers of a different kind. They were tinkers who stole clothes from washing lines, tinkers who broke fences and put other peoples dinners in their cooking pots and other peoples possessions in their pockets. When they were in the village nothing was safe, unless it was locked up or hidden.

The tinkers thought it a lovely joke to frighten so many people all at the same time and they were always raiding the village. Things got so bad that soon no one dared to hang washing out at all. Potatoes couldn't be dug and left to dry in the sun anymore. Chickens could no longer be allowed to peck freely in the long grass.

"Something has to be done about this," fumed Old John, when one day the tinkers crept into the village unnoticed and stole the very chair he was sitting on. "We must consult the wizard."

"Are you sure that will be safe?" asked one of Old John's friends.

"Not for those rascally tinkers I hope," said Old John.

The wizard had lived in the village for many years. The villagers always took great care not to upset him for they didn't quite know what he could do in the way of spells. But he had always been friendly and he had helped them out of trouble before, so Old John and the village elders went to consult him.

"I know why you have come," said the wizard before they could utter a word. "Turn round and go home. Next time the tinkers come to the village close your windows and lock your doors and leave the rest to me."

The village elders went home, not having said a word, but knowing somehow that the wizard understood their problem and would help.

"I can never understand how he knows things without being told," said Old John's wife. "Makes me feel kind of creepy, that does. . ."

It made Old John feel a bit uneasy too.

But not as uneasy as the tinkers felt a few days later. They descended on the village in a noisy, rowdy band. Windows were closed and doors locked in the twinkling of an eye.

"Ha. .ha. .ha. ." laughed the tinker chief. "Someone was in such a hurry he forgot his cheese."

And indeed, standing right where the tinkers couldn't fail to see it, on a three-legged stool to raise it from the ground, was a round, ripe and beautiful cheese.

There was a lot of whispering going on behind locked doors.

"Whose cheese is that?"

"How did that cheese get there?"

"The cheese is mine," said the wizard hobbling from his house, pretending to be afraid. . .which he wasn't.

"Oh no it isn't. . .not any more," said the tinker chief.

"Just let me take one slice," said the wizard, quickly sinking his knife into it's creamy skin.

"Away from there!" shouted the tinker in a temper.

He roughly pushed the wizard to one side, but not before the wizard had whispered something to the cheese.

From the hole which he had just cut rose a thousand humming, buzzing, angry bees, that buzzed and threatened and stung. . .and stung. . .and stung. . .and stung. . .

"Ow . . . ow . . . ow . . ." screeched the tinkers as they took to their heels and ran, with the bees following close behind. The bees may be chasing the tinkers still because neither the bees, nor the tinkers, were ever seen in the village again.

As for the wizard, he went back to his cottage and bothered nobody, and nobody bothered him until there was another problem to solve. That way everyone was happy. Except those rascally tinkers of course.

CLACKETY CLACK

There is an old woman
Who spins in the sky.
Clackety, clackety, clack.
She spins all day long,
And all night-time too.
Clackety, clackety, clack.

She spins clouds in wisps.
She spins clouds in billows.
She spins them in sheets,
And fluffs them like pillows.
She spins puffs of white,
And blankets of grey.
She spins yellow and gold
At the end of the day.

There is an old woman
Who spins on a wheel.
Clackety, clackety, clack.
Without her the sky
Would be empty and still.
Clackety, clackety, clack.

THE ROLLING DRUM

Jason Brown was walking along the lane one sunny morning, wondering what he could do to pass the time, when he met a man carrying a drum. The drum was simply enormous, and the man was rather short, and Jason couldn't decide whether the pair of them looked more like a drum which had grown a head and two legs, or a man with a drum where his tummy should have been.

"Are you laughing at me?" asked the man crossly.

"Of course not," said Jason.

"It's no laughing matter when you have something as big and as awkward as this to carry," said the man.

"Then why don't you put it on a cart and push it?" asked Jason.

"Because no one will lend me a cart," said the man.

"Then put it on the ground and roll it along," said Jason.

"I've already tried that. I couldn't see where I was going. I pushed it into a tree and made a dent in it. Now stop pestering me and let me get on my way."

"I'll help you if you like," said Jason. "If you roll the drum along the road I'll walk in front and call out directions. I won't let you bump into anything . . . I promise."

The man was tired. The drum was heavy and his arms ached. He supposed it was worth a try. He lowered the drum to the ground and rubbed the stiffness from his arms.

"I've got a better idea," he said. "YOU push, and I'll guide you."

Jason didn't mind pushing. He thought it might be rather fun. So off they set, with Jason pushing and the man guiding.

"To the left . . . to the left . . ." shouted the man, dancing about all over the road like a little leprechaun. "Now . . . a little to the right . . . you're going too fast . . . you're going too slow . . . push straighter . . . mind that stone . . . look out, there's a pot-hole . . . further to the left . . . further to the right . . ."

Jason was getting confused.

"No . . . no . . . I said left . . . LOOK OUT . . . you'll hit that tree . . . can't you push straight? . . ."

"It's all very well for you . . . You can see where I'm going . . . I can't," grumbled Jason.

"Stop mumbling, boy . . . and keep pushing . . ." shouted the man excitedly. He was enjoying himself. It wasn't often he had a boy to order around. He shouted so many different instructions, so quickly, one after the other, that Jason's poor head began to spin.

Jason decided enough was enough. He stopped pushing and put his hands over his ears.

"What's this . . . what's this?" cried the man hopping all round Jason and the stationary drum. "Surely you're not tired already?"

"Of course I'm not tired . . ." said Jason, trying his hardest to be polite. "But please stop shouting at me all the time."

"If I don't shout, you won't hear me," said the man.

"If you DO shout, I won't push anymore," said Jason.

"I'll tell you what I'll do," said the man, who was enjoying himself too much to let his helper walk away. "When I want you to steer to the left, I'll bang on the left side of the drum, and when I want you to steer to the right, I'll bang on the right side of the drum. I'll have to walk backwards I know, but I'm clever enough to manage that. Now come on . . . push . . . or it will be nightfall before I reach my destination."

Off they set again and what a commotion they made. The drum rattled and bonked along over the stony road and the man banged on it's sides with a merry rat-a-tat-tat-thump-bang-bang every two seconds. Jason's head began to feel like a drum itself, and very soon he couldn't tell which side of the real drum the man was banging.

A gang of boys who had been exploring along the hedge came to see what all the noise was about, and joined their cheers to the hub-bub.

"The circus is coming . . ." they shouted.

"No it isn't . . ." shouted the man as he rat-a-tat-tatted on the drum.

A dog came from the wood where he'd been chasing rabbits and ran after them.

"Yap . . . yap . . ." barked the dog.

"Caw . . . caw . . ." joined in the rooks, who until then had been sitting quietly in the trees.

"Z.Z.Z.Z . . ." buzzed the bees, forgetting all about their empty pollen sacks.

"Eeee awwww . . ." brayed a donkey.

"Baaa . . . baaa . . ." bleated the lambs.

"Moooo . . ." mooed the cows.

Jason was so confused he didn't hear one of the boys shout a warning. Neither did anyone else for that matter.

Suddenly Jason found he wasn't pushing any more. The drum was rolling by itself . . . down hill. And it was chasing the man. It's hard enough to run backwards at the best of times and this wasn't the best of times. The man's heels caught up with his toes, his legs tied themselves into a knot, and down he fell. The drum rolled on . . . over his feet . . . over his legs . . . as it rolled over his tummy he flung his arms round it and held it tightly. It didn't stop rolling, as everyone expected it to. It carried on down the hill, with the man wrapped round it like a rubber tyre.

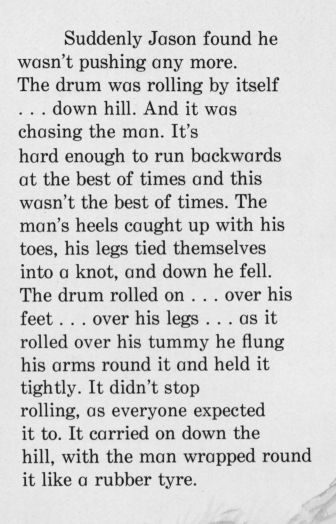

"Stop me . . . stop me . . ." he shouted. But he didn't stop until the drum stopped, and the drum didn't stop until it ran off the road at the bottom of the hill, and splashed into the duck pond.

"Quack . . . quack . . ." squawked the ducks noisily. One of them stood on top of the drum and looked down into the man's face.

"Get me out of here . . ." he shouted, "before I'm eaten alive."

Jason shooed the ducks away and the boys waded into the pond and pulled him out. Then they waded back and pulled out the drum.

"We'll push it for you mister," said the boys eagerly.

"No, you won't," shouted the man. "I don't want any more help from any more boys. I'll carry it myself."

And he did. He picked up his drum and carried it to wherever he was taking it, with water streaming from his pockets, mud squelching from his boots, and water-weed dangling from his ears. He didn't say thank you and he didn't look back once.

And Jason? He went exploring with the boys. He'd done his good deed for the day. Now it was time to have some fun.

OSCAR

A puppy named Oscar had very long ears,
They earned him unpleasant remarks, and the sneers
Of Jenny and Penny, his two lady friends,
Who swore that his ears had no shape and no ends.

He walked up and down, shedding many a tear,
And then he was struck with a splendid idea.
He went to the mirror, and with a huge grin
Tied a neat bow with them under his chin.

Now Jenny and Penny admire his good features,
They think him the very divinest of creatures.
And all the young dogs are a-wearing of bows
On ear, and on chin, and on tail, and on nose.

THE MEDDLER

A group of children were playing ball on the village green when suddenly the ball took it upon itself to fly up into the sky and over the rooftops. Up . . . up . . . it went, till it was just a tiny speck and then, that too, vanished.

"It's that horrid witch," sobbed little Catherine, whose ball it was, and nothing anyone said, or did, would comfort her.

The horrid witch lived in the cave just outside the village and was always meddling. When the housewives were cooking and the pastry was rising in golden domes over their pies, it would suddenly flop, sink into the gravy and go soggy. Cakes which were rising and promised to be as light as a feather would come out of the oven like lumps of clay. As soon as a broken fence was repaired it would fall down again. As soon as a cabbage with a sound heart was cut in the field it would be invaded by nibbling caterpillars. The village fountain spouted water sideways instead of upwards. The bottoms were always falling out of loaded buckets. Eggs were always addling the moment they were laid. And what was far worse, children were always crying when they should have been laughing.

And it was all the witch's doing.

Not that anyone in the village had ever done anything to upset her. But once, long ago, long before anyone in the village had been born, someone had made her get out of bed on the wrong side, and she had been a meddlesome old witch ever since. Even the birds in the trees stopped singing for fear she would notice them and make their tail feathers fall out . . . a favourite trick of hers. Cats took care not to miaow in her hearing, lest they suddenly discovered their tails tied into knots. Tiles fell off roofs, hinges fell off doors, keys got stuck in locks. Life, for everyone, was very miserable. No one laughed any more.

But how DOES one get rid of an unwanted witch?

The villagers couldn't very well ask her to move away. There was no telling what she might do with her magic. They began to wonder if they should move themselves and leave the village empty and deserted, but how could they be sure the witch wouldn't leave her cave and follow them?

At last, in despair, the Village Elders went to see the Abbot of a distant monastery.

"You should have come sooner," he said, when they had explained the problem.

The villagers could hardly believe their eyes when the Elders returned, accompanied by a thin, spindly monk, who looked as though he wouldn't dare say boo to a gosling, let alone a goose!

"What can HE do against a witch?" they tutted in their disappointment. "He'll run a mile, rather than face her." They had already seen the village blacksmith, a man with brawny arms and a strong broad back, run and hide like a frightened rabbit when he thought he heard the witch coming.

But the meek-looking monk was braver than they thought. He went to the cave alone, because nobody was brave enough to go with him.

His sandalled feet didn't make a sound, but at the entrance to the cave, his sleeve brushed against a rock and sent it tumbling with a clatter. The villagers, who had followed at a safe distance, gasped, and each held his breath.

The witch came cackling from her hiding place, already planning mischief. And then, something quite unexpected happened. The witch took one look at the brown-robed monk . . . and shrieked.

"Look at her . . . she's frightened . . . why is SHE frightened of HIM?" whispered the villagers in amazement. They crept a little nearer.

"She is trying to run away . . . look, SHE is running away from HIM . . ."

The monk calmly sprinkled water on the witch's fleeing back . . . and before their startled eyes she turned into stone. The villagers gazed with awe at the monk, and with more than a little fear. If the witch was afraid of him, then perhaps they should be too, but he quickly reassured them.

"Good has triumphed over evil," he said. "When the witch saw me she knew her magic would have no effect . . . that is why she tried to run . . . now, my friends, enjoy the peace . . . she will meddle no more."

And she didn't.

She stands in the cave to this day. Just a pillar of stone, unless you happen to know better.

JUMPING JACK

Jack started jumping as soon as he could walk; little jumps at first, then bigger and bigger. By the time he had grown into a young man he found it easier and quicker to jump everywhere. People were rather weary of him. "There goes 'Jumping Jack'," they would say. "It's no good trying to keep up with him." His sudden jumps were startling, and his neighbours grew to dislike him. Jack became lonely; an outsider.

One day, he made up his mind to leave the village where he had lived all his life and go off into the world. He'd walk and walk, for miles and miles; he'd cure himself of jumping. Then, he'd make friends – be an ordinary person. He said goodbye to his parents.

"Don't stay away long, Jack," said his mother. "We shall miss you."

Jack tried to cheer her up. "I'll be back, mother! . . . I'll make my fortune, and get rid of this jumping disease. I don't want to be called 'Jumping Jack' all my life."

His father wished him luck, and they both waved him off on his travels.

After several miles, Jack was tired and quite glad to see a stretch of water in front of him. Leaving his shoes and stockings on the bank, he paddled in the cool waves. Imagine his horror when he saw, swimming towards him, a huge crocodile! . . . What could he do? The creature was so close.

There was only one thing he could do – he jumped!

Landing the other side, on his bare feet, Jack looked around. There were beautiful flower beds, paths, seats and fountains.

"Good gracious! I've jumped out of one trouble into another!" he said out loud. "This looks like a royal garden!"

Sure enough, soldiers advanced from all directions, each armed with a sword. He took another jump – right over their heads! They gazed up in amazement. Jack looked down towards the courtyard where he would land; it was straight in front of a splendid palace.

More soldiers rushed, grabbed him and marched him off to the king. Jack begged His Majesty's pardon for trespassing and explained that he'd only jumped because he'd been in great danger.

"Quite! Quite!" agreed the king. "You're the first one Camilla has missed."

Jack gave a shudder at the thought of that terrible crocodile.

Just then, the beautiful Princess Arabella entered and spoke to her father. He turned to Jack:

"We have other visitors here, competing for my daughter's hand in marriage. Would you care to join them?"

Jack bowed, first to the princess and then to the king.

"I would be honoured, Your Majesty."

A contest was arranged for that very evening. Jack would have
to fence with a prince, in front of the royal family and hundreds of
people. He had never learned the art of fencing; it would be
difficult and very dangerous.

At first, Jack pranced around keeping himself safe. Then he
gave some jumps. The crowd thought him clever – and funny. People
began to laugh. Soon they were all doubled up with laughter. The
king held his sides. He nearly collapsed when Jack leapt over the
prince's head.

"Stop! Stop!" he cried. "That's enough! . . . I can't laugh
any more!"

Would the king have Jack thrown to Camilla for making the prince look stupid? No; Arabella gave him her hand and they danced round the ball-room. She glanced at his feet.

"They're very nimble, but wouldn't they be more comfortable in shoes?"

Jack felt ashamed, but then he saw her smile.

"Come!" he said and they danced faster and faster. Up the staircase, out of the palace, through the courtyard and garden; on and on they danced to the water's edge. There, Jack lifted Arabella up in his arms and made a flying leap. Camilla's eye gleamed in the light of the moon as she watched them pass over. They landed safely, by the side of Jack's shoes and stockings. He put them on and once more jumped his princess over the water.

Back in the palace, the king made a speech announcing the wedding. Invitations were to be sent to Jack's parents. Jack was to receive a title and the king asked him what name he would like to be called.

"Any name you wish, Your Majesty. I am so happy you could even call me, 'Jumping Jack'!"

WHY WINTER WAS LATE ONE YEAR

The East Wind had a cold. He should have stayed in bed of course, but the East Wind was very stubborn and once he had made up his mind about something, nothing and nobody could change it for him. Or so he thought.

"I haven't been out to blow for weeks," he complained to North, South and West, who were doing their best to make him stay in bed. "Every time I go out to make the leaves shiver and the ponds freeze, one of you has got there before me. If I don't start blowing soon Old Man Winter will never wake up."

"One more day of sleep won't hurt him," said South Wind, trying to push him back into bed.

"Take your hands off me . . . you . . . you . . . warm wind you! . . ." snapped East Wind, with more than a hint of ice in his voice.

"At least put your scarf on," said West Wind and began to wind yards and yards of striped scarf round East Wind's neck, and yards and yards more of the same scarf, which was very long indeed, round East Wind's middle, and then the rest of it round his ears. The scarf was so long it stretched further than the eye could see when it was laid out straight. and when it was all wrapped round East Wind, his nose, his toes, and his knobbly knees, were the only parts of him which showed.

"How do you expect me to blow properly with this . . . this thing, wrapped round my person?" snapped East Wind icily.

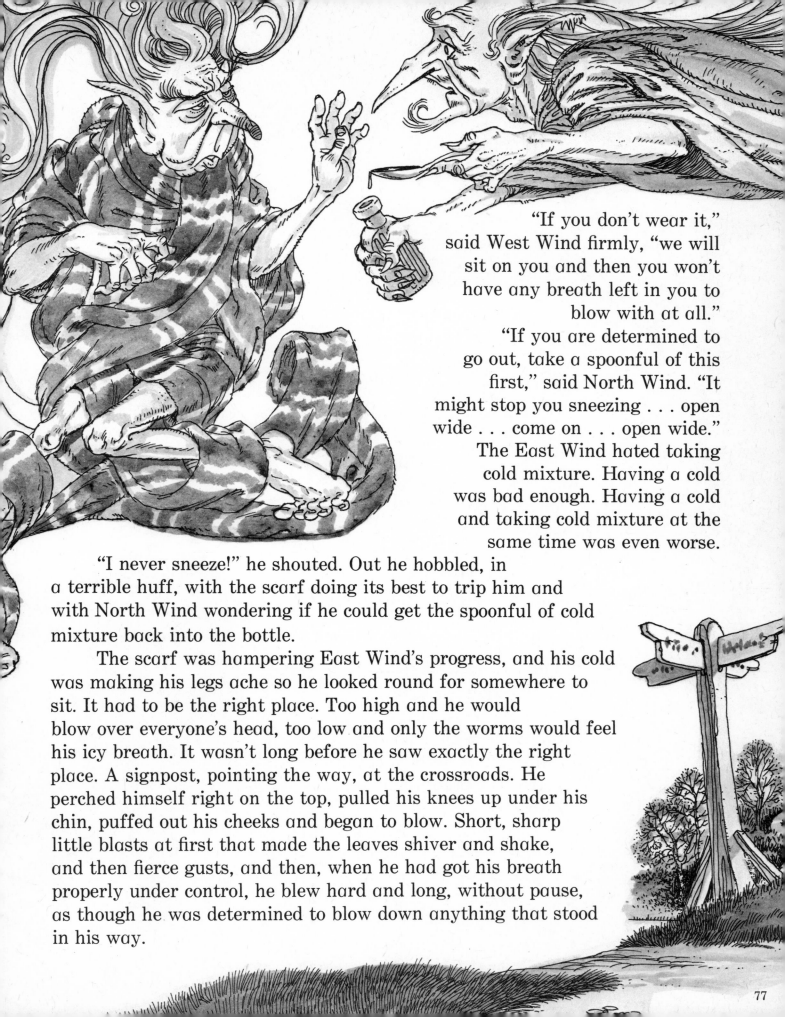

"If you don't wear it," said West Wind firmly, "we will sit on you and then you won't have any breath left in you to blow with at all."

"If you are determined to go out, take a spoonful of this first," said North Wind. "It might stop you sneezing . . . open wide . . . come on . . . open wide." The East Wind hated taking cold mixture. Having a cold was bad enough. Having a cold and taking cold mixture at the same time was even worse.

"I never sneeze!" he shouted. Out he hobbled, in a terrible huff, with the scarf doing its best to trip him and with North Wind wondering if he could get the spoonful of cold mixture back into the bottle.

The scarf was hampering East Wind's progress, and his cold was making his legs ache so he looked round for somewhere to sit. It had to be the right place. Too high and he would blow over everyone's head, too low and only the worms would feel his icy breath. It wasn't long before he saw exactly the right place. A signpost, pointing the way, at the crossroads. He perched himself right on the top, pulled his knees up under his chin, puffed out his cheeks and began to blow. Short, sharp little blasts at first that made the leaves shiver and shake, and then fierce gusts, and then, when he had got his breath properly under control, he blew hard and long, without pause, as though he was determined to blow down anything that stood in his way.

"Brr, what an icy wind! It is getting cold," said the people passing by.

"Wouldn't be surprised if it snows."

That was the kind of talk East Wind liked to hear. He almost smiled, in spite of his cold and his tickling nose and his sore throat. He blew harder . . . and harder . . . and then . . . he did something which he said he never did do . . . he sneezed.

He sneezed so hard, he fell off the signpost and landed with a thud on the ground. It quite knocked the breath out of him.

"Thank goodness that nasty East Wind has dropped," said people passing by. "And what a good thing too!"

Now that was the kind of talk the East Wind didn't like to hear.

"I'll show them . . . I'll make them complain," he grumbled. He climbed back onto the signpost, pulled up his knees, loosened his scarf and got ready to blow the longest, iciest, meanest blow, he'd ever blown. He was so cross he failed to notice that the end of his scarf was coming unwound and that yards and yards of it were already dangling beside the signpost. He blew harder, and harder still. His breath was white, and frosty with ice. The loose end of his scarf somehow got caught in the lash of his breath and it began to wind itself round and round the signpost.

There was already a layer of ice on the ponds.

"Brrr . . . winter's on its way . . ." shivered people as they hurried past.

The East Wind blew harder and harder . . . until he did, again, what he said he never did do. He sneezed. It was such a sudden, jerky sneeze, it tugged the end of the scarf which was wound round the signpost and started to unwind it. Once it started to unwind it would not . . . could not . . . stop.

It spun the signpost round just like a spinning top. Round and round and round. Quicker and quicker and quicker, till it was just a whizzing blur. The East Wind, who was spinning round too, and whose breath was spinning round inside him, was so surprised and confused he forgot to stop blowing.

Hats blew into the air in spirals, and everything that could move was blown first in one direction and then in another.

"What's happened to the wind? It's gone mad!" cried the people, with so many bumps and collisions and narrow misses going on round their ears.

The signpost continued it's crazy twirl until the scarf had completely unwound, and then it wobbled to a stop. East Wind immediately lost his balance and fell to the ground. He lay there, waiting for his breath to stop spinning inside him and thought about the advice his friends had given him.

"They were quite right. I should have stayed in bed. I should have taken the cold mixture," he said. "I shall go home and I shall stay in bed until I'm better. Winter will have to sleep a little longer this year."

And that is exactly what he did do, leaving some very puzzled people and a very wobbly signpost behind him.

Ever after that, whenever the East Wind blew, the signpost at the crossroads got confused and spun round and round on the spot like a spinning top. It was always sending people off in the wrong direction and getting the blame for something which wasn't really its fault.

HUMPTY DUMPTY

Humpty Dumpty climbed over the wall;
He'd really no business there at all;
He cut his hand,
He tore his trews
And scuffed the toes of his newest shoes.

He slithered down onto grassy ground
Then brushed himself off and looked around;
Soldiers approached
And grabbed at him:
"Young man, you must come and see the King!"

They marched him then to the High Court room;
He trembled to think upon his doom;
The King looked up,
Eyes opened wide,
He laughed and laughed till he almost cried.

"Pray, what on earth do you call yourself?
Should you not be on the dairy shelf?
Aren't you an egg
Fresh laid·– surely?
And for heaven's sake, why come to me!"

At the name, 'Humpty Dumpty', the King
Laughed again: "You're an 'eggstra' strange thing;
A mascot, eh?
To cheer my men!
Clean him up and I'll see him again."

Humpty was dressed in uniform fine
And there he marched at the head of the line.
When he was tired
They held him up
And bore him along in the King's egg-cup.

His fame it spread wide from land to land;
He'd a special tune and a special band;
Such special care
They had to take
For never; oh, never, must Humpty break!

NED OF THE TODDIN AGAIN

Ned of the Toddin was a very unusual ginger kitten. He lived on an emerald green bank between an old stone farmhouse and a brambly wood. His mother's name was Waowhler, and his father's name was Skaratch. His round eyes sparkled with curiosity, because all cats are curious, as you know.

One day, Ned went out towards the brambly wood to catch a mouse for his dinner. He went down the emerald green bank, across the field, and into the bramble bushes. They didn't scratch him because he was so small. Now he hadn't gone very far when he heard a noise. PID A PAD. PID A PAD. Just like that. Round the corner came a big black cat. His coat was black, his nose was black, and his whiskers were black. His eyes gleamed like little bonfires. His name was Clawface The Magnificent, and he was the most dreaded cat in all the neighbourhood.

"Out of my way, little kitten," said Clawface the Magnificent. "This is my brambly wood. You have no business to be here."

"No, I won't get out of the way," said Ned. "I am looking for my dinner."

"Go home to your mother at once," said Clawface, "or I'll have you for MY dinner."

"No, I won't," said Ned, who wasn't afraid of anybody.

"MIAAAAAAAOUW!" cried Clawface The Magnificent. "Do as you're told or I'll spank you hard."

"If you do," said Ned, "I'll crumple your whiskers with my twitchy tail."

Now, Clawface was not used to being spoken to like that by a little kitten. Without more ado he sprang towards Ned, and he would certainly have spanked him very hard indeed, but Ned turned round and hit him on the nose with his twitchy tail. PLONK. Just like that. Clawface The Magnificent became so angry he didn't know what to do. His black fur stood on end, his black tail waved about, and he hissed.

SSSSSSSS!

But Ned of the Toddin sat very calmly and licked his furry paws, for all the world as if there was nothing going on at all.

Suddenly, Clawface the Magnificent sprang again, but Ned jumped out of the way at once. Then he caught hold of poor Clawface's front legs with his twitchy tail. He pulled Clawface's legs hard, and Clawface fell on his nose in a patch of damp grass.

"SSSSS!" he said, "SSSSSSS!"

Ned left Clawface where he was, and went on his way to look for his dinner. He had not gone far when he heard a rustling noise coming from the wavy corn. Before he knew where he was, there stood a brown hare. The hare had long ears, long back legs, and little short front legs. His name was Mauleverer Hopquick. He was the fastest hare in all the neighbourhood.

"Hallo little kitten," said Mauleverer Hopquick. "Would you like a race round the field?"

"If you like," said Ned.

"I bet you can't run as fast as I can," said Mauleverer Hopquick. So, I will give you a start."

But before he had time to say any more, Ned was off. He ran round the field so fast you couldn't see his legs at all, and although Mauleverer Hopquick ran as fast as he could, he could not catch up with him.

"That wasn't fair, little kitten," said Mauleverer. "You didn't wait for me to start. This time I will count."

So Mauleverer Hopquick counted. ONE, TWO, THREE! Just like that. Yet, although he ran faster than he had ever run before, he could not catch up with furry Ned. Round and round the field they went, and I'm afraid they knocked over a great many ears of corn,

until poor Mauleverer sat down under a shady tree.

"Phew!" he cried. "I didn't know kittens could run as fast as that."

"Some of them can," said Ned. He began to wash his whiskers, for all the world as if he had just been out for a walk in the dappled sunshine.

They had not been sitting there long when they heard a strange noise. H.H.H.H.H.H.H.H! Just like that. As soon as they heard it, they knew there was a dog coming. H.H.H.H.H! The noise came nearer and nearer until it was just behind the shady tree.

"Goodbye, little kitten," said Mauleverer Hopquick. "I must be off." He ran across the field like greased lightning, which as you know is very fast indeed.

H.H.H.H! The noise came right round the tree, and there stood an enormous dog. He had sharp teeth, sharp ears, a sharp nose and sharp claws. His name was Woofus Woofusson. He was the fiercest dog for miles.

"RRRRR," he said. "Little kitten I'm going to bite your tail off."

"Oh, no, you're not," said Ned.

Quick as a flash, he jumped onto Woofus Woofusson's back. There he sat, and although Woofus Woofusson danced about, and did everything he could think of to get him down, he simply stayed there, for all the world as if he were stuck on with glue.

"Come off my back, little kitten," cried Woofus Woofusson, "and I'll let you go home to your mother."

Now, furry Ned knew he wouldn't do anything of the sort, but he jumped nimbly down, and started to walk away. Woofus Woofusson came after him immediately to try to bite him, but Ned caught hold of his collar with his twitchy tail and threw him high into the branches of a shady tree. His leather collar caught on a twig, and he hung there, gently swaying to and fro in the breeze.

"Rrrr," he said, feeling very sorry for himself. Just then Woofus's master came by on his way to the old stone farmhouse.

"You're in a fine state, aren't you my lad?" he said.

Woofus's master reached up to the tree to get Woofus down. As he put his arms up, something fell out of his pocket. It was a packet of CHEESE SANDWICHES.

As soon as Woofus and his master had gone on their way to the farmhouse Ned ran up to the sandwiches. He undid the packet with his twitchy tail and ate them up for his dinner. MUNCH. MUNCH. MUNCH. Just like that.

"I do like cheese sandwiches," said Ned.

Then, because he had eaten his dinner, he lay down in a patch of warm sunshine and fell fast asleep, for all the world like an ordinary little kitten who had never even heard of cheese.

"PRRRRR," he said. "PRRRRR."

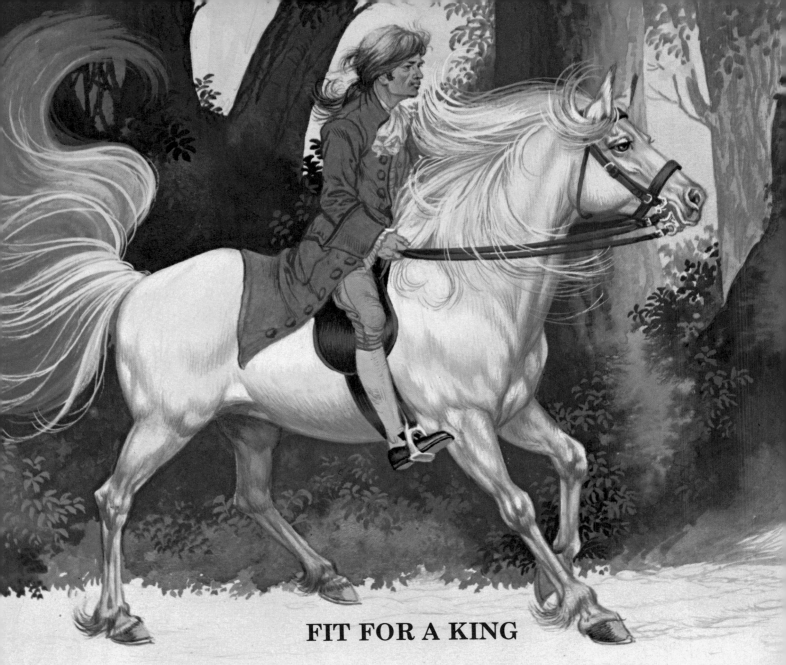

FIT FOR A KING

"Wife. . ." said Samuel Duggett one fine Spring morning. "I'm going to the market today to sell the white mare."

"Then be sure to get a good price for her," said his wife. "She's a beautiful horse, fit for a king to ride upon."

The way to the market led through the wood. Sam Duggett sat high on the mare's back and felt like a king himself as he jogged along through the dappled sunlight. Deep in the wood, where the brambles were most tangled and the shadows the deepest, he was hailed by an old man with a long white beard.

"Will you stop a moment? I have something to ask you."

"Whoa there, my beauty!" called Sam to the white mare. She stopped, with a soft whinny, before he even had time to tighten his grip on the bridle.

"Hallo old man. Is there something I can do for you?" asked Sam, his cheerful voice echoing through the wood like a rumble of muffled thunder.

The old man's voice was quiet. but surprisingly strong in one who looked so frail and old.

"You have a beautiful mare," he said, fondling the mare's muzzle. "If she is for sale, I will buy her."

Sam took one look at the old man's homespun robe with the worn elbows and another at his dusty feet, and laughed long and heartily.

"She is for sale, but not to the likes of you, I'm afraid. I'm taking her to market for some fine gentleman to buy. She will fetch me a very good price, of that I am sure."

And with that, he doffed his cap, bid the old man a courteous goodbye, and galloped off.

The old man watched the dust flying from the horse's hoofs and said no more, but he smiled quietly as though there was a secret which only he knew.

The market was crowded and business was good that fresh Spring morning. There were many fine gentlemen about in their tailored coats and silk cravats. Several indeed, were looking for a fine horse to buy.

Everyone, even those who wanted to buy pigs, and cows, and sacks of grain, admired Sam Duggett's fine white mare.

"She really is a beauty, Sam."

"She's magnificent. Haven't seen a mare like her for years."

Sam rubbed his hands and thought of the gold he would be taking home to his wife.

"Who is going to have the privilege of buying my lovely mare?" he asked.

But the day came, and the day went. The market filled and the market emptied.

"What . . . not sold that mare yet?" asked a man who had sold every one of his pigs.

"I don't understand it," said Sam. "You can see for yourself what a beauty she is. I've nearly sold her a dozen times . . . but nearly isn't good enough . . ."

"She's too beautiful . . . that's her trouble," said the man who had sold every pig. "I should take her home again if I were you."

That was all Sam could do. The market place was empty, there was no point in staying any longer.

He took the mare's bridle in his hand and began the slow walk home. He wanted to delay the moment when he would meet his wife for as long as possible. He knew she would scold him and say it was his fault the mare wasn't sold. To his surprise, as he was passing through the wood he met the old man again.

"I see you still have your white mare," said the old man. "Come with me, if you please."

Sam was so miserable and so anxious not to get home too soon, that he followed the old man with no argument at all. He didn't even bother to ask where they were going, or why.

After a few minutes they came to a sandstone cliff. As far as Sam could see there was no path up it, over it, or round it. Before he had time to ask any of the many questions which suddenly popped into his head, the old man struck the cliff with his fist.

Before Sam could laugh, and say, as was in his mind, "You'll never move a cliff that way, old man," two enormous gates appeared and flew open with a thunderous noise that sent the birds screeching into the sky, and the rabbits hopping to their burrows.

The old man beckoned Sam forward. Now, feeling very frightened indeed, so frightened that he was afraid not to do as the old man asked, Sam followed him into the cave which lay behind the gates.

An unbelievable sight met his eyes. King Arthur of the Round Table, and his Knights, lay sleeping in the darkness.

"King Arthur and his Knights will sleep for a long time yet," said the old man, who, it seemed to Sam, had suddenly grown very tall and straight, "but the day will come when England has need of her Ancient Kings, and then King Arthur and his Knights will wake and ride forth to battle on white horses. They need one more

white horse . . . a horse fit for a king to ride upon . . . now . . . will you sell me your white mare?"

Sam Duggett didn't say a word. He handed the mare's bridle to Merlin, for the old man was indeed, Merlin, the Wizard who had lived at the Court of King Arthur and who now kept watch over him as he slept. He took the purse of gold which Merlin gave him . . .
. . . and ran.

At the entrance to
the cave, he turned
for a moment. He saw
Merlin leading the white
mare into the darkness,
and then he found he had
his nose pressed against
the golden coloured stone
of the sandstone cliff.
No one believed his story,
of course.
The sandstone cliff
still stood in the wood
but no amount of banging
and thumping ever made
the gates reappear.
In time Sam himself found
it hard to believe what
had happened. But, there
was one thing of which
everyone was certain;
the white mare had
vanished, without trace.

NONSENSE

Jane's umbrella blew inside out
And lifted her up from the ground.
"I'll send you a postcard,"
She said with a shout.
"When I know where I am, when I'm found."

A BUSY BUZZING BUMBLE BEE

A busy, buzzing, bumble bee,
Came buzzing very close to me.
I stood quite still so he could see
I would not hurt him. No Siree!
I looked at him. He looked at me.
I wasn't afraid. And neither was he.
He flew around and looked me over.
It was easy to see I wasn't clover.
He buzzed around then flew away.
Perhaps we'll meet another day.

SPROGGET AND I GO TO SCHOOL

I'm growing up; I go to school – Sprogget, he comes too;
Only I can see him and the magic he can do;
Because, of course, he's special and I am very glad
To have a friend so useful in case things turn out bad.

Glad to have him with me – he remembers what to do;
He knows exactly where things are – he finds my other shoe;
For shoes, you see, have got a trick of disappearing fast;
It makes me feel so silly, if I'm slow and finish last.

In class he guides my wobbly hand – I try to write my name;
He gets me out of trouble in a rough and tumble game;
He makes me get a move on when it's time to wash for lunch;
Then helps the timid children – they stand huddled in a bunch.

For some of them seem very lost when first they go to school;
They must be brave – not scared of things – a most important rule.
The constant changing worries them – it gets me down a bit;
Take off; put on; wear this, now that – sometimes my own won't fit.

I've made a friend of Susie, she sits right next to me;
When something's wrong we work it out – much easier you see.
My Sprogget, he is still quite close – he doesn't mind at all;
He too, is fond of Susie and he's always there 'on call'.

On music days we form a band and I beat on a drum;
My Sprogget, he just loves it – he never fails to come.
He dances there – a fine routine; he even flings his cap;
I time my 'Bongs!' to come between his 'tippy-tippy-tap'.

He's not so good at reading – that's one of the 'Three Rs';
He'd really rather be outside – on climbing frames or cars;
He fidgets and he tickles – that feather comes in handy;
I tell him off – then promise him a bigger piece of candy.

It's waiting there at home for us; who needs it most? . . . we'll see;
With lessons done; we up and run; Sprogget and his friend, me.
Don't get it wrong – my school is great; Sprogget likes it too:
If only schooldays wouldn't come when I've better things to do!

THE BELLS

It was a warm night. The stars were twinkling and the moon kept popping in and out of the clouds.

"Ho de hi o hum hum hum!" sang Bartholomew Green at the very top of his voice as he ambled along the lane past the churchyard.

"Hoohoo!" hooted an owl from within a hollow tree.

"Hoo hoo to yooo tooo!" sang out Bartholomew Green. He had been to a party which he had enjoyed very much and now he was on his way home. He didn't care that everyone else was in bed and asleep. He wanted everyone to be as happy as he was.

"Hi de ho hum hum hum!" he sang as he stumbled along the dark path by the vicarage gate.

Inside the vicarage, the vicar put his head under the bedclothes and pretended he couldn't hear the noise going on beneath his bedroom window. He knew who the reveller was . . . it was Bartholomew Green. He would have recognized that voice anywhere. He wished Bartholomew Green would go to bed at the same time as everyone else.

But the vicar couldn't possibly pretend the
noise wasn't there. There was a rattle at the window.

Bartholomew Green was throwing gravel.

There was a much heavier rattle against the window.
Bartholomew Green was throwing tiny stones. If he
wasn't careful he would break the glass.

The vicar opened the window wearily, and leant out.

"Go away . . ." he said. "Please . . . go away."

"Ring the bells," called Bartholomew Green. "Ring
the bells . . . I want to hear the bells . . ."

"No," said the vicar. "I will not ring the bells."
And he closed his bedroom window with such a bang that
Bartholomew Green knew he meant what he said.

Now, it so happened that
Bartholomew wasn't the only
person out that night. There
was a wizard slinking around
dark, night-time corners and
dipping into dark, night-time
pools, looking for spell-making
ingredients. He came upon
Bartholomew Green sitting on a
tombstone, crying slow silent
tears that rolled like raindrops
down the side of his nose.

"What's wrong?" asked
the wizard, who had found all
that he had wanted to find and
was in a good mood.

"He won't ring the bells!"
said Bartholomew Green. "I
asked, but Vicar won't ring
the bells . . ."

"Then I will ring them for you," said the wizard, who felt like playing a joke on someone. He fumbled in his pocket and took out some red powder mixed with pocket fluff, and flicked it towards the vicar's bedroom window.

"There." he said. "That should do it."

"I can't hear anything," said Bartholomew Green. He could see something though. The light had gone on in the vicar's bedroom and the vicar was dancing about with his hands over his ears.

The wizard laughed. "He should have done as you asked," he said.

The next day there were rumours all over the village.

"Have you heard? The vicarage is haunted. Bells have been ringing."

"I haven't heard anything," said Bartholomew Green.

"You wouldn't . . . they're only heard in the bedroom. Maisie told us about it . . . she dusts and cleans for the vicar you know. The vicar didn't have a wink of sleep last night."

Bartholomew had some hazy memory of asking the vicar to ring the bells the night before, and he also had a hazy memory of meeting a friendly person in a long robe in the churchyard . . . but he couldn't remember anything else. So he went to the vicarage to hear for himself.

The rumours were perfectly true. Outside the vicarage it was so quiet he could hear the grasshoppers chirping. Inside the house it was so quiet he could hear the bread singing in the oven. But in the vicar's bedroom, which by then was crowded with people who had come to hear for themselves, there was a merry jangle of noise.

Clang! Clang! Clang! Clang! Clang!

Bartholomew couldn't help feeling that somehow it was his fault, though he couldn't for the life of him think why.

The bells continued to ring in the vicar's bedroom for years and years. He got quite used to them in the end and could sleep in spite of the noise. Then one night, on the same night that the wizard died, as it happened, though nobody noticed the coincidence, they stopped ringing as mysteriously as they had begun. The vicar almost missed their cheerful company. As for Bartholomew, he never quite lost that strange guilty feeling he had. It was something he often found himself wondering about, even when he was an old, old man.

THE MIRROR
AND THE MOON

Long ago a lady fair
Combed her wavy golden hair;
She sat upon the silver sand,
A silver mirror in her hand.
Then up came the wind
With a whoosh and a whoo;
He laughed and grinned
With a 'How d'you do?'
And a wheel and a whoop
And a loop of the loop.

With a mighty puff and roar
He raced along the shore;
He pulled the golden hair;
The mirror flew in the air.
The wind laughed "Ho ho ho.
You'll see your mirror soon
In the sky with a silver glow
As a shining silver moon."
"What is a moon?" she cried.
"A bit of glass," he replied.

THE GREEDY KING

One day, in the land of Jingle Jangle, the King stood before his people and told them that he had no money left to build schools and hospitals, and that made them very, very angry. They were not sorry for him, for they called him King Need-a-lot because he was always spending, spending, spending money.

The King went back to his palace and every day the postman brought bills and more bills to be paid, and every night, the King could not sleep, for thinking how he was going to pay them. He even tried to hide himself away in the palace, but the postman always found him and gave him more and more bills.

"I'm getting tired of all these bills," said the King to his old servant. "I think I will run away." And one day he did, and his old servant followed him. As they ran through the town, they passed the Butcher's shop and the Butcher saw them.

"The King is running away and he hasn't paid my bills," he cried. "He must not get away, I'll follow him." So he began to run behind the old servant.

Then they passed the Baker's shop and the Baker saw them.

"The King is running away and he hasn't paid my bills," he cried. "He must not get away, I'll follow him." So he began to run behind the Butcher.

Then they passed the Shoe-maker's shop and the Shoe-maker saw them.

"The King is running away and he hasn't paid my bills," he cried. "He must not get away, I'll follow him." So he began to run behind the Baker.

King Need-a-lot ran on and on
and on and on. He ran over the fields
and through the woods until he
reached the seashore. He was
puffing and blowing and he could
not run quickly now. He glanced
over his shoulder and saw his old
servant, the Butcher, the Baker and
the Shoe-maker following him, but
as he looked back, he stumbled over
a sack on the beach and was just
too tired to get up again. When
the old servant reached him, he
thought the King had hurt himself.
He looked round and found a little
boat nearby, so he put the King in
the boat and ran back to get help.

On the way he met the Butcher,
the Baker and the Shoe-maker.

"Stop!" he cried, "The King
has hurt himself, we must help him."

He turned round again and ran back to the beach followed by the
Butcher, the Baker and the Shoe-maker, but when they reached the
seashore, all they could see was the little boat sailing away from the
shore and in it was King Need-a-lot fast asleep.

The four of them waited for many, many hours until the tide came in again bringing with it the little boat, and the King was still fast asleep. The Butcher helped the old servant to carry the King back to the woods, while the Baker and the Shoe-maker lifted the sack from the boat and from a hole in one corner dropped a piece of gold and then . . . another and another.

"Why, it's a sack of gold," cried the Baker. "We must carry it carefully and not lose any more."

Away they went to join the others in the woods and there they rested until the King awakened. When he did wake up and saw the Butcher, the Baker and the Shoe-maker sitting beside him, he cried, "I cannot pay you. I've spent all the money and have no more left."

"Oh, yes you have!" they said, and they showed him the sack of gold. "It's yours, you found it."

The King looked puzzled, so his old servant told him all that had happened. He thanked them for taking care of him, then he paid the Butcher's bills, the Baker's bills and the Shoe-maker's bills and they all marched back to town.

The King then paid ALL his bills, gave a big party for everybody who lived in his kingdom and still had enough left to build hospitals and schools for his people.

He never spent all his money ever again and now his people call him King Save-a-lot, because he does.

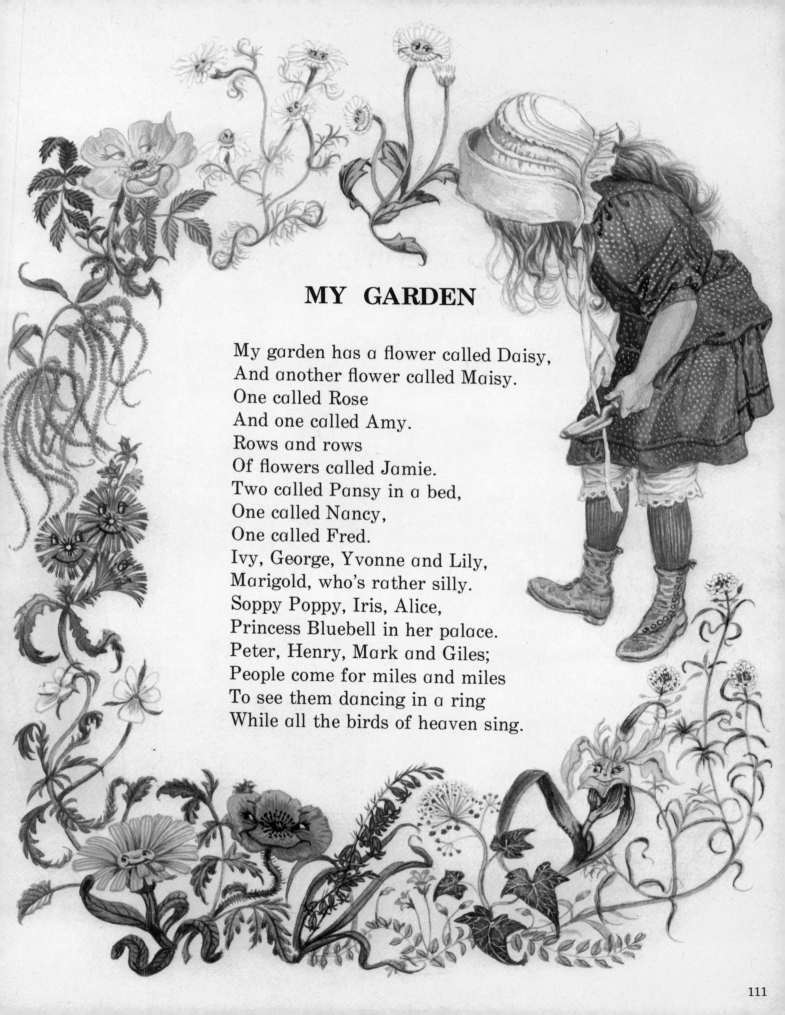

MY GARDEN

My garden has a flower called Daisy,
And another flower called Maisy.
One called Rose
And one called Amy.
Rows and rows
Of flowers called Jamie.
Two called Pansy in a bed,
One called Nancy,
One called Fred.
Ivy, George, Yvonne and Lily,
Marigold, who's rather silly.
Soppy Poppy, Iris, Alice,
Princess Bluebell in her palace.
Peter, Henry, Mark and Giles;
People come for miles and miles
To see them dancing in a ring
While all the birds of heaven sing.

THE BRAVE LITTLE ENGINE

"For goodness' sake, keep still and go to sleep, Bonny!" said the big locomotive.

"I won't get a wink of sleep again tonight if you go on with that fidgeting and shuffling," grumbled a green tanker.

Bonny sighed. He didn't want to keep the other engines in the shed awake. During the day, all he did was to pull a branch line train between a few stations, and he had so much energy left at the end of the day that he simply couldn't go to sleep.

"Bonny's just the engine for the job," said the voice of his driver. The great door of the engine-shed slid open and Joe and the depot manager hurried in.

"It's an emergency," Joe told Bonny. "Two trucks of coal have got to be taken to the power-station tonight. The bridge over the river has been damaged and we daren't risk taking the big goods-engine over it. You are light enough to do it."

Soon Bonny was out of the engine-shed and coupled up to two huge coal-trucks. Never had he had such a load behind him. He puffed and groaned as he felt the weight of the coal-trucks, but he kept pulling, and as he moved forward, the strain eased and he then increased speed. Soon he was rolling along at a smart pace.

"Well done!" said Joe, "I knew you'd do it!"

Bonny had never been out at night before. The moon came out and flooded the track with yellow light. The stars winked down at him and the trees rose like ghosts through the gloom, nodding their branches at him as he rumbled by. Suddenly a great black mouth loomed up in front of him. He let out a screech of fear. He thought he was going to be swallowed up!

"Take it easy!" said Joe. "It's a tunnel, the Cosset Tunnel, half a mile of it."

Bonny had never gone through a tunnel before and the utter darkness of it inside almost sent him into a panic. But he was a plucky little engine, and he gave a blast on his siren, as much as to say, "I'm not afraid of the dark, so here I come!"

Only tiny gleams of light from lamps fixed at long intervals in the sides of the tunnel broke the deep darkness, and presently Bonny became so hot that he thought he would burst his boiler. Then at last he felt a breath of fresh air, and suddenly he came out at the other end of the tunnel.

"Now for the bridge," said Joe. "Be very, very careful.
We don't want to end up in the river!"

Bonny saw two red discs ahead. He knew they were danger
signals. The unsafe bridge stretched right across a wide river.
Joe slowed him down to a crawl, and then Bonny began to roll
across the river. He could see the moonlit water below him on
either side, and he felt the bridge move under the weight of the
trucks behind him.

"Keep going!" muttered Joe, who was very anxious and tense. Very, very slowly, Bonny moved across the bridge, the trucks rumbling behind him. The parapet of the bridge had broken away, but Bonny kept going forward and presently, he heard Joe say, "We're over! Well done, Bonny!"

Bonny let out a whistle of relief, but there was another shock in store for him. Just as if it was attracted by the whistle, a white bird flew suddenly out of a tree beside the track almost right into his funnel! Bonny nearly jumped off the rails!

Joe laughed. "Well, I'm blessed! A snowy owl! It must have thought you were something to eat, Bonny!"

Soon after, they reached the power-station, where the coal-trucks were uncoupled in a siding.

"You've saved all the nearby towns from being blacked out tomorrow," said the power-station manager to Joe. "This coal will keep us going until another load gets here from the north. Thanks for coming!"

Joe patted Bonny. "I've got a first-class engine here," he said. "Now we'd better get back home, Bonny."

Bonny had never been on the main line before. Joe let him have his head – Bonny fairly raced through the night. When he saw the tunnel ahead, he gave a loud shriek and tore into it; he didn't give a hoot for tunnels. He didn't give a hoot for owls, either, even if THEY hooted! But no owls flew his way now. Any birds that were about, took care to keep out of his way as he roared along the line. A herd of cows in a field looked up and called out 'Moo!' to him as he raced past.

"I should think you've broken the speed record tonight, Bonny," said Joe, as he drove him into the engine-shed at the end of his journey. "I shall ask the depot manager if we can have a change from our branch line and pull a train or two on the main line – at least until the bridge is repaired."

In the engine-shed all the engines started to talk at once.
"What happened, Bonny?"
"Where have you been?"
"What was the emergency?"

Bonny gave a great big yawn. "I'll tell you tomorrow," he mumbled. "I'm – too – tired – to – talk – tonight. So – sorry!"

And he fell fast asleep.

THE DRAGON OF WANTLEY

The Dragon of Wantley lay sleeping in his rocky den. From time to time, a puff of smoke came floating from his bright green nostrils, but apart from that, he was completely still. The only noise came from the dragon's pet white mouse, Wilfred, who was putting coal on the fire to make a hot breakfast for the dragon. The entrance to the dragon's coal-mine stood nearby.

As soon as the fire was glowing hot, Wilfred seized a grey goose's feather and began to tickle the dragon's nose. "Time to wake up, master," he called.

With a great fiery sneeze the Dragon of Wantley woke up. He yawned a little, stretched his legs and flapped his great wings.

"Is it breakfast time, Wilfred?" he asked, sniffing the smoke from the fire. "Yes, master. Eat up while the coal is still hot."

The dragon began to tuck into the glowing coals with a hearty appetite. He liked hot coals for breakfast – dark smouldering red. When he had finished, he went down to the stream for a long drink of water so that he would be able to make plenty of steam during the day. Finally, he reached for the morning paper, which Wilfred had laid out carefully for him on a rock. "Same old news, I suppose," he said with another yawn.

The newspaper contained many reports of battles between various kings who lived in the land. The dragon glanced at the reports without paying much attention to them.

"I see the King of Noke has beaten the King of Bagby," he said. Wilfred did not answer because he was busy with a nice piece of cheese. Then, the dragon's eye was caught by a small paragraph which told how a terrible deed had been done by the wicked Black Knight. Not content with stealing all the King's gold, the Black Knight had carried off the Princess of Stoke Poges to his castle in the forest.

At once the dragon began to read more carefully, because he was a kindly dragon, who was always rescuing princesses and restoring gold to kings who had lost it.

'The princess,' said the newspaper, 'was on her way to be married to the Prince of Nether Stowey when the Black Knight rushed out of his castle and carried her off. The King of Stoke Poges has offered a reward of half his kingdom to anyone who rescues the princess.'

'Half a kingdom,' said the dragon to himself. 'That is not much of a reward for rescuing a princess. But as I never ask for a reward, I suppose it doesn't matter.'

As soon as Wilfred had finished with his cheese, the dragon called out to him. "Wilfred," he said, "we are going to Stoke Poges to rescue another princess. You had better climb on my back."

"I hope she is beautiful," said Wilfred.

"Of course she is," replied the dragon. "All princesses are beautiful."

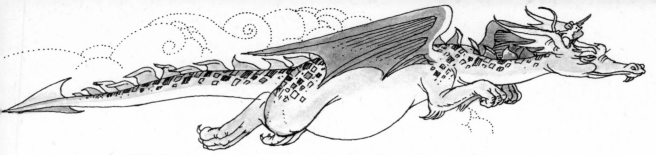

Wilfred ran along the dragon's scaly tail until he came to his favourite perch, just between the dragon's pointed ears. With a great swish of his wings, the dragon rose into the air and set his course by the sun for Stoke Poges.

Below them as they flew through the air they could see the many towns and villages of England, all with their kings and castles. Some of the castles were being besieged, and in other places, the kings were fighting each other with great armies. But the Dragon of Wantley flew steadily on his course through the sky. A great many people who were not fighting came out to see him go by, but as they had been taught that dragons did not exist, they refused to believe what they saw.

At last, just after one o'clock, the dragon arrived at Stoke Poges. They went straight to the castle to see the king, who was having his lunch. The dragon and Wilfred bowed before the royal throne.

"I have come to rescue the princess and restore your gold, sire," said the dragon. The king looked extremely pleased.

"Thank you, my boy," he said. "I hope you will have some lunch first."

"Certainly, sire," replied the dragon. "I will have a little fresh coal if I may. My mouse would like some cheese if you have any."

The king clapped his hands. Immediately the royal servants brought in a hundred sacks of coal and a huge block of cheese for the guests. While they ate, the king explained the way to the Black Knight's castle.

"If you take the road into the forest," said the king, "you will see the Black Knight's castle on the left as you go past the thousandth oak tree. Knock on the gate and state your business. He will then come out to fight with you, and may the best man win."

"Thank you, sire," said the dragon. "I will be on my way now, if I may."

"By all means, my boy," said the king. "I will see you to the door."

Wilfred climbed back between the dragon's ears and they left the castle, taking the forest road as instructed.

"Let us both count the oak trees," said the dragon, "to make sure we do not miss the castle."

They set off through the forest. At the thousandth oak tree, the dragon stopped.

"How many oak trees have you counted?" he asked.

"Eight hundred and sixty four," replied Wilfred.

"I see," said the dragon. "We had better begin again."

They went back to the edge of the forest and began to count again. For the second time they counted differently, and once more they went back to the beginning. The third time they managed to agree on the thousandth oak tree, and there, sure enough, was the castle on the left. The dragon marched up to it boldly and knocked at the gate.

"Who goes there?" cried a gruff voice.

"The Dragon of Wantley. I have come to rescue the Princess of Stoke Poges and return the gold you have stolen from her father."

"Wait there a moment while I fetch my armour," answered the gruff voice.

After a delay of about ten minutes, the Black Knight charged over the drawbridge of his castle on a magnificent black horse. He lowered his lance and began to gallop towards the dragon, who knew exactly how to deal with a situation like this.

When the knight was almost close enough to touch, the dragon let out a small flame with a big puff of smoke. At once the knight pulled up in amazement.

"Where is your lance?" he shouted. "I cannot fight you unless you have a lance, or at least a sword."

For reply, the Dragon of Wantley simply let out a long stream of flame.

"This is disgraceful," shouted the knight. "Fight properly or not at all!"

Once again the dragon let out a flame. Then he made a terrible roar which frightened the knight's horse. The horse ran away, taking the knight with him.

"Well done, master," said Wilfred. "He will not return yet."

"I don't understand why he was so frightened of me," said the dragon. "I would never hurt him, no matter how many princesses he had captured."

They went into the castle and found the dungeon where the princess was kept. The dragon burnt down the door with a long flame, and out stepped the princess. To their amazement, she was not beautiful at all. In fact, she was fat and rather ugly with ordinary brown hair. However, the dragon bowed low just the same.

"I have come to save you from the Black Knight," he said.

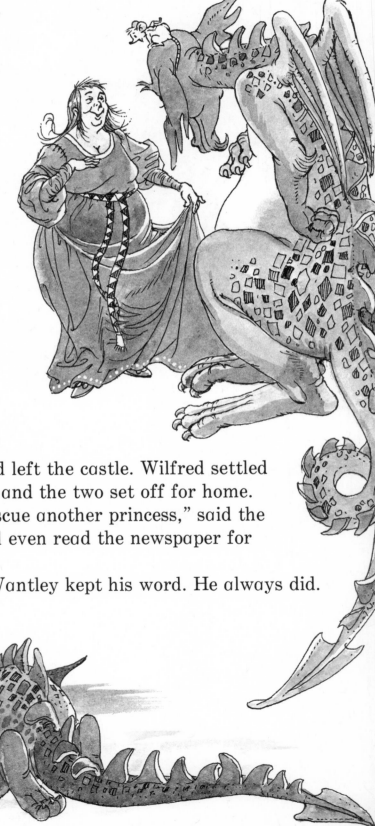

"There was no need to bother," replied the princess. "I do not want to be rescued at all. If I am rescued, I shall have to marry the horrid Prince of Nether Stowey. Please let me stay here."

The dragon could see that the fat princess would cry if he carried her back to the king, so he decided to leave her with the Black Knight after all.

"Would you like me to rescue your father's gold?" he asked.

"No, thank you," she replied. "It is not real gold. It is only painted wood. My father would never let anyone steal his real gold."

The dragon gave a low bow and left the castle. Wilfred settled down comfortably between his ears, and the two set off for home.

"I shall think twice before I rescue another princess," said the dragon. "In fact, I don't think I shall even read the newspaper for weeks and weeks."

What is more, the Dragon of Wantley kept his word. He always did.

THE STRAW HAT

Once upon a time, there was a hat. An ordinary, plain little hat made from yellow straw. She lay in a dusty hat box at the back of a cupboard and her only friends were the spiders who had crawled through a hole in the box and woven their webs around her. The spiders were kind, and she liked watching their babies play, but it seemed such a long time since she had seen the sunshine, and she always felt sad.

Then one day, when even the spiders had deserted her, she was taken from the box.

"Oh dear . . . oh dear . . ." she trembled as she felt the sharp bristles of a brush scratching at her straw. "I don't like this at all. This is awful . . . oh dear . . . oh dear . . ."

"Hmmmmmm" said a voice. "I think it will do."

The hat found herself plonked, without ceremony, onto a head; she knew from long ago what it felt like to be on a head, and then she found herself looking into a mirror. It had been so long since she had looked into a mirror, she had almost forgotten what she looked like. She didn't like what she saw. She remembered enough to know she had once been as fresh and as neat as a daisy. Now she was shabby and there was a hole in her brim where a mouse had once had a nibble. Fortunately the mouse hadn't liked the taste of her yellow straw very much or she might have had no brim left at all.

The face looking back at her, from under her own brim, was young and had sparkling blue eyes.

"It will need brightening up," said another girl who was looking over her shoulder. "Try this round it." She tied a wide piece of red ribbon round the hat's crown. It really was quite surprising the difference it made. The hat felt brighter and better at once. In fact, she almost felt pretty again.

"Yes, definitely . . . it will do," said the girl, and she took off the hat and laid it on the dressing table.

'Do for what?' thought the hat. Oh, she did hope it was for something important. A special outing. Or a wedding perhaps. She pulled in all her ragged ends, and did some exercises to stiffen her brim.

Later that day, the girl returned and before long, the hat found herself balancing on springy curls and taken along a sunny street with the breeze fluttering her new ribbon. It was like being on holiday.

"Like your hat Sally!" someone called. The hat glowed with pride and began to feel beautiful.

That afternoon was the most wonderful of her life. The sun warmed her, the breeze freshened her, and the scent of the girl's hair nestled into her straw so that she smelt of summer herbs too. They walked by the river, and they were smiled upon, often.

"I do hope we come here every day," thought the happy hat.

And then . . . it happened. They met a group of Sally's friends.

"You did it then!" they whooped, running towards her and laughing. "We didn't think you would dare!"

"I told you I would!" shouted Sally, and pulling the hat from her curls, she threw it into the air and caught it by its ribbon. "I always take a dare . . . I told you I'd wear the oldest hat I could find. I found this one in an old hat box at the bottom of a cupboard. It belonged to my great-aunt Lucy. Isn't it awful?"

The poor little hat wanted to die. She felt so old and so ragged and so shabby. If a hat could cry, she would have cried, sad, sad tears.

When they got home she was flung onto a chair and sat on. And there she was left, crumpled and flattened and very unhappy.

But that is not the end of the story, because Sally's little sister happened to find the hat and she straightened her out. Jane was five and didn't mind a bit about ragged ends and mouse nibbles.

"I do like this hat," she said. "Do you think I could have it?"

The hat trembled and waited for something else awful to happen, but this time was quite different. Jane had a teddy bear she loved very much and she wanted the hat for him. It didn't fit very well it was true, but the red ribbon tied under his chin kept it from falling off.

The hat liked being Teddy's hat. He was NEVER unkind. Sometimes Jane took Teddy, and the hat, out into the garden to enjoy the sun, and in the summer she took them both on holiday.

Jane kept her teddy always, even when she was grown up, and Teddy always wore his hat. He didn't mind ragged ends and mouse nibbles either.

And so the little hat made from yellow straw never went back into the dusty cupboard and I am glad to say the rest of her days were happy days.

SPROGGET AND HIS PETS

I didn't understand it – couldn't make it out at all;
My magic friend, my Sprogget, gave no answer to my call.
I wouldn't ask about him, for grown-ups only say:
"You talk a lot of rubbish – there's no Sprogget anyway!"

I searched the house from roof to floor; no Sprogget to be seen;
Then out of doors to search some more, for clues where he had been.
His special tree was empty – the one we climb together;
Then, right up on the sloping bank I found his orange feather.

He'd planted it to point the way; I followed up the trail;
And there among the rabbits sat Sprogget looking pale.
He'd been there several days and nights without a wink of sleep;
He'd minded baby rabbits and he wanted them to keep.

Mother doe, her leg was hurt, Sprog helped then took her place;
He cuddled all her children and taught them how to race
Back down their hole if danger came, to wait – then re-appear;
They've enemies like cat and owl and slinky fox to fear.

I know just how my Sprogget feels – he loves each furry one;
He watches them and guards them – he laughs when they have fun.
He likes to see them washing – so busy with their paws;
Then off they hop to feed again before they run indoors.

So, Sprogget has a family – eight of them all told;
He spends his time out there with them – even when it's cold.
He's named each one and calls to them; Peter, Ben and Fluff;
There's Tommy, Titch and Traddles; Slow-down and That's Enough.

Slow-down runs round at such a speed – trips and turns right over;
And That's Enough just eats and eats – sneaking all the clover.
Titch is small and likes to snooze – there on Sprogget's lap;
All the others gather round when called to take their nap.

Sprogget lets me help him; we have to train each rabbit
To grow up strong and perfect – correct in every habit.
But Sprogget he has promised to come back when they are grown;
To leave his pets – for they are wild and happy on their own.

JUMPING FROGS

Once there was a young frog who would not jump. His mother tried to make him jump. His father tried to make him jump. His brothers tried. His sisters tried. But whenever they jumped, or hopped, he walked. And of course, that meant everyone was always having to stop and wait for him, because, as everyone knows, to walk somewhere takes longer than to jump there. His mother was always begging him to hurry. So were his brothers and sisters.

"Jump . . . Francis . . . JUMP!" they would call impatiently, every time they had to stop and wait for him.

"I don't want to jump," Francis would reply.

"Why don't you want to jump?" asked Father Frog one day. He couldn't bear to walk himself, and never did unless it was absolutely necessary.

"Because it's undignified," said Francis.

"Undignified," giggled his brothers and sisters. "You should just see yourself trying to walk."

"Frogs are supposed to jump," said Father Frog. "It's undignified for a frog NOT to jump."

"Perhaps he can't jump," said Mother Frog. She took him along to see the frog doctor. He made Francis lie on the couch and examined his legs carefully.

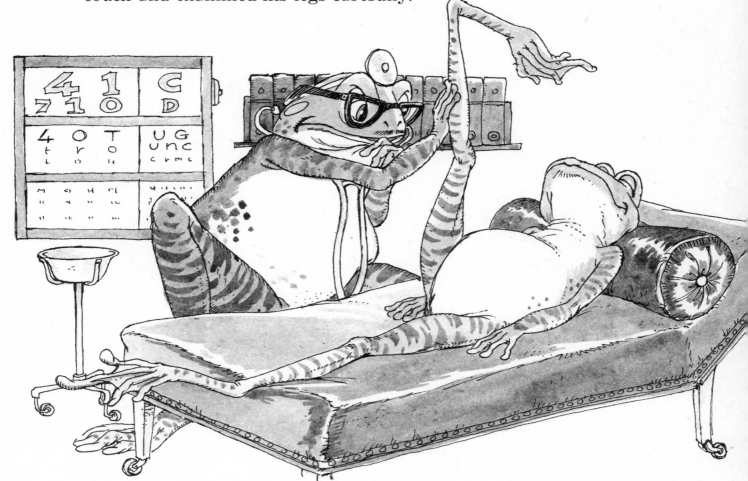

"Stretch . . . bend . . . stretch . . . bend . . ." he said.

Francis did it perfectly. Or rather his legs did. Then the doctor tapped his knees with a rubber hammer to make sure his legs jerked properly. They did. They jerked perfectly.

"Nothing wrong with him at all," said the doctor.

"I knew there wasn't," said Francis.

"Then WHY won't you JUMP?" asked his mother tearfully.

"Because I don't want to," said Francis.

"Because he doesn't want to," said the frog doctor and shook his head wisely. "I'm afraid there's no medicine to cure 'Don't want to's'."

That evening the frog family sent Francis out on an errand and had a family conference.

"This state of affairs cannot go on," said Father Frog. "A frog who CANNOT jump deserves our sympathy . . . but a frog who WILL NOT jump is just being stubborn." Father Frog was getting himself quite worked up. His chins, of which he had several, were beginning to wobble dangerously.

Mother Frog tried to calm him. "Now, now, dear," she said.

"Don't now, now me," grumbled Father Frog. "Just you make that boy jump or I'll never jump again myself . . . and you wouldn't like that would you?"

"Oh no, dear, I wouldn't," said Mother Frog, and then she added thoughtfully, "But I wonder . . ."

"Wonder what?" interrupted Father Frog crossly.

"I wonder what would happen if we ALL walked everywhere . . ." said Mother Frog quickly because Father Frog's fourth chin was beginning to wobble now.

"We would look silly – everyone would laugh at us," said Father Frog. "And I would lose my temper . . . in fact, I think I'm going to lose it anyway . . ."

"Now, now, dear," said Mother Frog soothingly. THAT did it, of course. Father Frog jumped up and down, stamping both feet at once, till HE ran out of breath and his legs ran out of spring.

"Feel better dear?" asked Mother Frog when at last he stopped. She had washed the supper dishes and the children had gone to bed.

"Yes . . ." said Father Frog. ". . . and I've been thinking. Make US look ridiculous would he? Well, we'll make HIM look ridiculous then perhaps he'll change his mind about walking everywhere.

"Now, now, dear," said Mother Frog, but that time, fortunately, Father Frog didn't appear to hear, or perhaps, if he did, he was just too tired to lose his temper again.

Father Frog told the family that they too, must walk everywhere. They found it a very difficult thing to do, for it is as natural for a frog to jump as it is for a tree to grow. They had to concentrate really hard and went about with deep frowns on their faces. Francis was quick to notice that no one was smiling, and that worried him, but then he noticed they weren't jumping either, and THAT pleased him.

"You're being sensible at last," he said happily. "Now I have a family I can be proud of."

Father Frog spluttered and got very red.

"It's not going to work . . ." he muttered under his breath. "If it doesn't . . . I'll . . . I'll . . ."

But in spite of Father Frog's doubts, the whole family tried. How hard it was, pretending not to hear the scornful laughter of the other frogs. How tired their legs got. How short their tempers became. Francis was used to walking. HIS legs never got tired, and although it still took him a long time to walk everywhere, he always got there much quicker than the rest of the family. Now it was HIS turn to stand and wait while everyone caught up with HIM.

"Oh do hurry up!" he said one morning, when there had been a shower of rain and everyone was on his way to the puddle patch. "The sun will dry up the puddles before we get there."

Father Frog signalled secretly to the rest of the family to slow down even more.

The sun was warm. Francis could feel it drying his back. He wanted to get into some nice, cool, wet, water.

"We'll all dry up, and frizzle away!" he grumbled. "If you can't walk any faster than that, why don't you jump?"

"What was that you said?" asked Father Frog, pretending he hadn't heard properly.

"Jump . . . JUMP!" shouted Francis, losing HIS temper, because he was dry and hot, and everyone else was being silly. "Look, like this . . . I'll show you . . . jump . . . JUMP . . ."

And there he was, jumping like a proper frog should.

"Thank goodness for that," sighed his mother and father.

"Hurrah!" shouted his brothers and sisters, and raced him to the puddle patch.

From that day onwards Francis jumped everywhere, as a frog should, and to his surprise he found he enjoyed it. He even won prizes for jumping, and THAT, as Father Frog said, is as dignified as a frog can get.

THE MAGIC SPECTACLES

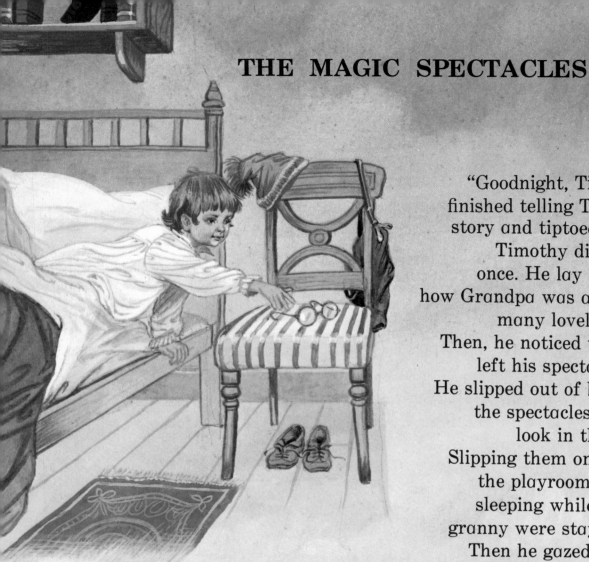

"Goodnight, Timothy!" Grandpa finished telling Timothy a bedtime story and tiptoed out of the room. Timothy didn't go to sleep at once. He lay awake, wondering how Grandpa was able to make up so many lovely bedtime stories. Then, he noticed that Grandpa had left his spectacles on the chair. He slipped out of bed and picked up the spectacles. "I wonder how I look in them," he laughed. Slipping them on, he looked round the playroom, in which he was sleeping while his grandpa and granny were staying in the house. Then he gazed in astonishment.

Through the spectacles he saw an extraordinary sight. In a corner of the playroom was a long table at which half a dozen elves were busy cutting up loaves, making pastry, stirring bowls and filling glasses. They chattered as they worked.

"Princess Primrose's wedding is at twelve, and the feast will begin very soon after," said one elf.

"We shall have to hurry," said another. "I haven't started icing the cakes yet."

Timothy could hear sounds outside, so he opened the playroom door, which led into the garden. Outside he could see people everywhere, little people. None of them was higher than his knee. There were gnomes too, and fairies at gaily decorated stalls full of flags and streamers. Children were dressed in their best clothes; flags and bunting decorated the streets. Above the main street rose a beautiful glass palace, with a red carpet laid along the courtyard in front. Uniformed soldiers paced to and fro before the steps.

Suddenly a great commotion arose. A bell rang out. It belonged to the Town Crier, who called out startling news. The handsome prince bridegroom could not get to the city to marry Princess Primrose at twelve o'clock. He was travelling by train from a far country, and wicked goblins had broken down the bridge between his country and the Land of Makebelieve, so that the train with all his guests could not cross the wide river.

Cries of dismay went up from all the people, and children began to cry.

'In the stories Grandpa tells me,' said Timothy to himself, 'goblins are always getting up to mischief.'

He knew there was a stream at the far end of his daddy's garden. Perhaps to tiny folk and gnomes and fairies, the stream would be a wide river. He would go and see!

He soon reached the stream. Sure enough, there was a train – a toy train to him – standing still on the other side of the stream. It couldn't go any farther. The wooden bridge over the water was wrecked. Stooping, Timothy lifted the little train, with all the people in it, over the stream and set it carefully on the rail on his side. Faces appeared at the windows of the train and arms waved. The train puffed happily away to the cheers of the passengers.

Timothy reached the city again before the train. He heard the Town Crier ring his bell and call out that news had come through that a kind giant had lifted the train over the wide river, and that the bridegroom was on his way to the wedding. The people cheered, the children waved their flags, and the band struck up rousing music.

When the train arrived, the handsome prince stepped out, and a troop of soldiers on horseback rode up to escort him to the church. But first the bride had to walk from the palace to the church. As the church bells rang out, she stepped down the palace stairs on the arm of her father, the King. She was about the step on to the red carpet when a dreadful thing happened. Rain began to fall in torrents. It came out of a clear sky. Princess Primrose shrank back. People ran for shelter. Nobody had an umbrella and it looked as if everybody would be soaked to the skin.

But Timothy saw what was happening. He ran to the far wall of the garden. A dozen goblins, chortling with glee, were holding a water hose which was attached to a tap in the wall. The goblins had climbed on each other's shoulders and turned on the tap. Now they were sending the water up in the air and over all the people.

"Stop it!" cried Timothy.

He grabbed the hose, but he didn't turn the water off. Instead, he turned it on the goblins, who ran away shouting and screaming angrily. They were soon wet through.

"I don't think we shall see them again today!" chuckled Timothy. Turning the tap off, he hurried back. He was just in time to see Princess Primrose walk along the red carpet to the church, with the children waving their flags and cheering.

'Why,' thought Timothy, 'Princess Primrose looks just like my sister's bride-doll!'

He stooped down to try to peer into the church, but the spectacles fell from his nose – and suddenly, the whole scene had gone! He was looking on the garden just as it had always been. Then he heard the voice of Grandpa, who had come in search of his spectacles.

"Ah, there you are, Timothy! Good! You've found my spectacles. Come back to bed now, there's a good boy."

As he tucked Timothy into bed, he said, "I won't tell you another story tonight, as it is getting late."

Timothy nodded and yawned. "I don't want another tonight," he murmured. "I've just been in one."

STAIRS

At night when I go up to bed,
I count the stairs for fun;
And in the morning coming down,
I uncount – down to none.

In any place where there are steps
I play this counting game;
But the escalator staircase
Well, that isn't quite the same.

I'd like to run up to the top
Counting all the way;
But Mummy says: "Be good! Stand still!
You'll not come another day!"

So, it is rather difficult
To get the numbers right
For when we reach the 'Children's Wear',
Each step slips out of sight.

I wonder what becomes of them
All sliding more and more?
What an awful lot of muddled steps
Each store keeps in its floors!

Perhaps they move right round again
To start up down below;
They never get a rest at all –
No wonder they are slow!

I'd like to build a staircase
Of all the steps I count,
And starting from the very first
I'd mount and mount and mount.

Up and up and up I'd go
Beyond earth to the stars;
In fact, I very well might be
The first to step on Mars!

CHUFFA'S MOON TRIP

Chuffa the engine is cheerful, chunky and charming. He is also dozy, dreamy and drowsy. Here he is at the end of the line, dozing in the silvery moonlight. And there on his funnel is Sebastian, the seagull who is one of Chuffa's best friends. Sebastian thinks he would like to be like Chuffa – sturdy, steely, strong and hardworking and only sometimes late. And Chuffa thinks he would like to be like Sebastian – flying, floating, skimming and swooping through the air. If only he, Chuffa, could fly. He dreams of flying like a bird – like Sebastian. He gives a big sigh, CH-uff, and dozes off to sleep.

Suddenly he hears Sebastian calling. Not just one Sebastian, but six Sebastians! Why they are lifting Chuffa up into the air. All six of them. How strong they are. Well, Sebastian always wanted to be strong, didn't he? And here he is making Chuffa's dreams come true – making Chuffa fly like a bird in the sky. Chuffa looks down and sees the whole world and one sleepy squirrel all silvery in the moonlight, while they soar up into the air.

Chuffa is not the least bit afraid even when they have left the earth far, far behind and are up in Cloud-land where the cherubs and the angels live in the clouds.

But even six strong Sebastians cannot go on lifting up a Chuffa engine without getting rather tired. There is even a danger that they might drop Chuffa! Oh, how terrible that would be! So Sebastian asks help from two dear little angels sitting on a golden cloud.

"Sure, we'll help," said the angels. "Hang on." So the six Sebastians hung on.

"You need to get airborne," said one angel. "Sure, you do, said the second. "It's no problem," said the angels, "We'll each lend you a wing. We'll only need one each if we join arms and fly together!"

So that is what they did. Each took off one wing. (No, I don't know how they did it.)

Then the angels fixed the wings on to Chuffa's cabin. He carefully flapped one and then the other. Then both at once. And hurrah! He could fly.

Chuffa, the first engine in space! And now for the Moon. Chuffa-chuffa-flap-flap up and up. Sebastian had to give up, it was too high for him. But not for Chuffa.

So the angels guided him to the great, round, dusty surface of the Moon, and on the way, they took turns riding on Chuffa – the very first train ride in space.

Then Chuffa felt himself being pulled like a fish is pulled on a line. But there was no line, just a pull, getting stronger and stronger, and down and down he went until he landed in a moon crater. But it wasn't a hard bump at all. It was as soft and gentle as when you land on your very own bed. No trouble at all. In fact, it was lovely. Chuffa felt as light as a feather.

He began to do kangaroo hops all round the Moon. He even felt like a game of golf or something but he hadn't brought a ball.

"Now, what shall we do next?" asked Chuffa.

"Well, how about a trip to the Great Station-in-the-Sky?" said one of the angels. "That's where all the good trains go, when they get very old. Just give a blast-off on your whistle," said his friends.

That blast-off was enough to launch Chuffa into Outer Space and away beyond that until, they came to a land of beautiful coloured clouds. First a fine blue cloud, where all the engines lived which had come to the end of the line. There, they lived happily ever after without a timetable or anything to worry them. They were very kind to Chuffa and promised that if he were good, one day he could come and live there too!

Then the angels took Chuffa to a rose, pink cloud where even more engines lived. Chuffa was so excited and flapped his wings to keep himself hovering in space. Suddenly, he saw the cutest little engine he had ever seen. She had the prettiest headlights, the sweetest little funnel and the cosiest cabin you ever saw. Which one was it, do you think? Well, we shall never, never know, because at that very moment . . . in spite of the warning voices of the angels, Chuffa decided to land on that rosy, pink cloud and make friends.

"Don't do it," cried the angels. "It won't hold you up. You are too heavy for it." But Chuffa wouldn't listen. WOOOSSH!

Right through that rosy, pink cloud went Chuffa. Down and down and down.

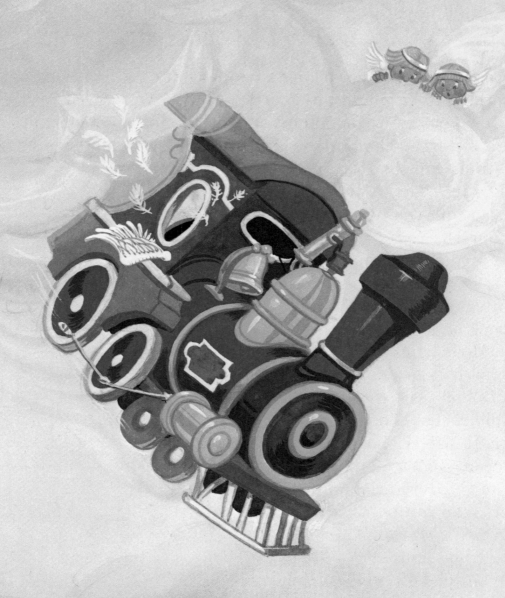

He fell through the pink cloud, past the blue cloud, through Outer Space and down and down.

And as he fell, a terrible thing happened. The speed of his fall loosened the feathers of the wings that could keep him up. One by one, then two by two, they came off and floated away into Outer Space.

Soon there was not a single feather left on either wing and there was nothing to keep him up. Poor old Chuffa was scared. Well, you know how you feel when you dream you are falling downstairs or off the top of a tall tree? That is how Chuffa felt. Down and down you go and nothing can save you.

But just as in a dream, when you fall, you never, never hurt yourself. So it was that Chuffa landed back on his rails without so much as a bump. Not even a teeny one. And there he was, back on Mother Earth with the old Moon shining overhead and old Sebastian fast asleep on his funnel. And there on the cabin roof was a single feather. It MIGHT have been one of Sebastian's feathers. But it might have been an angel's feather. Who can tell? Did Chuffa really go to the Moon, or was it just a dream?

What do you think?

COME TO THE FAIR

I'll see you at the fair.
It's great fun to be there,
With merry shouts
From the roundabouts,
And the big wheel in the air.

It isn't very far;
We'll drive a dodgem car,
With a bang and a smash
And a prang and a crash,
And win a goldfish in a jar.

We'll have a good try
At the coconut shy;
We'll throw with a ring,
We'll ride on a swing
And make it go up to the sky.

I'll see you at the fair.
It's great fun to be there,
With merry shouts
From the roundabouts,
And the big wheel in the air.

153

CHUFFA AND THE BANDIT

Way up in the North there is a great big fir forest, and in the
forest there are many wild creatures like birds and bees, and butterflies
and rabbits, and badgers and beavers and bears. There is also a railway
line for carrying logs from the fir forest. And on this line goes
Chuffa the train, driven by old Mr Driver. He is always ready to
give anyone a lift and all the animals love him. And Chuffa too!
Chuff chuff chuffa-chuffa-chuffa.

Now, one day some little birds flew up and said, "Oh, Mr Driver,
do come and have a look at Bruin the Bear. He is very poorly."

Mr Driver jammed on the brakes. ('I wish he wouldn't do that,' thought Chuffa.) Old Mr Driver got down from the train and the birds led him into the forest. There was Bruin the Bear propped up against a fir tree looking, very, very poorly.

"Why, what's up Bruin?" asked Mr Driver.

But Bruin could only sigh. "Just hand me your paw," said old Mr Driver, and he took out his watch and felt Bruin's pulse.

"My, my, that's very fast, or else my watch is slow. You certainly are a poorly bear. We shall have to get you to old Doc. Sawbones. He'll fix you up in a jiffy."

Well, it wasn't all that easy getting Bruin on the train. He was weak and limp and floppy and they had to pull him and push him and lift him.

"Gee, I feel poorly," said Bruin.

"Never you mind, old fellow," said old Mr Driver. "Just a few more steps and you'll soon be on the train and on your way to the Doctor." At last they managed to shove him and push him and pull him into an empty truck.

"Ready?" said Mr Driver to Chuffa.

"Wooo-oo-oo," replied Chuffa and off they went. Chuffa-chuff-achuff-achuff-achuffa.

And of course they were late! The Station Master at Dallas was as cross as can be. "Just look at the time," he shouted. "Half an hour late! Half an hour!"

"I'm sorry. I couldn't help it," said Mr Driver. "I found a poorly bear." And he showed the Station Master poor old Bruin. But that didn't please the Station Master either.

"Get that darned bear out of here," he yelled.

"I cannot," said Mr Driver. "He cannot walk and I cannot lift him. He is too poorly to walk."

"Then put him on a trolley. Do anything but get him out of here. Do you hear?"

"Yes," said old Mr Driver.

Doctor Sawbones was very wise and he didn't mind seeing a great, big bear in his surgery. He looked at Bruin and he sounded his chest and checked his tongue and felt his pulse and took his temperature. Then he said, "Hmm," very wisely. "Hmm, had any honey lately?"

The bear groaned. "Honey?" he said weakly. "Did you say honey? Well, perhaps just a taste."

"How much?" asked the Doctor.

"Well, w-e-l-l, about two pounds, maybe three," said the poor, sick bear.

"Right, into bed for three days. That'll put you right. And no more honey for a month."

And just as the Doctor said, in a few days the bear was quite well again and fit enough to go back to the forest. So old Mr Driver fetched Chuffa along and they set off for the fir forest. Chuff chuff chuffa chuffa-chuffa . . .

When they got there, the bear climbed down and said to kind-hearted Mr Driver, "Thank you very much for helping me when I was poorly. If ever you are in this forest and want any help, just call out 'Bruin' and I'll be there at once."

"Well, that is very kind of you," said Mr Driver. "I do hope I shall not need to call for help."

"So do I," said Bruin, "but you never can tell."

Back at the railway station, the Sheriff had a job for Mr Driver and Chuffa.

"Just listen to the Sheriff," said the Station Master. (But someone else was listening to the Sheriff. Who could it be?)

"I want you to take this bag of money to Woodville, see?" said the Sheriff. (But someone else saw as well. Who could it be?)

"See no one steals it. Understand?" (But someone else understood as well! Who could it be?) Mr Driver said he would take the money for the Sheriff.

He took the money in the bag and hid it under some logs in the train. Then he pulled the lever and off they went. C-h-u-f-f chuff chuffa chuffa-chuffa . . .

All was going well as they went whisking through the forest, when suddenly Chuffa saw a great pile of logs ahead right on the railway line. He whistled like anything and Mr Driver jammed on the brakes. ('I wish he wouldn't do that,' thought Chuffa.)

Mr Driver got down and looked at the logs. "Something strange going on down here," he said wisely. Then he began to shift the logs from the line. Suddenly he heard a most terrible shout.

"STICK 'EM UP!" roared a voice.

And there beside the track was a bold, bad Bandit. With a bandit's horse. And a bandit's mask. And a bandit's gun! Poor Mr Driver had to put his hands up in the air.

"Now, where's that money?" shouted the Bandit.

"In the wood," said Mr Driver.

"And where's the wood?" cried the Bandit.

"Under the trees," said Mr Driver truthfully.

"Then I'll give you three seconds to find it," said that horrid Bandit, "Then, I'll fire."

So what could Mr Driver do but get the bag from under the wood.

"If you steal it, it won't do you any good you know," he said to the Bandit. "If you're a thief, you'll always find there's trouble brewing."

And as he said that, up popped Bruin the Bear! Like a flash he seized the bad Bandit's hat and pulled it down over his eyes.

At the sight of the bear, the bad Bandit's horse bolted, and the
Bandit's gun went off BANG! But Bruin held on tight until Mr Driver
brought a rope. Then they tied him up so that he could not escape
and set him on top of some logs in one of the trucks.

"Come on Chuffa, my lad," said old Mr Driver. "Off we go to
Woodville as quick as quick." Bruin said, "I think I'll get on as
well, to keep an eye on this gentleman here." (He meant the Bandit.)
So he got up on the next truck and kept a sharp eye on the Bandit
who was too scared to move.

"Just as well you remembered to call out 'Bruin' like I said,"
said the bear.

"Wasn't it!" said Mr Driver who didn't know what he was talking
about.

"Do you suppose there is a reward for this bandit?" Chuffa said.
"Woo-oo-oo woo-oo-oo chuffa chuffa . . ."

When they reached Woodville, Mr Driver handed the money over to
the Bank Manager. "Capital, capital," cried the Bank Manager.
Then Mr Driver handed the Bandit over to the Sheriff. "Splendid,
splendid," cried the Sheriff. Everyone in Woodville was delighted
and there WAS a reward for the bold, bad Bandit. And the next day,
Mr Driver and Bruin were given Sheriff's Deputy badges.

"I owe it all to Bruin," said Mr Driver.

"And I owe it all to Chuffa," said Bruin.

"And so do I," said Mr Driver, proudly patting Chuffa.

"Well done, Chuffa. Well done indeed."

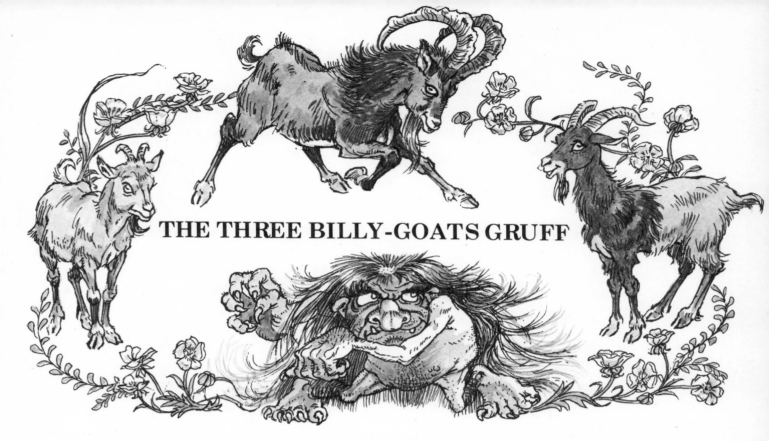

THE THREE BILLY-GOATS GRUFF

Once upon a time and far, far, away, in a land of beautiful mountains, fine green fields and sparkling streams, there lived three billy-goats. They were all named Gruff.

The eldest and largest was called Big Billy-Goat Gruff; the next was called Middle Billy-Goat Gruff; and the youngest and smallest was called Tiny Billy-Goat Gruff.

They had eaten all the grass in their field; they were hungry and getting thinner every day. So, they set off to find a better place where they could eat and grow fat.

In the distance, on the other side of a wide stream, they saw a fine green field. The grass was thick and long; it looked absolutely delicious.

"We'd get fat on that," said Tiny Billy-Goat Gruff in his tiny voice.

"We certainly would," added Middle Billy-Goat Gruff in his middle-toned voice.

"We'll go!" declared Big Billy-Goat Gruff in his big gruff voice.

But, there was a bridge to be crossed and under that bridge there lived a troll. Now, trolls were the most objectionable creatures you could imagine. They were squat, with large ugly heads. They had great big staring eyes and enormous noses; their mouths were snarling and greedy; instead of finger nails and toe nails they had long sharp claws . . . Quite terrifying!

And the Troll under this bridge was the worst of all. No villagers or children ever tried to cross over. They were afraid of being gobbled up.

The three billy-goats looked at the bridge.

"How about the Troll?" asked Tiny Billy-Goat Gruff in his tiny voice.

"Yes, how about him?" added Middle Billy-Goat Gruff in his middle-toned voice.

"I have a plan," declared Big Billy-Goat Gruff in his big gruff voice. All three goats put their heads close together and they whispered to one another.

Tiny Billy-Goat Gruff was the first to reach the bridge. Trip, trip! went his tiny hooves on the wooden boards.

Out came the Troll.

"Who's that?" he roared. "Who's that tripping over my bridge?"

"Oh!" cried Tiny Billy-Goat Gruff in his tiny voice, "I'm Tiny, the smallest Billy-Goat Gruff. I'm going to the field to eat and grow fat."

"Ha!" roared the Troll again. "AND I'M GOING TO EAT YOU!"

Poor Tiny Goat trembled all over.

"Oh, no! Don't you bother with me . . . I'm very small and so thin! Why not wait for the next Billy-Goat Gruff; he's much bigger and fatter."

The Troll stopped to think.

"Very well!" he shouted. "Be off with you!"

So, Tiny Billy-Goat Gruff tripped over the bridge and into the fine green field.

Before long, up came Middle Billy-Goat Gruff. Trip, trot! Trip, trot! went his hooves on the wooden boards. Out came the Troll.

"Who's that?" he roared. "Who's that trotting over my bridge?"

"Oh!" cried Middle Billy-Goat Gruff in his middle-toned voice, "I'm Middle, the second Billy-Goat Gruff. I'm going to the field to eat and grow fat."

"Ha!" roared the Troll again. "AND I'M GOING TO EAT YOU!"

Poor Middle Goat trembled all over.

"Oh, no! Don't you bother with me . . . I'm only middle-sized and quite thin. Why not wait for Big Billy-Goat Gruff; he's really big and very much fatter."

The Troll stopped to think.

"Very well!" he shouted. "Be off with you!"

So, Middle Billy-Goat Gruff trotted over the bridge and into the fine green field.

Then came Big Billy-Goat Gruff. Trip, trot, tramp! Trip, trot, tramp! went his big hooves on the wooden boards. Out came the Troll.

"Who's that?" he roared louder than ever. "Who's that tramping over my bridge?"

"Ah!" answered Big Billy-Goat Gruff in his biggest, gruffest voice. "I'm Big, the biggest Billy-Goat Gruff . . . AND I'M TRAMPING OVER THIS BRIDGE!"

164

The Troll nearly roared his head off. "Then I'm coming to get you!" and he moved a few steps towards the goat.

"Oh, no you won't!" bellowed Big Billy-Goat Gruff. "I'M COMING TO GET YOU!"

He lowered his head and stamped his hooves. Tramp, tramp, TRAMP! Tramp, tramp, TRAMP!

They met and the battle began.

Big Billy prodded the Troll with his sharp horns, picked him up and tossed him into the air. The Troll turned three somersaults before he splashed down below into the deep water. He was never seen again.

So, Big Billy-Goat Gruff tramped across the bridge and into the fine green field.

All three billy-goats ate the sweet grass and grew fatter and fatter.

All the villagers and children were happy again. They could use the bridge, for the Troll was not there to gobble them up.

And all you children can sleep safe and sound, for there is not one single troll left -- not anywhere.

THE WEDDING

One day, a little field mouse sat in the middle of a cornfield and waited for her friend Tom. He had a secret to tell, which he whispered in her ear, before they ran off together.

At the edge of the field, grew Red Poppy, now wide awake in the warm September sun. "Good morning," she said to the corn. "You do look well today, quite golden brown in fact."

"I know," said the corn. "And soon I shall be cut down and sent to the miller to be made into flour, but not before the wedding I hope."

"The wedding!" cried Red Poppy looking up at him.

"I use my ears, you know," he said. "Why, only last week I heard Tom Field Mouse telling Milly Field Mouse, that when the moon was full and round in the sky, they would be married the next day, at two o'clock."

"Why, that's today," said Red Poppy, dancing in the breeze.

The little blue harebells, standing on their thin stems said, "We shall ring for them this afternoon."

The little sparrows, sitting on top of the corn ears said, "We shall sing for them this afternoon."

"What can we do for them, Red Poppy?" asked the grass growing in the field,

"I'll ask the breeze to help you," she replied.

All week the little field mice had been collecting seeds and berries to eat at the Wedding Day party, and they had asked their cousins from town to come to the wedding and now, all was ready.

The village clock struck two -- Tom and Milly Field Mouse were married. As they walked down the path by Red Poppy, the harebells began to ring, the sparrows began to sing and the breeze blew grass-seed confetti all over them.

Then the party began. There was plenty to eat and then everyone played Hide and Seek, Hunt the Acorn and even had a climbing race to the top of the corn stalks.

"What a lovely wedding we have had," said Milly Field Mouse. "I wonder though, who told our secret."

"Oh, you can't have a secret here, my dear, remember the corn has ears," said Tom and quickly they ran away.

Now, the sun was going down and it was very quiet.

"Goodnight, Red Poppy," said the corn. "I wonder what I shall hear tomorrow?" Red Poppy did not answer, she was fast asleep.

DIFFY

Mrs Duck was very happy. She was listening to the little creaks and cracks that meant her eggs were breaking open and soon there would be a family of baby ducklings. One of the eggs kept rolling away and that one did not make any sound at all.

"Now WHY?" Mrs Duck asked herself, staring hard at it.

CREAK! CRACK! POP! went all the other eggs and out popped the fluffy yellow ducklings.

"BEAUTIFUL!" sighed Mrs Duck, happily. She glared at the egg that was left unopened as it rolled away uncracked.

SNAP! Without any warning at all the last egg BURST open and the duckling inside it SHOT out. He went up into the air as if he were a bird who could fly but not swim, instead of a bird that could swim but not fly. Mrs Duck watched open-beaked as the youngest duckling soared into space.

"NOT a budding space-duck!" wailed Mrs Duck, who sometimes watched the Farmer's television.

But the little fellow soon came down to earth again because, of course, he could NOT fly, and he landed upside-down next to his brothers and sisters.

Mrs Duck eyed her son fondly.

"I thought YOU would be different," she said, not knowing whether to be proud or put-out.

"DIFFERENT!" gurgled the little duckling. "What a lovely name. Call me DIFFY!"

The very first thing Diffy wanted to do was to leave home.

"You can't!" snapped Mrs Duck. "You've only just got here."

"I have a SPIRIT OF ADVENTURE," explained Diffy. He had a very good turn of speech, or rather, QUACK, for such a young duckling.

"Save it until you are grown up," shrieked Mrs Duck. She had to shriek because little Diffy was already on his way.

The first place brave Diffy came to was not as adventurous as he thought it might be. HE thought that after all that walking he must have reached foreign parts but he hadn't. He had only got as far as the farmhouse.

The farmer's wife was cleaning the kitchen. She did not like the job and so she was doing it as quickly as she could to get it over. She was rather short-sighted and so when Diffy perched on the handle of a wooden spoon for a rest, she thought he was a feather-duster.

"I had forgotten I had this," she told herself, as she picked up the DIFFYDUCKYWOODENSPOONFEATHERDUSTER.

Diffy had to cling hard to that wooden spoon because first the farmer's wife shot him UP to dust the pictures. Then she pushed him SIDEWAYS to dust the clock and even DOWN to dust inside a vase.

Diffy could have been named DUSTY before she had finished with him. He raced away from the wooden spoon as soon as she put it down. He meant to make for the door, but with all that dust in his eyes he went the wrong way and ended up against the wall.

Just then her son, Fred, came in through the door from school. Fred did not see Diffy sitting on the floor trying to brush the dust out of his eyes. Fred took off his hat as soon as he came in, as he always did. He tossed it across the room to try and get it on the hook in the wall above where Diffy was, as he always did. Fred missed, as he always did. The hat fell on the floor as it always did. But never before had there been a baby duckling sitting there, as there was this time. The hat fell over Diffy and at once it did something it had NEVER done before. THE HAT RAN ACROSS THE FLOOR!

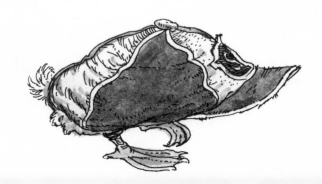

It was only Diffy really, who thought the roof had fallen on top of him and was running to try and shake it off. Fred thought that he was seeing MAGIC and he just stood and watched with eyes like saucers. He closed his eyes so that he could yell louder and at that very moment Diffy reached — and fell over — the doorstep. The hat stayed behind and Diffy was able to scuttle away. When Fred opened his eyes again after his yell, Diffy was gone.

For ever after, Fred was sure that he was the only person in the world who had seen a hat run across a floor. As a matter of fact, he wrote an essay about it at school the next day and got top marks for imagination.

Diffy left his SPIRIT OF ADVENTURE behind him in the farmhouse. He knew that his beak was pointed towards his duckpond home, because he could hear his mother telling his brothers and sisters what to do as she took them for their first swim.

Diffy decided to join them and go back later for his lost SPIRIT OF ADVENTURE. It was sad, in a way, because Mrs Duck could not count and she didn't have time to notice that Diffy was back again. She went on boasting dreadfully to friends and relations about her youngest son, who, she told them, was TRAVELLING THE WORLD WITH A SPIRIT OF ADVENTURE. None of the family and friends could count and so THEY did not know either that Diffy was back, which was a pity for them, because they did get so horribly bored just HEARING about him.

As for Diffy HE never tired of hearing about himself and as he listened hard ALL the time, he grew up feeling that he really was DIFFERENT!

THE MOUSE

A little mouse hid himself under a chair,
He knew, of course, who was sitting there;
A gracious lady -- so calm and serene,
Robed and bejewelled -- a beautiful Queen.

He wanted to see all the people who came;
All were important -- some of great fame;
The colours and costumes! A splendid sight!
But then the mouse had a terrible fright.

For someone had joined him, the Right Royal Cat:
"What do you think you are playing at?
A mouse -- in the palace! It will not do!
My duty is plain -- I'm kept to kill you."

The brave little mouse tried to smile a faint smile:
"Your Highness, could you not wait awhile?
I'm really quite thin -- a very poor snack;
I'm afraid I shall scream when you attack."

"Very well," said the cat, "we'll see out the ball;
Can't let a mouse cause chaos, at all:
But when it's done and the Queen goes to bed;
I tell you, mouse, you'll be deader than dead!"

The cat settled down and the mouse looked around;
A way to escape, it must be found!
The hem of Her Majesty's gown of lace,
He chewed the stitches and squeezed in the space.

So when the dear Queen thought she'd had quite enough,
Mouse went too – leaving cat in a huff.
"A fine stately ride! Three squeaks for that!
The Queen! God Bless Her! We fooled the cat!"

THE NEW COAT

Pimm Pixie was rolling up cobweb thread in the brambles one day, when his coat caught on a thorn, and tore from the collar right down to the hem. It was as open down the back as it was down the front.

"I suppose I could put some buttons on it," he said, "but then everyone would think I had my head on back to front."

When he got home he mended the tear but he knew the coat would never be the same.

"I can't see the mend myself," he said, "but everyone else can. Everyone will be looking at my stitches, which I know are very uneven. I think it's time I had a new coat."

He went to see the pixie tailor.

"Good morning Pimm," said the tailor. "What can I do for you?"

"I want a new coat, exactly like this one," said Pimm. The torn coat had a deep collar to turn up round his ears when the wind blew, it was long enough to keep his knees warm, and it had deep pockets for carrying things in. He felt comfortable in it. He liked wearing it and saw no reason why his new coat should be any different.

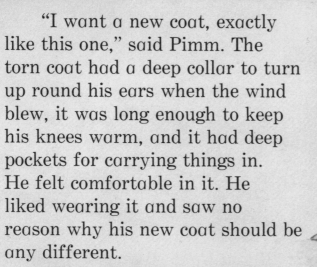

"I'll be glad to make it for you," said the tailor, who had made Pimm's first coat and was glad he liked it so much. He took Pimm's measurements, just to make sure they were still the same, which they were, pixies not being in the habit of growing very much.

"There is one small change I would like you to make," said Pimm, who had been looking at the tailor's own coat.

"Yes?" said the tailor, waiting with his pencil held over his note pad.

"I would like it made up in a different shade of green this time . . . I like the shade you are wearing."

The tailor wrote, 'colour, emerald green' on his note pad.

"When will it be ready?" asked Pimm. His own sewing was not very good. The draughts were finding their way in, in between his clumsy stitches and his back was getting cold.

"Tomorrow, if I start straight away," said the tailor, and he went to the shelf and took down a roll of emerald green cloth.

"Ummmm" said Pimm thoughtfully, as the tailor started to snip with his scissors. Pixie tailors can start cutting straight away, they don't have to bother with paper patterns. "Perhaps that blue would be better."

"But I've already started cutting," said the tailor.

"It's my coat. I'm the one who will have to wear it. The colour MUST be right."

The tailor put down his scissors. "If you want your coat finished by tomorrow," he said, "you must make up your mind quickly. I will give you until eleven o'clock."

"I'll go away, and think about it, and then come back and tell you what I have decided," said Pimm. Before he reached the door he turned and said, "I've thought already. Make it in crimson."

"Very well . . . if you're QUITE sure," said the tailor.

Pimm said he WAS sure, but five minutes later he was back.

"I've changed my mind. I'll have it made in yellow."

Ten minutes later he had decided on indigo. And ten minutes after that, he had decided on purple.

"I do wish you'd make up your mind," sighed the tailor.

"I am making up my mind," said Pimm. "I've made it up six times already."

The tailor put ALL the rolls of cloth on the table.

"Now which is it to be?" he said, beginning to look almost as sharp and scratchy as his pins. "I can't have you changing your mind any more. I have other customers to think about."

"The trouble is," wailed Pimm, "I like ALL the colours. It really is very difficult to choose just one."

"Then leave the choice to me," said the tailor. It seemed to Pimm that perhaps that might be the best idea.

"Come back in the morning," said the tailor. "If I see your nose peeping round that door before morning, I'll snip it off with my scissors." He didn't mean that, of course, but he had to keep Pimm out of his way somehow. "Now be off with you!"

Pimm hardly slept a wink all night wondering what colour cloth the tailor would use.

Next morning, as soon as it was light, he went and stood on the tailor's doorstep. It was hours before the tailor opened the door. He knew Pimm was there, but he had his breakfast first, swept the floor and tidied the shelves. He didn't think it would do Pimm any harm to keep him waiting. At nine o'clock precisely, by the dandelion clock, he unbolted the door and let Pimm in.

"Is it finished? What colour did you use? Let me see it. Oh, I do hope you used the RIGHT colour!"

"Which colour IS the right colour?" asked the tailor.

"I don't know . . . if only I DID know . . ." wailed Pimm.

He could hardly bear to look as the tailor uncovered the coat. What could he say if he didn't like the colour the tailor had chosen? But what a surprise he had. He gasped! He clapped his hands together in glee! He jumped onto the table and danced a jig! He beamed from ear to ear! The point on his hat curled and uncurled by itself! The tailor looked pleased.

"Did I use the right colour?" he asked, dodging out of the way as Pimm bounced up and down like a ball.

"Oh you did! You did!" exclaimed Pimm. "What a clever tailor you are!"

The tailor blushed with pleasure.

"Try it on for size," he said. It fitted perfectly, as he knew it would because he had taken the measurements himself.

"Thank you . . . thank you . . . thank you . . ." sang Pimm as he danced off down the street. The clever tailor had used a piece of cloth from each roll and had made him a coat that was ALL the colours of the rainbow!

SOLDIERS

Ten wooden pegs,
Smooth and brown,
On the table,
Lying down.

Black for boots,
And black for hats,
Red for tunics,
Front and back.
Dark blue legs,
With stripes of white.
Spots of gold,
For buttons bright.

Ten soldiers made
From wooden pegs,
March up and down
On painted legs.

FLY AWAY TERRY

Terry Towel was tired of being washed, and hung on the line to dry, every Monday morning. Soap made him sneeze, hot water made him limp, the spin dryer made him dizzy and the pegs pinched him. One Monday morning, when he had sneezed more than usual, and the pegs were pinching extra hard, he decided he could bear it no longer. He began to pull at the horrid pegs which were holding him so tightly to the line.

"Help me . . . help me . . ." he called to the wind. He pulled and he tugged and he wriggled. The wind was doing his best to help. He could feel one of the pegs loosening.

Ping! The loose peg flew off the line and lay in the grass.

'Nearly free . . . one more hard tug should do it,' thought Terry. He waited until the wind puffed out another gust, and then he pulled with all his might . . . and away he sailed, up, up, up, into the sky.

"I'm free . . . I'm free!" he called at the top of his voice.

Two birds flying by were taken completely by surprise.

"What do you suppose THAT was?" one of them chirped, turning his head to get a better look and bumping into his friend as he did so.

"Look where you're going . . ." twittered his friend with feathers all ruffled. "It's only a piece of blown-away-washing."

Terry didn't like being called a piece of blown-away-washing.

"Oh no I'm not . . . I'm King of the Sky!" he shouted.

"You're not!" twittered the birds.

"I am . . ." shouted Terry. "I am . . . I am . . . I am . . ." And he twisted and turned in loops and circles, and he dived and soared like a kite to show them how clever he was. "Look at me! Look at me!"

"Do stop showing off . . ." twittered the birds, who knew they could do everything Terry was doing, only better.

"I'm not showing off! I'm King of the Sky. You must all bow when I pass."

The birds ignored him, as he deserved, and flew away.

"It's only because you're jealous of me!" shouted Terry.

The wind, who had been listening, suddenly stopped blowing. The birds carried on flying of course, because they had their wings to carry THEM, but Terry went limp and fell to the ground.

"How dare you let me fall . . ." shouted Terry. "I'm King of the Sky. Blow wind . . . blow!"

"Only if you stop boasting," said the wind.

"I will . . . I will," said Terry. So the good-natured wind, puffed up his cheeks and blew Terry back into the air. Away danced Terry, skipping and hopping and looping over the grass.

"Moo . . . " hiccupped a cow, as Terry danced in front of her and dazzled her. "What's that?"

"A piece of blown-away-washing!" twittered the birds.

"Maa . . . ammma . . . wait for me . . . maa . . . baaaa . . . " bleated a tiny lamb, mistaking Terry for her mother, and running after him.

"Baaa . . . come back at once . . . " bleated the lamb's mother. "Can't you tell the difference between your own mother and a piece of blown-away-washing?"

Terry laughed. He was having fun.

He danced right across the field and into the shady wood. He danced in and out of the trees, startling the rabbits, and frightening the squirrels. Presently he heard voices. There were children walking amongst the bluebells. One of the children saw him, and screamed.

"It's a ghost!"

"Look! Look!"

"It's a ghost!"

The children ran as fast as
their legs would take them.
Every time they glanced over their
shoulders to see if the ghost was
following, Terry was a short way
behind, dancing and wafting and
willowing, as he imagined a ghost
would. That made them scream
louder, and run faster.

"Stop frightening those poor
little children!" hooted an owl.

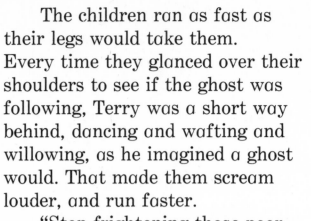

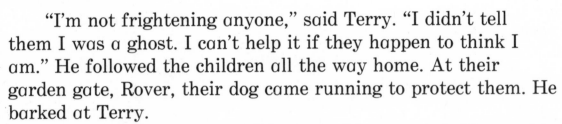

"I'm not frightening anyone," said Terry. "I didn't tell
them I was a ghost. I can't help it if they happen to think I
am." He followed the children all the way home. At their
garden gate, Rover, their dog came running to protect them. He
barked at Terry.

"Stop frightening my children . . ." he growled. He caught
hold of one of Terry's corners with his teeth and shook him.

"Put me down . . . put me down . . . " gasped Terry.

"Only if you behave yourself," said Rover, without letting
go.

184

"Look," said the children. "It wasn't a ghost at all. It's a piece of blown-away-washing. Let it go, Rover, there's a good boy. We're not afraid anymore."

Rover let go at once, and Terry fell to the ground with a sigh. Being shaken THAT hard didn't agree with him at all. The children came and picked him up. His back and his front were covered with dirty streaks where he had been playing in the field, and green streaks where he had rubbed against mossy bark in the wood. He looked a sorry sight. He felt a sorry sight.

The childrens' mother came into the garden.

"You've found my towel," she said. "It blew off the line this morning. I wondered where it had got to."

Once more, Terry found himself sneezing in the washing machine and getting dizzy in the spin dryer. But this time, as he hung on the line with the pegs pinching his corners, he decided that being soft, and clean, and fluffy, wasn't so bad after all, and when the wind asked him if he wanted to go for another fly around the sky, he said,

"No thank you. I've had my adventure, and I enjoyed it. I'm quite content to be myself now."

He danced on the line until he was dry, making quite sure he didn't pull at the pegs TOO hard. And then he was folded and put away in a warm cupboard -- a cleaner, and wiser towel.

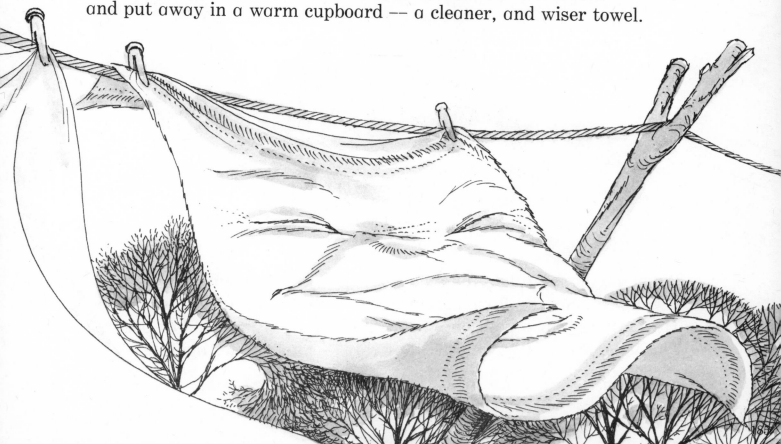

85

SPROGGET ON HOLIDAY

One day I called my special friend, Sprogget, the magic one;
Nobody knows about him, but he is lots of fun.
"Come, Sprog, the car is waiting! Please hurry or you'll find
That we have gone on holiday -- and you are left behind."

But Sprogget came and we set off through towns and country fine.
We climbed the hills; we followed streams; passed forests of dark pine.
At last we stopped at Granny's -- she opened up the gate.
"You'll love the farm," I whispered. "Oh, Sprog, it's really great!"

We had a meal -- a proper feast -- like in a fairy book;
Gran remembers things I like -- she knows just what to cook.
Then, out to see the animals -- a calf and a new foal;
I helped to feed the chickens and I filled their drinking bowl.

We slept that night in my small room -- kept specially for me;
I woke to hear the farm sounds -- saw Sprogget up a tree;
He'd swung himself out on a branch that tapped my window pane;
Throughout our stay, he used that way -- many times again.

We rode the Shetland pony and the donkey called Grey-Moke;
When I fell off, my Sprogget laughed -- he thought it was a joke.
I warned him, "Just you watch it! You might fall yourself one day!"
He winked at me and helped me up; then off we ran to play.

The day we went to market I thought my friend was lost;
He didn't join me shopping -- didn't help me check the cost.
Then suddenly he came along astride a baby goat;
He'd saved it from the river with a rope slipped round its throat.

Of course, no one could see or hear my magic Sprogget man;
Folk asked a lot of questions and marched me off to Gran;
The little kid was never claimed; Gran kept it on the farm
It's pretty -- we all love it and it's safe from any harm.

Our holiday is over , Why can't it last and last?
I've never known so many days go whizzing by so fast.
Granny's asked us back quite soon, to have a longer stay;
Sprogget grins and we both shout: "Hip, hip! Hip, hip! Hurray!"

TOM THE GIANT

Once upon a time, there was a giant. His name was Tom, and he lived all by himself in the mountains. His cabin was made of tall trees, his cup was as big as a barrel and his boots were as large as boats.

Tom was a very friendly giant, but the people who lived in the town nearby were afraid of him because he looked so big and fierce.

One day, Tom went into the town to buy some green wool to make himself a hat. As soon as the people saw him coming, they shut the gates of the town and ran into their houses to hide. Tom stepped over the wall, but when he walked along the street all the people shouted at him from their windows.

"Go away," they cried. "You are much too big to come into our town. You will tread on us and squash us flat."

At last, poor Tom had to go away without the wool for his hat, because none of the shopkeepers would sell him any. When he got home he took off his boots and lay down to sleep in his giant bed. Before long he was fast asleep, with his giant cat Toby curled up on the blanket beside him.

During the night, a terrible storm arose. The thunder rolled, the lightning flashed and the rain poured down like a waterfall. Then a terrible wind came which blew away all the black rain clouds and when there were no clouds left, it blew away the stars.

The stars fell down a hundred at a time. They sparkled through the air and landed as quietly as snow. They lay twinkling where they had fallen -- on the grass, in the fields, on the trees, in the streets and on all the rooftops in the town.

All the people were amazed when they saw the stars. They looked up into the dark and empty sky.

"How shall we put the stars back?" they said.

The next morning, the town crier went round the town ringing his bell. "Oyez, Oyez, Oyez," he cried. "If anyone can put the stars back into the sky he shall have a hundred pieces of gold as his reward."

Everyone tried to think of a way to put the stars back, but nobody had the faintest idea of what to do. No one thought of asking Tom the Giant.

"What on earth shall we do?" said the Lord Mayor.

"I don't know, I'm sure," said the town crier.

Just then, they heard the heavy footsteps of Tom the Giant.

"Don't be afraid," called Tom. "I have come to put the stars back, if you will help me."

One by one the people came out of their houses and stood on the walls to talk to Tom.

"What do you want us to do?" asked the Lord Mayor.

"Everyone must take a bag and pick up all the stars he can find," said Tom. "When all the stars have been picked up, bring them to me and I will take them away in my big leather sack ready to put them back in the sky."

No sooner said than done.
The people searched everywhere for
the fallen stars. They looked
under the bushes and in the flower
beds; they looked down the chimneys
and at the bottom of the wells,
until at last they had found every
single star. Then Tom emptied all
the bags of stars into his big sack.
He picked it up, and set out for the
mountains. All the people stood
on the walls and waved as he walked
away.

As soon as he reached his
cabin, Tom took down his long
ladder. Then he stood the ladder
against the clouds and climbed up
with the sack of stars on his
back. One by one he put all the
stars back into the sky. When
night came the stars twinkled as
merrily as ever, just as if nothing
had ever happened.

The next day, Tom went down to the town to see the people. They gave a loud cheer when they saw him.

"Here are your hundred pieces of gold," said the Lord Mayor.

"I do not want the gold," said Tom. "All I want is some green wool to make a hat."

The people took the wool from fifty sheep until they had enough to make a hat for Tom. They worked all day, and by that evening, a new green hat was ready for him.

"Thank you," said Tom.

With the green hat on his head, he walked proudly back to his home in the mountains. The people were never afraid of him again.

AMANDA AND THE ANIMALS

Once upon a time, there was a little girl called Amanda, who lived in a pretty white house in the country with her mother and father.

One sunny day, as it was her birthday, and so, of course, a very special day, they took her to the zoo. Amanda was so excited, for it was the first time she had ever been there and she adored animals.

She gazed in wonder at the huge lions, laughed at the antics of the cheeky monkeys, and stroked the heads of the gentle deer. She had a wonderful time!

Later that day, tired but happy, she sat on her garden swing while her mother prepared supper -- a special birthday supper -- with a birthday cake as well.

Amanda swung slowly backwards and forwards, her mind full of all the animals she'd seen at the zoo, some so big; some so small; and all the time she swung, backwards and forwards, backwards and forwards . . .

'In the jungle, I'm a king,'
Remarked the Lion full of pride,
'I'm not afraid of anything,
At least, not much,' he said aside.

'I know the big savannah well,
There, many animals retreat.
But I must find out where they dwell,
For when I'm hungry, I must eat.'

   Amanda's blue eyes widened as she looked at the lion. He
certainly was beautiful, with his thick golden mane and his
flashing eyes. As a matter of fact, he was sitting on her
father's prize roses, but she didn't like to tell him, in case
he was offended. He went on . . .

'My claws are very sharp, you know,
Because they have to grasp and tear.
My sense of smell is not so good,
But there's very little I don't hear.

At night, I see as well as day,
And I can run quite fast along,
Though rarely do I chase my prey,
For I am very, very strong.'

Another voice broke in then, and Amanda saw a giraffe looking down at the lion, who was now busily washing his paws!

'What of me?' asked the Giraffe,
I'm very tall, quite eighteen feet.
My neck is long,' he gave a laugh,
'So from the tall trees I can eat.

My eyes are fringed against the sun.
I've two horns on my head.
I have no voice at all -- just none,
I cannot even howl instead!

I live in Africa -- it's hot,
The sun is always big and bright,
It seems to shine an awful lot,
The only time it's cool is night.

It's quite a problem when I drink,
I have to put my legs astride,
Yet though I'm tall, I really think
I'm quite content and satisfied.'

Amanda chuckled at this, then stared in surprise at the zebra who was standing there listening with much attention.

'My stripes blend in with the trees,
And with the background where I live.
I come and go just as I please,
Though lots of care to this I give!'

On one point I should like some light
About these stripes upon my back.
Now what is which, I don't know quite—
Black stripe on white or white on black?'

Amanda nearly fell off her seat with laughter, for the zebra really did look quite puzzled. A loud trumpeting sound made her jump. A big, grey elephant was standing near the greenhouse. Amanda hoped he wouldn't lean on it, in case he knocked it down!

'In size I'm larger than you all,
For quite six tons — that's what I weigh.
I trumpet loudly when I call,
So they can hear me far away.

You'd think my trunk was in the way,
And yet without it lost I'd be,
For when I'm hungry through the day,
I pick leaves from the highest tree.

Some of my friends, they work for man,
They pull and lift the trunks of trees,
That's not for me, for if I can
I'd rather do just what I please.'

The elephant thought hard for a moment, swinging his trunk from side to side, until Amanda knew she'd simply burst if she didn't laugh soon, but she didn't dare!

The elephant continued,

'My ears are big; my hide is grey,
I have two tusks of ivory;
I've nothing really more to say,
Except I'm rather glad I'm me!'

Here he was interrupted by a sniffly, snuffly sort of voice.

'I know I am an ugly beast,
But all Hippos are just like me;
And I don't mind it in the least,
There's nothing else I'd rather be!

You'd see that just my head appears
When I am swimming, which I love;
For I also close my nose and ears,
That's all you notice from above.'

The hippopotamus stopped short then, his words almost drowned when he opened his enormous mouth to have a big, comfortable yawn! Amanda couldn't believe her eyes. How could any animal have such a huge mouth?

'I'm twelve feet long, that's quite a lot,
I weigh four tons, or so it's said.
My feet are webbed, so I can trot
Along the muddy river-bed.

I like to chew the leaves and flowers,
And other greenery, of course.
While sugar I could eat for hours.
My other name's the River Horse!'

Amanda was surprised to hear this, and thought it was a lovely name. The Hippo looked at her, his little eyes twinkling, gave another yawn, and promptly went to sleep!

There was a sudden thud, and a kangaroo appeared from nowhere!

'I know I'm not as big as you,
Nor quite as heavy, nor as plump;
But there's one thing that you can't do,
That I can do, and that is JUMP!

I leap as far as twenty feet,
The farmers wish I could be banned,
Because you see, I love to eat
The grass that grows upon their land.

When I was born, you'd never dream
That I was very, very small,
So very tiny, it would seem
I wasn't really there at all!

Within my mother's pouch I kept,
Though that's a long time past, I own.
Inside it, nice and warm I slept,
But now I'm big and fully-grown.'

Even as he finished, all the other animals who had been listening, started to make such a noise, each one claiming that he was the finest animal. Amanda put her hands on her ears to shut out the noise, but it grew louder and louder, until suddenly she heard above it all, someone calling her name.

"Amanda, supper's ready!" It was her mother calling. She turned to look at the animals again, but they all seemed to have disappeared somewhere.

"What a shame," she said, "I was so enjoying myself!" She raced down the garden path and went into the house.

"Mummy, I've just seen some of the animals that we saw at the zoo today!" Amanda told her excitedly.

Her mother smiled down at her. "Oh, Amanda," she laughed, "have you been playing make-believe again?" Amanda opened her mouth to argue, but shut it again. She knew it wasn't any good anyway, because whenever she'd had an adventure before, and told her mother, she'd always said Amanda had been playing make-believe. Grown-ups didn't know everything, did they?